O9-AHW-142

BICYCLING THE BACKROADS
OF NORTHWEST WASHINGTON

by Erin and Bill Woods

Fourth Edition

Cartoons by Dale Martin

The Mountaineers, Seattle

 Published by
The Mountaineers
1001 SW Klickitat Way, Suite 201
Seattle, Washington 98134

© 1976, 1984, 1992, 1997 by Erin and Bill Woods

1 0 9 8 7
5 4 3 2 1

No part of this book may be reproduced in any form, or by any electronic, mechanical, or other means, without permission in writing from the publisher.

Published simultaneously in Great Britain by Cordee, 3a DeMontfort Street, Leicester, England, LE1 7HD

Manufactured in the United States of America

Edited by Nicky Leach
Maps by Helen Sherman and Bill Woods
Cartoons by Dale Martin
Cover design by Patrick Lanfear and Helen Cherullo
Book design by Bill Woods, Erin Woods, and Marge Mueller

Cover photograph: Bicycling down a path in the tulip fields of Mt. Vernon, Washington. Photo © Bert Sagara, Tony Stone Images

Library of Congress Cataloging-in-Publication Data
Woods, Erin
    Bicycling the backroads of northwest Washington / by Erin and Bill Woods ; cartoons by Dale Martin. — 4th ed.
       p.   cm.
    Includes indexes.
    ISBN 0-89886-507-7
    1. Bicycle touring—Washington (State)—Guidebooks. 2. Bicycle touring—British Columbia—Guidebooks. 3. Washington (State)—Guidebooks.
4. British Columbia—Guidebooks. I. Woods, Bill, 1925– II. Title.
GV1045.5.W18W66   1997
796.6'4'09797—dc21   96–52803
                                                             CIP

 Printed on recycled paper

NOTE ABOUT RIDE NUMBERING

Do not look for missing pages. The tours in this book start at number 55 to follow in sequence those in *Bicycling the Backroads Around Puget Sound* (The Mountaineers, Seattle, Washington). This numbering system was adopted to facilitate cross-referencing and compilation using tours from both books. Tours numbered 54 and under, when cited, refer to the publication above.

CONTENTS

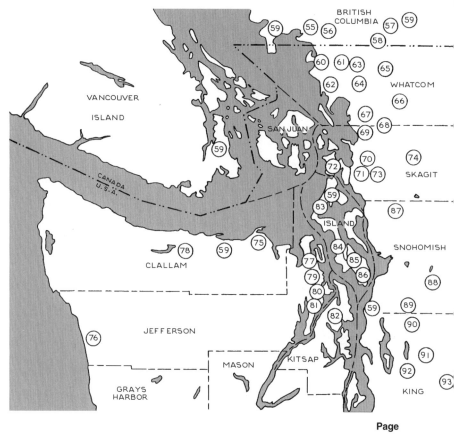

MAP LEGEND

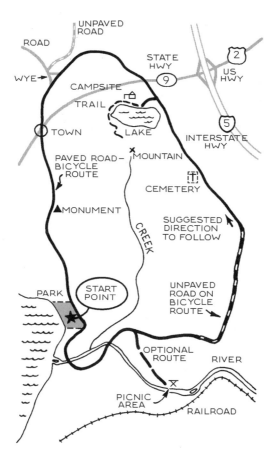

"Since when were they built just for bicycles?"

INTRODUCTION

As a companion to *Bicycling the Backroads Around Puget Sound* and *Bicycling the Backroads of Southwest Washington*, this book provides the bicycle touring buff an expanded choice of day, weekend, and longer rides. As always, we have an aversion to heavy automobile traffic and go to great lengths to avoid it. In covering what we feel are the remaining enjoyable, low traffic, rural and semi-rural bicycle loop tours in northwestern Washington, we have omitted several popular rides in metropolitan and suburban areas and routes on busy state and federal highways. For maps and route descriptions of several popular highway routes, such as the Olympic Highway loop, Hood Canal loop, and North Cascades Highway, bicycle strip-map booklets can be obtained from the Washington State Highway Department.

In picking up where the previous "backroads" book left off, this volume offers a few rides in the Seattle–Puget Sound area but, in general, ranges farther afield. Many rides offered in Skagit, Whatcom, Clallam, and other counties entail long driving distances for most Puget Sound area cyclists. To make the longer drives worthwhile, the tours are of moderate length, usually 30 to 60 miles, and offer satisfying workouts for the intermediate to advanced cyclist. This is not, however, at the expense of enjoyable scenery and interesting stopping places. The ideal conditions sought when scouting and selecting the tours in this book were as follows:

Length: 30 to 65 miles per day. Shorter loops or side trips were included where they can be added to another ride for a longer tour. For the less ardent cyclist, many of the tours can be shortened by short-cutting loops.

Roads: Primarily paved rural county roads. Short stretches of gravel and low-traffic state highways were included where unavoidable. Hills are unimportant on low-traffic byways. Long stretches of steep gravel are to be avoided, as is even a short uphill grind in heavy traffic.

Starting Point: A public parking area, such as a park, school, or small-town side street. Public restrooms nearby are important but not mandatory if available soon along the route.

Lunch Stop: A park, preferably, with shelter, tables, and restrooms. Where a park was not available, a pleasant lake or stream bank or a public fishing access may have been substituted. For those who would rather buy than take along their food, cafes and grocery stores nearby are desirable.

Points of Interest: Nearby museums, historic monuments, industrial plants, zoos, and parks. These were sought out and investigated for details of availability to touring bicyclists. Distinctive flora and fauna along the way were identified, if possible, and unusual features pointed out.

Ride Complexity: Avoidance of busy highways and gravel roads may necessarily complicate the route, but capricious complexity is undesirable.

Private Property: Where private property or other questionable access is encountered, permission for bicycle access must be obtained.

Not all the rides in this book meet all the above conditions. Those that do not are retained for their scenic or other unusual aspects. Several rides that initially appeared attractive were removed from this collection because they failed to meet one or more conditions.

The rides in this book were scouted primarily during winter months, when the bicycle clubs with which the authors are associated are relatively inactive. The layout of rides for scouting was accomplished with state, county, and USGS quadrangle maps. Prospective routes were laid out for distance, probable traffic density, and hills. Parks were located and the routes modified to intercept them if possible. Bicycles were hauled by automobile to the nominal starting point and the adventure begun. Although many of the rides were repeated during spring and summer months, time did not allow this treatment for all of the tours. As a result, many of the summer flora and fauna have been missed, leaving some write-ups with a wintry flavor. Other than a possible increase in traffic density, the environment in summer should be equally enjoyable, especially when it is so interesting in wintertime.

...diverting attention at a critical moment.

Popular multi-day tours, such as the Puget Sound–Fraser Valley tour, were scouted for the most part by making day tours along the route. Portions of these short tours were then connected to make up the longer tour. The combined sets of rides presented in this book and in *Bicycling the Backroads Around Puget Sound* offer a high degree of connectivity for creating multi-day tours throughout western Washington, and their use in this manner is encouraged. To facilitate this task, a list of cities, towns, and communities encountered along rides in the books is offered in the "Tour Junctions" appendix. As in many texts, "further exercises are left to the student."

Now a word about safety. As the number of bicyclists increases, so does the number of serious bicycle accidents. In our experience with group touring, the most frequent causes of serious bicycle accidents are dogs, negligent bicycle driving, and negligent automobile driving, in that order. Dog bites, though not rare, are usually the least of dog problems. Dogs get in the way, hit bicycles, and cause sudden braking and jam-ups in groups of cyclists, with resulting crashes. Often just their presence causes a bicyclist to divert attention from road hazards at a critical instant. Negligent bicycling includes riding on the left-hand side of the road, following another bicycle too closely, failure to signal, a sudden stop or turn in the presence of others, and operation of a bicycle at an excessive speed for road conditions.

The price of accident-free touring is vigilance and adherence to rules of the road. Even with careful attention, however, sooner or later almost anyone who does a lot of riding will have an accident of some sort. To lessen the consequences, certain bicycling accessories are recommended. The first is a safety helmet. King County has a bicycle helmet law. The best helmets available are those designed and manufactured specifically for bicycling. They are hot in summer, a nuisance to wear, and some whistle in the wind, but one look at a helmet with a crushed liner or distended strap supports after it has been removed from an undamaged head is enough to make one a true believer. Other accident victims without helmets have not been so fortunate.

Aside from mechanical protection of the brainbin, primary safety devices are those that help you to see and be seen. A rear-view mirror that attaches to the glasses, helmet, or wrist allows the rider to see what is coming from the rear without losing sight of the roadway ahead. Mirrors are now being offered by several mail-order vendors advertising in national bicycling magazines. Lights and reflectors for riding in hours of dusk and darkness are a must. Generator or battery headlights and taillights can be augmented by transistorized strobe lights. These are lightweight, low-battery-drain attention-getters.

Last but not least, a few tips on maintenance. We do not intend to give a course on how to maintain a bicycle but do offer our experience on repair or replacement intervals as follows:

Tires (clincher): Cord failure after 300 to 4000 miles, depending upon the tire. For longer mileage at lower friction levels, buy high-pressure tires and keep them inflated to rated pressures.

Chain: Lubricate often with special chain lubricants or with popular pressure spray-can lubricants. Lubricate after every wet ride. With care, chains will last 3000 to 4000 miles.

Chain Wheels: Replace when visibly worn or when a new chain will not run smoothly under power. Front chain wheels can be expected to run 12,000 miles (aluminum alloy) to 20,000 miles (steel). Rear chain wheels are good for 1000 to 10,000 miles, depending upon usage.

Bearings: Properly hardened and maintained bearings will last almost indefinitely when given periodic cleaning and lubrication. Sealed bearings are popular for their lack of required maintenance.

General Maintenance: Give the bicycle a complete overhaul once a year "whether it needs it or not." This will not preclude breakdowns on a ride but may make them less frequent. Every once in a while everything seems to go wrong at once. If the riders are good enough bicycle mechanics and are well enough prepared, a trip can almost always be finished with only minor handicaps. Unless a "higher class" bicycle is in the plans, don't give up in disgust. If the frame is intact, a few new parts and a bit of effort will produce a smooth-running bicycle again. The bicyclists who learn to maintain, adjust, and repair their own bicycles under all conditions will have operational bicycles more of the time and be able to enjoy the tours more, knowing that, come what may, they will make it under their own power. Learn how.

Now that the reader has suffered through the boring details of tour scouting, been preached at, and been admonished to do this and that, here's hoping that he or she enjoys touring these rides in northwest Washington.

ERIN and BILL WOODS

SAFETY CONSIDERATIONS

Safety is an important concern in all outdoor activities. No guidebook can alert you to every hazard or anticipate the limitations of every reader, so the descriptions in this book are not representations that a particular trip is safe for your party. When you take a trip, you assume responsibility for your own safety. Some of the trips described in this book may require you to do no more than look both ways before crossing the street; on others, more attention to safety may be required due to terrain, traffic, weather, the capabilities of your party, or other factors. Keeping informed on current conditions and exercising common sense are the keys to a safe, enjoyable outing. On all trips, be sure to wear a helmet and urge your companions to do so as well.

Additionally, many of the lands in this book may be subject to development and/or change of ownership. Conditions may have changed since this book was written, making your use of some of these routes unwise. Always check for current conditions, respect posted private property signs, and avoid confrontations with property owners and managers.

U.S.–CANADA
INTERNATIONAL GROUP

A listing of bicycle tours of western Washington would not be complete without inclusion of some of the more scenic routes of our neighbors to the north. The Fraser River delta country, fashioned by 50 million years of glaciation, siltation, and flooding, offers many miles of flat, low-traffic roads through fertile delta farmland. At the edges of the valley, mountains rise steeply and offer challenging hills to climb for back-country scenery.

In addition to agricultural and scenic values, the river furnishes a transportation artery. In the early nineteenth century, the Hudson's Bay Company established trading posts along the river to the upper limits of navigation at Fort Langley. Transportation for logging and shipping industries is still an important river function. Industry, commerce, and cities have grown up along the river, with residential communities spreading inland on both sides. The expansion of these functions has been limited in agricultural areas by the 1973 British Columbia Land Commission Act, which restricts removal of farmland from crop production for any other use without strong justification. This has the effect of preserving rural roads for enjoyable cycling.

Unusual cultural features apparent to the cyclist in British Columbia include tiered, locker-type mailboxes in green steel cabinets at road intersections. Residences display a wide range of architectural styles, from Spanish arch-and-stucco to pillared southern mansion. Concrete serpents and lions guard the doorways. Some public schools, on the other hand, are designed not unlike army barracks.

Along the international boundary stand numbered survey monuments with inscriptions commemorating the U.S.–Canadian boundary treaty and survey dates. In some areas along the border, a monument and a few feet of grass are all that separate parallel roads in the two countries. The observant bicyclist will spot several of the monuments on the international tours in this book.

When touring in British Columbia, cyclists are seldom far from a supply of food. The corner grocery store is an institution to be found at close intervals along almost every route. The bakeries in each town are sought out for high-energy bicycle fuel. When buying food, however, bear in mind that carrying oranges uneaten across the border into the United States is a "No-No." Other customs hang-ups on both sides include firearms and booze. Anti-dog sprays ("Halt" or "Dog Shield") may be confiscated when crossing into Canada. Some form of identification, such as an automobile driver's license, a birth certificate, or naturalization papers, should be carried, although it is seldom asked for. With these simple precautions, crossing the U.S.–Canadian border by bicycle is pleasantly easy and rapid. Take any one or all of these tours, and enjoy the title of International Bicycle Tourist.

55 BLAINE– POINT ROBERTS

STARTING POINT: Blaine, Whatcom County. Take exit 276 (Blaine–Peace Arch Park) from I-5 and turn left toward Blaine at end of exit road. Go under I-5 and bear right on Marine Drive by marine warning flag tower toward Blaine Harbor Marina. Park in marina parking area.

DISTANCE: Total, 95 miles: first day, 51 miles; second day, 44 miles.
TERRAIN: Hilly, some flat.
TOTAL CUMULATIVE ELEVATION GAIN: 2300 feet: first day, 1280 feet; second day, 1020 feet.
RECOMMENDED TIME OF YEAR: May through September.

RECOMMENDED STARTING TIME: 9:30 A.M. from Blaine.
ALLOW: 2 days.
POINTS OF INTEREST
Whatcom County's Lighthouse Marine Park
George C. Reifel Migratory Bird Sanctuary

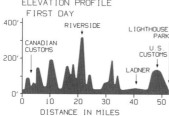

Low-traffic backroad route finding between Blaine, Washington, and Point Roberts, Washington, is not easy. Twelve miles of Puget Sound, 25 miles of highway, or 50 miles of Canadian backroads separate the two Whatcom County communities lying along the 49th parallel. The bicycle route chosen is long and devious to avoid the very heavy traffic on the main roads.

The pleasant rural atmosphere includes dairy and beef cattle herds grazing the green fields near Hazelmere, truck farms specializing in produce that thrives in the black soil along the Nicomekl River, small suburban farms hugging the hillsides, and corn, peas, and beans flourishing on the delta farmland near Ladner.

Small corner grocery stores at convenient points along the route provide welcome snacks. The aroma of delicious pastries acts as a homing signal and entices the bicyclist to a bakery in Tsawwassen.

Bird life abounds—herons and ducks of many varieties, northern harriers, swallows, and robins. Big, white snowy owls dot the winter landscape in years of scarce lemming supply to the north. For those bicycle tourists who are also bird buffs, the George C. Reifel Migratory Bird Sanctuary on Westham Island near Ladner supplies a fascinating diversion.

Magnificent views of the B.C. mountain ranges to the north and Mt. Baker to the south present themselves along the route in clear weather.

Whatcom County's Lighthouse Park at Point Roberts is the nominal overnight destination of this tour. A motel in Tsawwassen offers alternative housing for those who like to travel light. Sweeping views from the tall observation tower in Lighthouse Park include purse seiners swinging in close to shore to place their nets as they race the advancing schools of salmon, and ferryboats plying the Strait of Georgia between Vancouver Island and the mainland, their lights twinkling across the waters until late at night. Romping, barking sea lions and pods of killer whales occasionally entertain in the waters off Point Roberts.

Near Tsawwassen, long unit trains rumble across the landscape heading for Roberts Bank Superport, carrying coal from eastern British Columbia to be loaded on ships headed for Japan. Bicyclists must cross the train tracks several times and caution is advised. Industrial traffic will be encountered west of Port Mann along the Fraser River, but a marked bikeway, glimpses of wildlife, waterscapes, and interesting boat activity ameliorate the negative aspects.

On the return trip the communities of Boundary Bay, Crescent Beach, and White Rock cater to the summer tourist trade. Broad, sandy beaches and sparkling waterscapes beckon the city dwellers from the north. Delta farmland gives way to hillside residential areas at the edges of the valley. This ride offers widely varying scenery and habitat.

MILEAGE LOG

FIRST DAY

0.0   Blaine Harbor Marina parking lot. Head east on **Marine Drive**.

0.4   Turn left on **Peace Portal Drive** and go under I-5. Now on **D Street**.

1.2   Turn left on **State Route 543**, go up over small hill, and continue down past U.S. Customs. Stop and report at Canadian Customs, then proceed north on **B.C. 15 (176 Street)**.

2.5   Turn right on **8 Avenue** by Campbell River Store.

3.5 Turn left on **184 Street** (**Halls Prairie Road**). Proceed north through rolling farmland. Pass Hazelmere Market at 4.4, cross Nicomekl River at 8.2 and railroad tracks at 9.1, then start uphill. At 9.6 cross No. 10 Highway (56 Avenue) and enter Cloverdale; and at 11.2 cross Fraser Highway (B.C. 1). At 11.3 Clayton Community Park is 0.2 mile right on 70 Avenue.

12.6 Turn left on **80 Avenue** as 184 Street ends.

12.9 Turn sharp right on **Harvie Road**.

13.5 Turn left on **184 Street**.

14.6 Turn left on **92 Avenue**.

14.9 Turn right on **182 Street**, which bears left as it is diverted by freeway and changes name to **96 Avenue**.

16.1 Turn right on **176 Street**. At 16.4 cross Canada 1 (Trans-Canada Highway) on an overpass. Pedestrian walkway, separated from roadway by a barricade, may be used to avoid traffic.

16.6 Turn left on **100 Avenue**, which shortly is renamed **Barnston Drive**. Road bends right at 17.6 and is renamed **168 Street**.

17.9 Turn left on **104 Avenue**. Grocery store at this corner.

18.9 Turn right on **160 Street** at freeway interchange.

19.3 Turn left at stop sign on **108 Avenue**. Road bends right at 20.0 and becomes **154 Street**.

20.3 Turn left on **110 Avenue**. Almost immediately, turn left toward 108 Avenue at stop sign on busy thoroughfare and cross over freeway. Traffic merges from freeway on right; stop and wait for traffic to clear from both exit lanes before crossing.

20.7 Bear right with **B.C. 99A** and **B.C. 1A** (**108 Avenue**) as 152 Street intersects. This is a busy, four-lane highway.

21.3 Turn right on **148 Street** at the traffic light and head downhill.

21.7 Bear left with **Wallace Drive** as Ellendale Drive goes right at a five-way stop. Continue downhill with thoroughfare as its name changes to **Surrey Road**. Good views of Port Mann Bridge.

22.5 Bear left into Port Mann on **116A Avenue** from Surrey Drive. An asphalt-surfaced road leads past an A-frame gate into an undeveloped park on the left at mile 22.6.

22.7 Turn left on **King Road** and climb steep hill as 116A Avenue continues uphill to a gas turbine emergency electrical power plant, which can be seen from Port Mann. Bear right with King Road at fork and descend the hill. Roadway swings left at bottom of hill and becomes **116 Avenue**. Cafes at miles 24.2 and 25.6. The road bends left at mile 25.2 and is renamed **Industrial Avenue**.

25.9 Turn right on **112 Street** at stop sign, then immediately left on **Bridge Road**. Continue under railroad trestle and across railroad tracks.

26.3 Turn right on **Old Yale Road** at stop sign, go under a railroad trestle, then turn left on **Timberland Road**.

26.8 Turn left on **Tannery Road**. Cross two sets of railroad tracks.

27.2 Turn right at yield sign on **Scott Road**, which shortly bends left and becomes **120 Street**. Crank up a short hill.

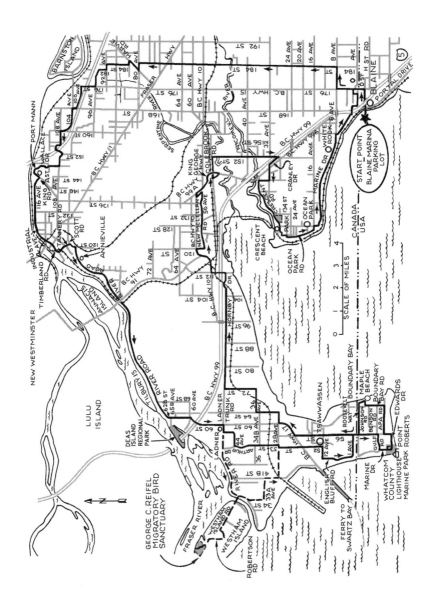

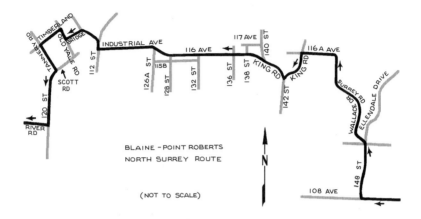

BLAINE – POINT ROBERTS
NORTH SURREY ROUTE

(NOT TO SCALE)

27.7 Turn right on **River Road**. Bear left at stop sign at mile 28.7 and continue with River Road as a major roadway merges from the right. Continue through community of Annieville at 29.6 (grocery, cafe) and along the Fraser River. Approximately five miles of improved shoulder relieve the traffic pressure. Cross railroad tracks and go under the B.C. 91 bridge at 31.3. Road bends away from river at 36.6 and becomes **62B Street**. Deas Island Regional Park appears on the right at mile 36.9; picnic areas, restrooms. swimming, group camp. Cross B.C. 99 on an overpass at mile 38.2 and continue on **B.C. 17 (60 Street)**. Hazardous merging traffic on right.

39.4 Turn right on **B.C. 10 (Ladner Trunk Road)**.

39.8 Turn left on **57 Street** at traffic light. 57 Street is blocked to automobile traffic, but a pedestrian lane circumvents the barricade. *Note: To visit the George C. Reifel Migratory Bird Sanctuary, continue on Ladner Trunk Road, 47A Avenue, River Road West, Westham Island Road, and Robertson Road, following signs to the refuge. Upon recrossing bridge from Westham Island, turn right on River Road West, bear left on 34 Street (Mason Road), left on 33A Avenue (Lewis Road), right on 41B Street, and left on 28 Avenue (Morley Road) to rejoin the regular route at mile 42.8 with a right turn on 52 Street. This side trip adds 10.6 miles to the route.*

40.2 Bear right on **44th Avenue**; left is marked to Ladner Municipal Services.

40.8 Turn left on **Arthur Drive** as 44th Avenue ends.

42.8 Turn right on **28 Avenue** as thoroughfare turns left, then turn left on **52 Street** and pass fruit stand.. At 44.1 cross B.C. 17, pass a golf course, and continue up a steep hill on 52 Street into Tsawwassen's residential district.

45.0 Turn right on **12 Avenue** as 52nd Street ends. *Note: Tsawwassen motels, cafes, and shops are left on 12 Avenue 0.5 mile.*

45.5 Turn left on **English Bluff Road**.

46.9 Turn left on **1 Avenue** as English Bluff Road is marked No Exit.

47.9 Turn right on **56 Street** by Diefenbaker Park.

48.1 Check in at U.S. Customs, cross border, and continue south on **Tyee Drive**. Grocery store on left at mile 49.2 is the last source of supplies before Lighthouse Marine Park.

49.2 Turn right on **Gulf Road**.

49.9 Turn left on **Marine Drive**. The Breakers Inn here offers food service.

50.6 Lighthouse Marine Park entrance. Boardwalk and picnic areas to the right, camping area on the left.

SECOND DAY

0.0 Leave Lighthouse Marine Park and turn right on **Marine Drive**, which bends left and becomes **Edwards Drive**. Road turns left at mile 0.6 by marina.

1.1 Turn right on **APA Road** from Tyee Drive. *Note: Route may be shortened 2.6 miles by continuing straight on Tyee Drive through customs to Tsawwassen.*

2.6 Turn left on **Boundary Bay Road**. Rural cycling through country lanes. Peaceful wooded roadsides with occasional houses. Coast down around a bend and into Boundary Bay.

4.0 Bear right on **Elm Street** in Boundary Bay as Meadow Lane goes left at bottom of hill.

4.1 Turn left on **Bayview Drive** and cycle along the water. Road bends left along border at 4.2 and is renamed **Roosevelt Way**.

5.7 Turn right on **Tyee Drive** through Canadian customs and continue downhill on **56 Street** into Tsawwassen. Cafes, bakery, and ice creamery at mile 7.3.

8.6 Bear right on **B.C. 17** through open delta country.

9.6 Turn right on **28th Avenue** just before B.C. 17 rises on a bridge over the railroad tracks.

10.1 Turn left on **64th Street** as 28th Avenue ends. At 10.5 cross railroad tracks. The 90-car, double-header unit trains run these tracks daily. That many hopper cars loaded with coal are not about to stop for you, so keep out of their way.

11.1 Turn right on **36 Avenue**. Cross railroad tracks again at 11.6.

12.1 Turn left on **72 Street** (**Benson Road**) as 36 Avenue ends. Cross railroad tracks at 13.1.

13.6 Turn right on **Ladner Trunk Road** (**B.C. 10**), a busy road with gradually narrowing shoulder. Endure it for three miles.

16.4 Turn right on **Hornby Drive** at traffic light as Ladner Trunk Road swings left across B.C. 99 on an overpass. Delta Air Park Restaurant right on 104 Street at mile 17.7. After two miles Hornby Drive swings left under railroad trestle and then right again.

18.8 Turn left on **112th Street** (**Oliver Road**) as Hornby Drive ends. Cross freeway on an overpass.

19.3 Turn right on **Ladner Trunk Road** (**B.C. 10**).

20.7 Turn right on **120 Street** at top of hill. Road bends left and becomes **New McLellan Road** at mile 21.0 and **56 Avenue** at mile 21.7.

23.6 Swing left with thoroughfare on **140 Street** and turn right on **No. 10 Highway**.

23.8 Bear right and downhill on **B.C. 99A** (**King George Highway**) across railroad overpass.

24.9 Turn right at bottom of hill and loop around on old roadway.

25.1 Turn right on **Colebrook Road** and go under B.C. 99A.

25.9 Turn right on **152 Street** as Colebrook Road turns to gravel.

28.8 Cross freeway (B.C. 99) on an overpass, then make a hard right turn on **Cranley Drive**. Road bears left at 29.0 and becomes **32 Avenue**.

29.2 Bear right with 32 Avenue as 32 Avenue Diversion continues on to traffic light. Cross King George Highway (B.C. 99A) at stop sign at mile 29.3. A historical marker indicates route of Semiahmoo Heritage Trail.

29.9 Turn right on **144 Street** at four-way stop.

30.3 Turn left at bottom of hill on **Crescent Road** as 144 Street ends. Canadian Museum of Flight and Transportation at mile 31.6. At 32.2 a sign points left to Crescent Park; picnic tables, shelters, restrooms.

32.8 Cross 128 Street and immediately bear left on **28 Avenue** toward Ocean Park. Road bends left and becomes **126 Street**.

33.2 Turn right on **27 Avenue**, then left on **124B Street**.

33.5 Turn right on **25 Avenue**, then turn left on **124 Street**. Road is renamed **Ocean Park Road**. Road bends left at 34.9 and becomes **16 Avenue**.

35.1 Turn right on **128 Street** by Ocean Park Shopping Centre.

35.4 Turn left on **Marine Drive**. At mile 36.4 enter White Rock. Descend on Marine Drive to beach level. At 36.7 the railroad divides the roadway from the beach but there is plenty of beach access. Grocery stores, cafes here. Go over a hill and return to beach level at 38.8; groceries, cafes. At 39.2 turn the corner and crank uphill out of White Rock; motels.

39.6 Turn right over the Campbell River on the Semiahmoo Footbridge as Stayte Road goes left. Continue two miles on the other side on **Beach Road**.

40.9 Cross the freeway by the north end of Canadian Customs, turn right along east shoulder, and turn left on **Peace Park Drive**. Continue on **Zero Avenue** past Peace Arch Park.

41.7 Turn left on **172 Street** as Zero Avenue is marked No Access.

41.9 Turn right on **2 Avenue**.

42.4 Turn right on **B.C. 15** (**176 Street**) at stop sign as 2 Avenue ends, and report through U.S. Customs. Bear right at 12 Street Exit Only sign and continue uphill on **12 Street**.

42.9 Turn right on **D Street** in Blaine.

43.7 Go under I-5 and bear right by marine warning flag tower on **Marine Drive**.

44.1 Back to the starting point at Blaine Harbor Marina parking lot.

56   BLAINE–FORT LANGLEY

STARTING POINT: Blaine, Whatcom County. Take exit 276 (Blaine–Peace Arch Park) from I-5 and turn left toward Blaine at end of exit road. Go under I-5 and bear right on Marine Drive toward Blaine Harbor Marina by marine warning flag tower. Park in marina parking area.

DISTANCE: 58 miles.
TERRAIN: Moderate to hilly.
TOTAL CUMULATIVE ELEVATION GAIN: 1250 feet.
RECOMMENDED TIME OF YEAR: All but inclement winter periods.
RECOMMENDED STARTING TIME: 9 A.M.
ALLOW: 6 to 8 hours; 1 day or overnight: camping, motel, or B&B.
POINTS OF INTEREST
Site of original Fort Langley
Fort Langley National Historical Park
Farm Machinery Museum
Centennial Museum
Telegraph Trail

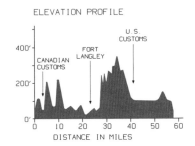

The highlight of this tour is Canada's Fort Langley National Historical Park. Established in 1827, Fort Langley was once an important trading post of the Hudson's Bay Company. By 1846 the fort was exporting several thousand barrels of salted salmon a year. It shipped food to Russian settlements in Alaska, cranberries to San Francisco, and hemp to England. Surrounded by a massive log palisade, the rustic fort sits on a hill by the bank of the Fraser River at what was, in those days, the upper limit of navigation. The park is open daily from 10 A.M. to 5 P.M. Inside the fort, officers' quarters, mess hall, commissary, and blacksmith shop are arranged around the square. Various workshops are operated by local craftsmen during the summer months. Neatly mowed green lawns extend within and without the fort; occasional bits of evidence indicate that the lawn mowers also bear wool. Farm implements, trapper supplies, staple foods, furs, and leather goods are exhibited in the commissary. A well-organized historical display utilizes the two floors of the officers' quarters. Ladies in period dress operate the registration table.

The bicycle route from Blaine covers many miles of hill-and-dale riding. Dairy farms occupy the valleys; upland farms harvest acres of strawberries, potatoes, and filbert nuts. Horses gallop along the fences, never quite sure what to make of the quiet, two-wheeled riders; conversation helps to reassure them.

A cedar lumber mill scents the air with aromatic odors near Port Kells. A few miles up the river, a large sign announces the presence of Imasco Lime Co. Ltd. Long freight trains roll along the north bank of the Fraser, signaling their approach with resonant, echoing blasts of their air horns. Opossums meander across the fields, tempting fare for large red-tailed hawks perched in the trees. Numerous swallows attack the airborne insect population, while great blue herons fly up from their favorite frog ditches.

After returning to the United States at the Lynden border crossing, the route skirts the edge of Whatcom County's rich agricultural land on the way back to Blaine. An obscure frontage road avoids busy traffic as it enters Blaine by the back door.

MILEAGE LOG

0.0 Blaine Harbor Marina parking lot. Head east on **Marine Drive**.

0.4 Turn left on **Peace Portal Drive**, go under I-5, and continue on **D Street**.

1.2 Turn left on **State Route 543**, go over a small hill, and continue down past U.S. Customs. Stop and report at Canadian Customs, then proceed north on **B.C. 15 (176 Street)**.

2.5 Turn right on **8 Avenue** by Campbell River Store.

3.5 Turn left on **184 Street**. Proceed north through rolling farmland past Hazelmere Market at 4.5, across Nicomekl River at 8.3 and railroad tracks at 9.1, then start uphill. At 9.6 cross No. 10 Highway and enter Cloverdale, and at 10.1 cross 60 Avenue. Three sets of polyphase power lines pass overhead. At 11.3 cross Fraser Highway (B.C. 1). At 11.4 Clayton Community Park is 0.2 mile right on 70 Avenue.

12.6 Turn right on **80 Avenue** as 184 Street ends.

13.1 Turn left on **188 Street** as a hill looms ahead on 80 Avenue.

14.0 Bear right on **Harvie Road** as 188 Street ends. Grocery at 88 Avenue crossing at mile 14.2.

14.8 Cross Trans-Canada Highway on an overpass and proceed north on **192 Street**, crossing 96 Avenue at mile 15.3; cafe.

15.6 Cross railroad tracks and turn right on **98A Avenue** as 192 Street ends. Follow thoroughfare as it is renamed **197 Street**, **101 Avenue**, **199B Street**, and **100A Avenue**.

17.1 Turn left on **201 Street**.

17.4 Turn right on **102B Avenue**.

18.2 Turn left on **208 Street** as 102B Avenue ends. Cross a levee.

18.8 Turn right on **Allard Crescent** as 208 Street is marked No Exit. Continue through forest and pastureland, then along the Fraser River. Derby Reach Regional Park, on the left at 20.2, offers a picnic area, running water, washrooms, and campsites along the river. A triangular, prismatic granite monument, guarded by a chain link fence on the left at mile 21.5, marks the site of the first permanent settlement in the lower Fraser Valley, the original Fort Langley. After passing the monument the road turns inland, undulating through rolling pastureland.

22.8 Turn left on **McKinnon Crescent** as Allard Crescent ends.

23.2 Turn left at wye and continue on **96 Avenue**. Angled railroad crossing at 23.7.

24.3 Turn left on **Glover Road** in Fort Langley. Groceries, restaurants. Bakery is right 0.2 mile in shopping center along Glover.

24.5 Turn right on **Mavis Avenue** and pedal uphill to Fort Langley National

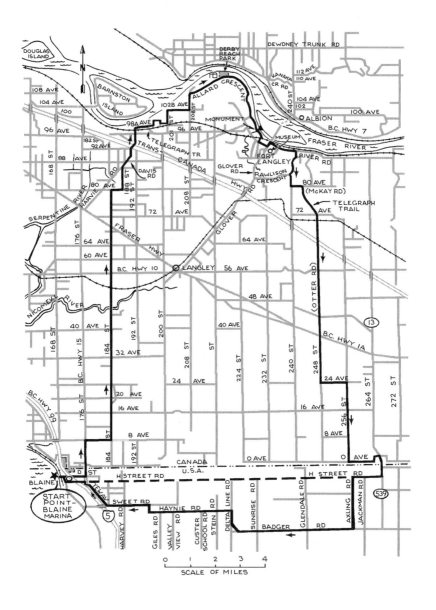

Historical Park. Centennial Museum and Farm Machinery Museum are just to the right on King Street. They are well worth a visit.

24.7   Fort Langley Museum. Park bicycles in the rack provided, and for a nominal fee, take a tour of the fort. Picnic tables by the parking lot make this an ideal spot for a picnic lunch.

24.9   Leave the fort parking lot, then make a sharp right turn from Mavis onto **River Road**. Bicycle along the river, pass below the fort, and emerge into open farmland.

25.9   Turn right on **240 Street** just after crossing acute-angled railroad tracks. The road bends left at mile 26.3 and is renamed **88 Avenue**.

26.7   Turn left on **240 Street** as Rawlison Crescent goes on. Crank uphill alongside a creek.

27.3   Turn left on **80 Avenue (McKay Road)**.

27.7   Turn right on **Telegraph Trail**. The road wanders in and out among old homesteads. Whistle down a steep hill, cross a creek, and climb a moderate grade on the other side. Telegraph Trail section ends as route crosses 72 Avenue at mile 29.0. Continue south on **248 Street (Otter Road)**, crossing railroad tracks at 29.2, the Trans-Canada Highway at 29.9, and 56 Avenue at 31.0; Four-Way General Store at corner. Cross 54 Avenue at mile 31.2 past Village Market on right, and B.C. 1A (Fraser Highway) at 33.4.

35.1   Turn left on **24 Avenue** and freewheel down a long hill.

36.1   Turn right on **256 Street**.

39.1   Turn left (east) on **0 Avenue** as 256 Street ends. The cleared strip of land on hill to the east marks the U.S.–Canadian border. Monument #19 alongside the road at 39.9 also marks the border. 0 Avenue is also called **Boundary Road**.

40.5   Turn right on **Diversion Road (B.C. 13)**. Report at U.S. Customs and continue south on **Guide Meridian Road (State Route 539)**.

41.2   Turn right on **H Street Road**.

42.5   Turn left on **Axling Road** as H Street Road starts uphill. *Note: Tour may be shortened by 3.7 miles by continuing on H Street Road to Blaine. Adds 400 feet elevation gain.*

44.5   Turn right on **W. Badger Road** as Axling Road ends. Pass grocery at mile 48.3.

49.2   Bear right at wye with thoroughfare on **Delta Line Road**.

49.7   Bear left at wye with thoroughfare on **Haynie Road**, which bends right at mile 52.7 and is renamed **Statvolt Road**.

53.4   Bend left at wye with thoroughfare on **Sweet Road**.

55.2   Turn right on **Yew Avenue** just before Hughes Road crosses I-5.

56.1   Turn left across State Route 543 on **Boblett Street**. Road bends right by elementary school and joins **Mitchell Avenue**.

56.6   Turn left on **H Street Road** as Mitchell Avenue ends. Cross I-5 on overpass.

57.1   Turn right on **Peace Portal Drive** as H Street ends in downtown Blaine.

57.3   Turn left on **Marine Drive** by marine warning flag tower.

57.7   End of ride, back at Blaine Harbor Marina parking lot.

57   HARRISON HOT SPRINGS

STARTING POINT: Huntingdon, British Columbia. Take exit 255 from I-5 in Bellingham. Head east on Mt. Baker Highway (State Route 542). Cross the Nooksack River and turn left at Nugent's Corner on State Route 9 to Sumas. Cross border and park cars along First Avenue just east of Canadian Customs. Public washrooms available at end of Canadian Customs building.

DISTANCE: Total, 95 miles: first day, 50 miles; second day, 45 miles.
TERRAIN: Flat to moderate.
TOTAL CUMULATIVE ELEVATION GAIN: 1360 feet: first day, 960 feet; second day, 400 feet.
RECOMMENDED TIME OF YEAR: Any time of year.

RECOMMENDED STARTING TIME: 9 A.M. from Sumas.
ALLOW: 2 days.
POINTS OF INTEREST
Westminster Abbey
Kilby Museum Provincial Historical Park
Bridal Veil Falls Provincial Park

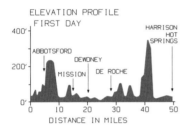

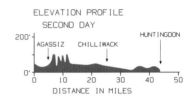

This two-day loop tour to Harrison Hot Springs takes cycle tourists along the base of foothills and through the broad, fertile delta of the Fraser River. Several points of interest near the route entice the rider on short side trips. Unless an extra day is allotted specifically for Harrison, however, not enough time will be available to enjoy these diversions and still appreciate the many attractions of this hot springs resort village. Accommodations in or near Harrison include tenting, recreational vehicle, bed-and-breakfast, hotel, and motel facilities. Advance reservations are recommended.

At the Sumas–Huntingdon border crossing, sounds of railway switchyard activity echo across the valley. The route from Huntingdon leaves the highway immediately and meanders north to the Fraser River on little-used side roads. Abbotsford, the first town along the route, is acclaimed for its annual August International Air Show. In the valley beyond, cows and calves stare from roadside fields.

The bridge across the Fraser to Mission City provides the cyclist with a sidewalk separated from automobile traffic by a high concrete barrier. It tends to accumulate broken glass, however, and care must be taken to avoid tire trouble. Strict attention to bicycle driving is necessary through Mission City. As the route heads east on a wide paved shoulder along the Lougheed Highway, vistas open up. Farmland stretches across the valley to steep hills that rise to catch the banks of fog floating up from the river, and snow-capped peaks stand guard at the east end of the valley. Westminster Abbey stands atop a hill and surveys the valley from the west.

A six-mile diversion on Nicomen Island offers closer observation of dairy farms; a boy on a bicycle herds cows down a narrow road. Swallows swoop around the barns, farm buildings, and fences covered with blackberries. Blue-winged teal paddle along a small slough while red-winged blackbirds sing and flash their epaulettes. Flower and vegetable gardens flourish in the rich soil.

Many varieties of wildflowers bloom along the roadsides near Lake Errock, adding touches of color for the summer bicyclist.

A side trip to Kilby Museum Provincial Historical Park presents a peek at the history of the local Harrison–Fraser River areas. Camping and picnicking areas on the sandy beach among the cottonwood trees at Kilby Park along Harrison Bay tempt a longer stay.

A climb up the shoulder of Mt. Agassiz brings the bicyclist to a spectacular viewpoint overlooking the broad, fertile delta of the Fraser River. After an exhilarating ride down to the valley floor, bicycles are diverted over backroads into Harrison Hot Springs at the south end of 30-mile-long Harrison Lake. Rugged, snow-capped, forest-clad peaks of the coast range surround and reflect in the clear, blue waters of the lake. Gold-rush prospectors discovered the bubbling 140°F hot springs that flow into the west side of the lake about a mile from downtown Harrison. Water from the springs is piped into town for use in the several pools and baths at the Harrison Hotel and also in the public swimming pool. An unpaved trail leading from the hotel continues past the springs and over the ridge to where the Harrison River begins its short trip down to Harrison Bay to join the Fraser River.

A number of fine restaurants, snack bars, a candy shop, and a grocery store offer tempting choices. Facilities for fishing, hunting, boating, golfing, and riding are also available. The optional four-mile trip to Sasquatch Provincial Park gives additional views of the beautiful lake setting.

On the return trip, busy highway traffic may be encountered near Agassiz, noted for its annual Fall Fair and Corn Festival on a Saturday in mid-September. Hot, buttered corn-on-the-cob is available at the fair and at fruit stands along the highway. Once across the Fraser River, many tourists make a side trip to Bridal Veil Falls Provincial Park, where a trail through dense forest leads to the misty spray of the aptly named waterfall.

An intricate network of hop vines covers many acres along Camp River Road. The shallow, slowly moving slough supports cattails, lily pads, ducks, and herons. Corn grows tall near Chilliwack, the center of the vast agricultural empire of the Fraser River delta. An expansive city park, Saturday market, bakeries, and cafes in Chilliwack invite cyclists for a lunch stop.

Winds sweep up and down the broad Fraser Valley and curl around Mt. Vedder. Easterly afternoon winds propel bicyclists through flat farmland reclaimed from Sumas Lake by an extensive series of ditches and canals. A short stretch of road along the international boundary with its historic survey monuments, many of which were replaced in 1985 by shiny aluminum obelisks, heralds the return to the starting point in Huntingdon.

"Watch this!"

MILEAGE LOG

FIRST DAY

0.0   Parking area along 1st Avenue in Huntingdon, British Columbia, near Canadian Customs. Head east on **1st Avenue**.

0.1   Turn left on **B Street**.

0.2   Turn left on **4 Street** and cross Sumas Way (B.C. 11) and railroad tracks.

0.6   Bear right at wye on **Riverside Road**. At 2.6 the Trans-Canada Highway passes overhead.

3.6   Bear right on **W. Railway Street** as Riverside ends.

4.1   Turn right at traffic light on **Essendene Avenue** in Abbotsford. Cross railroad tracks, go through second traffic light, pass Old Age Pensioners building, and immediately turn left on **Cyril Street**.

4.2   Turn right on **Hazel Street** as Cyril Street ends.

4.6   Turn left on **Ash Street** toward Ledgeview Golf Course and pedal through a pleasant residential area.

4.8 Bear right on **Old Clayburn Road** and ride through Abbotsford's new suburbia. Continue on **Clayburn Road** as road is renamed at bottom of hill at mile 7.5.

8.6 Turn right on **Bell Road** and head north past farms and country homes. Jog right on **Township Line Road** at 9.0, then immediately left again on **Bell Road**. Cross railroad tracks at mile 10.8.

11.3 Turn left on **Page Road** as Bell Road ends.

12.2 Cross railroad tracks. Stop and turn left on **Riverside Road**.

12.5 Turn right onto bridge approach and merge with **B.C. 11**. Go through notch in curbing and use sidewalk on bridge over the Fraser River. Watch for broken glass.

13.6 Sidewalk ends. Go through notch to the shoulder of the roadway and coast down into Mission City.

14.3 Turn left on **Horne Street**.

14.4 Turn right up and over railroad overpass. Very steep approach.

14.6 Turn right with **B.C. 7 (Lougheed Highway)**. Busy traffic through here. *Note: At 14.9 a sign points left uphill toward Westminster Abbey on Stave Lake Street.* Route heads up mild grade, overlooking Fraser River and valley. Information Center on the left with public washrooms at 15.4. Hatzic Store on the left at 16.9. At mile 20.0, cross railroad tracks, turn right with highway, and pass Dewdney General Store and cafe (good pies). Cross Nicomen Slough at 20.2.

21.5 Turn right on **Nicomen Island Trunk Road**. This is the first through road to the right. Watch carefully for it. Follow along a small slough. Enjoy six miles of relaxing bicycle riding. Wild blackberries are delicious on warm summer days.

23.4 Turn right at small wye as Waring Road comes in from the left. No street sign.

24.1 Keep left as Howell Road forks right.

27.5 Turn right on **B.C. 7** as Nicomen Island Trunk Road ends. Recross Nicomen Slough at mile 28.1. Signs proclaim resting areas for swans; no hunting. At 28.3 cross railroad tracks, then turn corner with the highway at DeRoche (grocery, cafe) and head east again, passing Lake Errock at mile 32.4. Vertical, slabby, granite cliffs on the left at mile 34.9 support asters and stonecrop. Harrison Bay stretches off to the right. Cafes just before crossing the Harrison River at 36.3 on a rotary drawbridge dated 1956.

37.4 Kilby Museum Provincial Historical Park (free admission) is to the right 1.2 miles down Kennedy Road. Old general store, built up on pilings above the main flood level, houses an interesting collection of memorabilia. Campground on beach of Harrison Bay.

40.4 At the left-hand side of the road, fresh drinking water from Dec Creek Spring, commercialized by a bottled-water company, is very welcome on a warm summer day. Scenic overlook at 40.7. A British Columbia "stop of interest" plaque tells the story of the Fraser River delta below. Toilets, trash receptacles, and terrazzo-faced concrete tables invite picnickers. Take in the view, check your brakes, then whistle down the hill around the curves and into the valley below.

43.0 Turn left on **Sutherland Road**.

43.5 Turn right on **Humphrey Road** as Sutherland Road ends.

44.2 Turn left on **Cameron Road** past marshy pastures invaded by tules. Road bends right at 44.6 and becomes **McCallum Road**.

45.9 Turn left on **Hardy Road**. Road bends right and is renamed **Golf Road**. B&B at this corner.

47.4 Turn left on **B.C. 9** (**Hot Springs Road**). Busy traffic. Camping facilities on both sides of road after one mile.

49.6 Hot Springs Road ends by Hot Springs Pool at Esplanade Drive along the shore of Harrison Lake. Harrison Hotel is to left with the hot springs one mile beyond. Public swimming pool at this corner. Sasquatch Provincial Park is to the right, four miles around the lake.

SECOND DAY

0.0 From the shore of Harrison Lake in the town of Harrison Hot Springs, head south out of town on **Hot Springs Road (B.C. 9)**.

4.0 Turn left with **B.C. 9** and **B.C. 7** toward Agassiz. Continue through Agassiz on the combined highways. B&B lodging in Agassiz.

5.0 Turn right with B.C. 9 as B.C. 7 continues on. Cross railroad tracks.

6.4 Bear right with **B.C. 9** as B.C. 7 access road goes left. Cross the Fraser River. *Note: The Agassiz Bridge over the Fraser River and the long causeways on either end have no shoulders or sidewalk and may carry heavy traffic.*

8.2 Get into left-turn lane and turn left on **Rosedale Ferry Road**. *Note: For a visit to Bridal Veil Falls Provincial Park, continue straight through blinking light on B.C. 9, past Minter Gardens. Cross Trans-Canada Highway on an overpass and continue around cloverleaf to left on **Bridal Falls Road** to park entrance and then right and uphill on **Page Road**. Grocery and cafe. Return to Rosedale Ferry Road after visit.* Continue with **Ferry Road** as it turns left under B.C. 9.

9.9 Road name changes to **Camp River Road** as McGrath Road goes left. Proceed along a slough among trees. Road is narrow, winding, and scenic with almost no traffic. A made-to-order "bicycle path." Hop farm on left at 11.4.

15.0 Turn left on **Hope River Road** as Camp River Road ends and Kitchen Road goes right. Country homes give way to a residential district.

17.6 Turn left on **Young Road North** at a small wye as Hope River Road ends. Ride through center of Chilliwack; park, B&B, bakeries, and bicycle shop. At 20.1 go under Trans-Canada Highway and continue on **Chilliwack River Road**.

23.7 Turn right on **Promontory Road** as Chilliwack River Road ends.

24.3 Cross busy Vedder Road and continue on **Watson Road**.

25.5 Turn left on **Carter Road**.

26.0 Turn right on **Keith Wilson Road** as Carter ends.

30.4 Cross Vedder Canal and turn left on **Boundary Road**. Jog right on **No. 3 Road** at mile 31.3, then left again on **Boundary Road**. *Note: Yarrow Central Road goes left 1.2 miles to Yarrow at mile 31.8; city*

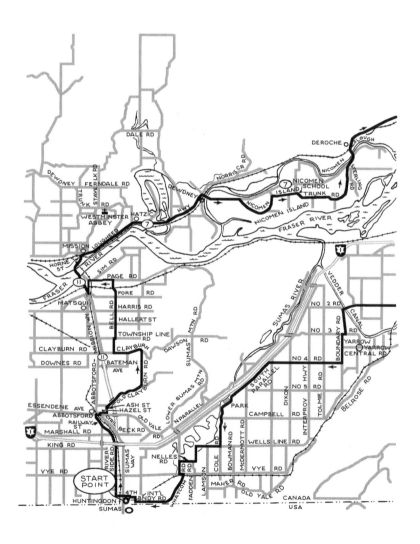

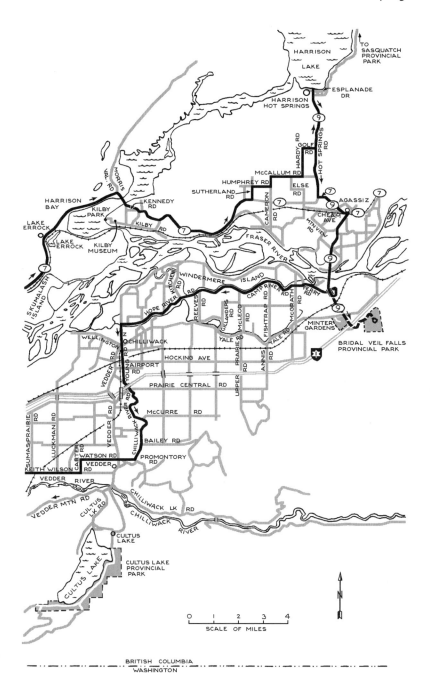

SCALE OF MILES

N

BRITISH COLUMBIA
WASHINGTON

29

park. deli, grocery, cafe. Enter the 33,000 acres of fertile farmland reclaimed from Sumas Lake.

32.3 Turn right on **No. 4 Road**.

35.4 Road bends left and becomes **South Parallel Road**.

37.2 Bear left on **Cole Road** as a freeway access goes right by a highway rest park.

37.6 Bear right into Hougen Park. Picnic tables, washrooms. Swimming in Sumas River for those who do not mind the sluggish, algae-colored water.

38.0 Pedal out of park in same direction. Now on **Cole Road**.

39.2 Turn right on **Wells Line Road**, following as it bends left at 40.2. Road bends right at 40.8 and is renamed **Nelles Road**. *Note: Dairy with great ice cream at this corner.*

41.2 Turn left on **Whatcom Road**.

41.8 Turn left on **Vye Road**, then right again on **Whatcom Road**. Road bends right and is renamed **International Boundary Road**. International Boundary Monument #34 at mile 42.0 commemorating Treaty of 1846. Monument #33 at 42.2, #32 at 43.1. Road bends right, then left, and is renamed **2 Avenue**.

44.6 Turn left on **B Street**.

44.7 Turn right on **First Avenue** and return to starting point.

"Any fresh fruit or vegetables?"

58 SUMAS VALLEY (Everson–Abbotsford)

STARTING POINT: City Park, Everson, Whatcom County. Take exit 256 from I-5 in Bellingham. Head north on State Route 539, then east on State Route 544 (East Pole Road) toward Everson. Take first left turn after crossing Nooksack River and follow road 0.2 mile to park entrance by sewage disposal facility. Park in south parking lot.

DISTANCE: 48 miles.
TERRAIN: Mostly flat.
TOTAL CUMULATIVE ELEVATION GAIN: 550 feet.
RECOMMENDED TIME OF YEAR: All seasons.
RECOMMENDED STARTING TIME: 9 A.M.
ALLOW: 6 hours.
POINTS OF INTEREST
U.S.–Canadian Boundary
Monuments

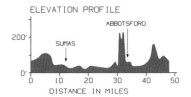

Between the Nooksack and Sumas rivers at their closest approach near Everson stands a divide roughly 15 feet high. The Nooksack continues west to empty into Puget Sound, while the waters of the Sumas meander sluggishly north to the Fraser River and thence west to the Strait of Georgia. The proximity of the two rivers supports the contention that the lower Nooksack is geologically an extension of the Fraser Valley. This bicycle tour traverses the U.S.–Canadian boundary in the valley of the Sumas River, starting from a park by the Nooksack and stopping for lunch at another small park in the heart of the Fraser delta farmland. Although this is basically a valley ride, occasional rolling hills on the edges of the valley provide adequate opportunity for vigorous exercise.

Stands of western white birch, typical of many Whatcom County areas, extend also into British Columbia and may be seen on hillsides near Abbotsford. In the Sumas River Waterfowl Refuge along Whatcom Road, a large old cedar snag provides a favored perch for the red-tailed hawk. Ducks of several varieties feed and nest in the sluggish river channel. History buffs will appreciate the informative legends on survey monuments along International Boundary Road.

Hougen Park, in an attractive setting along the Sumas River, provides a pleasant picnic lunch site on a summer day. In cold or inclement weather, however, the inns and cafes of Abbotsford may be more appealing. The several miles of hills separating Abbotsford from Hougen Park will generate a good appetite.

The route returns to Everson through glacially contoured uplands devoted to horse and cattle pasturage. A final, long downgrade comes to an end by the rodeo grounds at the northern edge of Everson's expansive riverfront park, just a few hundred yards from the tour's starting point.

MILEAGE LOG

0.0 Leave the city park on **Park Drive** and continue as it bends left and is renamed **West Main Street**. At 0.2 continue on **Main Street** as Everson Road goes right.

0.3 Turn right on **South Harkness Street**.

0.4 Turn left on **Lincoln Street** and proceed around a little park-playground.

0.5 Turn right on **South Washington Street** as Lincoln Street ends. Road bends left at 0.7, is renamed **Reeds Lane**, then bends right again as **Emerson Road**. Pass large dairy farm.

1.5 Emerson Road bends left and is renamed **Massey Road**. Now out into farmland with fields of raspberries, corn, and blueberries. At 2.2 cross railroad tracks, S.R. 9, and the slowly moving Sumas River and continue east on Massey Road. Woodlots of fir, birch, cedar, and some alder.

3.7 Turn left on **Goodwin Road** and ride up incline. At 4.0 cross creek and pass partially cleared stump ranches. An old schoolhouse gains a new lease on life as a community clubhouse at junction with South Pass Road at mile 4.7. Continue north through pastureland.

5.7 Turn right on **Sorenson Road** as Goodwin Road ends.

5.9 Turn left on **Telegraph Road** as Sorenson is marked Dead End. Cross Sumas River again at mile 6.9.

9.0 Go straight on **Hovel Road** as Telegraph turns right and Morgan Road goes left.

10.2 Turn left on **Rock Road** as Hovel Road ends. Rock Road changes name to **Front Street** as it enters Sumas.

10.4 Turn right on **Sumas Street** and cross a creek.

10.9 Turn left on **Garfield Street**, then right on **Cherry Street (State Route 9)**.

11.3 Pass through Canadian Customs and immediately turn right on **First Avenue** from C Street. Take next left turn on **B Street** as First goes on to dead end.

11.4 Turn right on **Second Avenue** and follow the road as it bends right, crosses railroad tracks, then bends left along the border and is renamed **International Boundary Road**. At 12.0, Monument #32 proclaims Treaty of 1846. Borderline established in 1857–61, surveyed and marked in 1903–07. Cross Sumas River just before road swings left through a waterfowl refuge along the river and is renamed **Whatcom Road**. Pipeline pumping station visible in the field to the right.

14.3 Cross railroad tracks, then turn right on **Vye Road** as Whatcom Road ends.

15.3 Turn right on **Lamson Road** and go under a railroad trestle.

15.8 Keep left on **Maher Road** as Lamson is marked No Exit. Road changes name to **Old Yale Road** at 16.5. Road snuggles up to hillside, bends north, ducks under a railroad trestle, and becomes **Marion Road**.

22.2 Turn left on **No. 5 Road**.

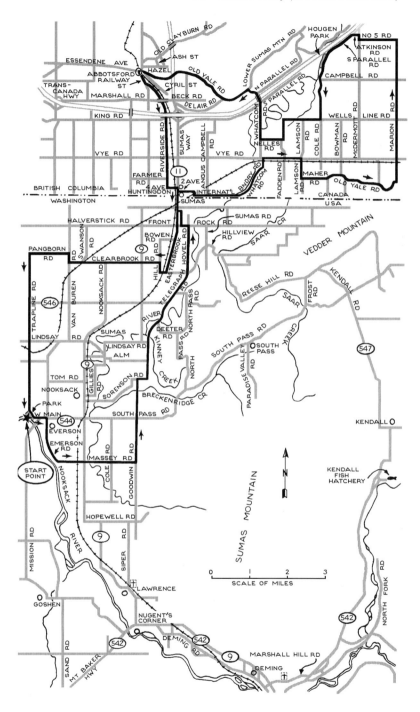

23.1   Turn right on **McDermott Road** as No. 5 Road ends.

23.3   Turn left on **Atkinson Road**, which bends left by freeway and becomes **South Parallel Road**.

24.1   Bear left on **Cole Road** as a freeway access goes right by a highway rest park.

24.5   Bear right into picturesque Hougen Park on the Sumas River. Picnic tables, swings, seesaws, green lawn, pit toilets, and change rooms for swimmers. Stop for a picnic lunch. Leave park and continue south on **Cole Road**.

26.0   Turn right on **Wells Line Road**, following it as it bends left at 27.0, then right again, and is renamed **Fadden Road** and **Nelles Road**.

28.1   Turn right on **Whatcom Road** as Nelles Road ends. Many raspberry vines. Cross Trans-Canada Highway on overpass at 29.2. Cross a creek and start up short, steep hill.

29.6   Turn left on **Lower Sumas Mountain Road** as Whatcom Road ends at top of hill. Glide downhill to valley floor, then pump uphill again.

30.3   Continue straight on **Old Yale Road** as Bel-Air Road goes left. Oceanspray and filbert trees overhang rocky bank. Reach a summit, then head downhill again on smooth-surfaced roadway. The road crests again in a residential area and heads downhill into Abbotsford, where it becomes **Essendene Avenue**.

33.0   Go through traffic light, cross railroad tracks, and turn left at second traffic light toward Sumas on **W. Railway Street**. Several restaurants and cafes available a block or two farther on Essendene.

34.0   Get into left-turn lane and turn left on **Riverside Road**. Go under Trans-Canada Highway at mile 34.5.

36.4   Bear left with main thoroughfare on **Fourth Avenue** and cross railroad tracks.

36.7   Turn right on **Sumas Way** (**B.C. 11**) and proceed through U.S. Customs. Continue south on **Cherry Street (State Route 9)** in Sumas.

37.6   Proceed straight on **Easterbrook Road** as S.R. 9 turns right on Bowen Road.

38.9   Turn right on **Morgan Road** as Easterbrook ends. Cross railroad tracks. Road bends right and becomes **Hill Road**.

39.3   Turn left on **Clearbrook Road**, cross S.R. 9 at mile 39.9, and continue west on Clearbrook Road over more railroad tracks at 41.6 and up a short rise.

41.8   Turn right on **Van Buren Road** and head uphill as Clearbrook ends.

42.1   Turn left on **Pangborn Road**.

43.0   Turn left on **Trapline Road** and head south through farmland.

47.1   Turn left on **Park Drive** as Trapline ends and Stickney Island Road goes right.

47.4   Turn right into park and back to the starting point.

59   PUGET SOUND–FRASER VALLEY INTERNATIONAL (PSFVI)

STARTING POINT: Parking along Admiral Street in Edmonds. Take exit 177 (State Route 104) when approaching from the south on I-5 or exit 181 (State Route 524) when approaching from I-5 north. Follow signs to the ferry terminal in Edmonds. Turn left on Dayton Street at signal by ferry ticket kiosk, cross railroad tracks, and bear left along Admiral Street.

DISTANCE: Total, 446 miles: first day, 45 miles; second day, 31 miles; third day, 46 miles; fourth day, 60 miles; fifth day, 47 miles; sixth day, 61 miles; seventh day, 47 miles; eighth day, 60 miles; ninth day, 49 miles.

TERRAIN: Mostly hilly, some flat.

TOTAL CUMULATIVE ELEVATION GAIN: 16,100 feet: first day, 2600 feet; second day, 800 feet; third day, 1800 feet; fourth day, 2200 feet; fifth day, 1300 feet; sixth day, 1500 feet; seventh day, 1200 feet; eighth day, 2200 feet; ninth day, 2500 feet.

RECOMMENDED TIME OF YEAR: May through September.

RECOMMENDED STARTING TIME: Catch early-morning ferry from Edmonds. On second day, take early-afternoon Blackball ferry from Port Angeles. Consult schedules.

ALLOW: 9 to 11 days.

POINTS OF INTEREST
First Day:
Port Gamble historic residences, store, and seashell museum

Second Day:
Olympic Game Farm
Dungeness Spit
Ediz Hook
Victoria tourist attractions
Third Day:
Sealand in Oak Bay
Fable Cottage
Butchart Gardens
Point Roberts Marine Park
Fourth Day:
Fort Langley museums
Fifth Day:
Stave Falls
Westminster Abbey
Kilby Museum
Harrison Hot Springs
Sixth Day:
Bridal Veil Falls Provincial Park
Minter Gardens
Seventh Day:
Chuckanut Drive
Eighth Day:
Coupeville blockhouse, canoes, and museum
Ebey's Landing and cemetery
Fort Casey
Ninth Day:
Old buildings in Langley

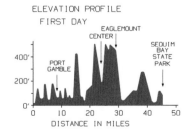

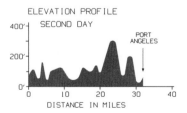

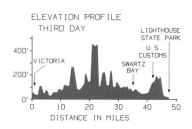

ELEVATION PROFILE
THIRD DAY

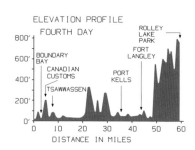

ELEVATION PROFILE
FOURTH DAY

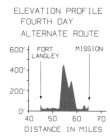

ELEVATION PROFILE
FOURTH DAY
ALTERNATE ROUTE

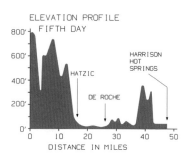

ELEVATION PROFILE
FIFTH DAY

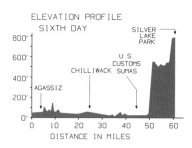

ELEVATION PROFILE
SIXTH DAY

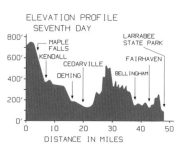

ELEVATION PROFILE
SEVENTH DAY

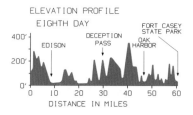

ELEVATION PROFILE
EIGHTH DAY

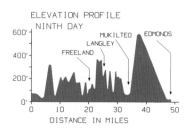

ELEVATION PROFILE
NINTH DAY

This tour was assembled in response to the demand for a major bicycle outing with a starting point in the vicinity of Seattle and available to that area's large urban population. Portions of several loop day rides described in the *Bicycling the Backroads* books are joined together with a few connecting links to produce a multi-day tour for the intermediate to advanced bicyclist. The long day mileages and the elevation gains presented are not recommended for the beginner.

The two high points of this tour are Victoria and Harrison Hot Springs, both major tourist attractions. Many cyclists have recommended allocations of an extra day for sightseeing in either one or both of these cities. The route has been chosen to utilize campgrounds wherever possible for overnight lodging and minimize costs to the cyclist. Backroads avoid the dense traffic situations while providing unusual scenic values. Hills, however, are part of the game.

This tour may be modified to include Seattle as a starting point, proceeding via Winslow and Agate Pass, and returning via Lowell, Bothell, and the Burke Gilman and Lake Union bicycle routes.

A synopsis of the tour is as follows:

First Day: Leave Edmonds, take ferry to Kingston, bicycle to historic Port Gamble. Cross Hood Canal Bridge, turn north on backroads to Eaglemount and west to U.S. 101 and the only cafe. Spend the night in Sequim Bay State Park.

Second Day: Head north on backroads past Olympic Game Farm. Views of Dungeness Spit, Mt. Angeles, open pastureland of Sequim area. Eventually forced out onto U.S. 101 for six miles; into Port Angeles for lunch. Take ferry across the Strait of Juan de Fuca to Victoria for an afternoon on the town. Stay overnight in Victoria's lodgings or bicycle north to Royal Oak Campground.

Third Day: After a leisurely ride along the marine drive of eastern Saanich Peninsula, cross to the western side on backroads. Ride up the west side of the peninsula to Swartz Bay to catch the Tsawwassen ferry. Stay overnight in Lighthouse Park on Point Roberts.

Fourth Day: After a short tour of Point Roberts, ride northeast to the Fraser River and follow its south bank to Fort Langley, site of an early Hudson's Bay post. Two museums and a replica of the fort to tour. Cross the Fraser on a small ferry and climb the northern slope to Rolley Lake Provincial Park.

Fifth Day: A quick descent to Stave Falls is followed by an equally steep but short ascent and scenic ride through rural countryside north of Mission. Pass the picturesque Westminster Abbey and descend to the Fraser Valley once more. A side road up Nicomen Island yields carefree cycling and interesting rural scenery. Kilby Museum, on a short side road, allows fascinating reminiscence of many decades. Early evening is spent soaking in Harrison Hot Springs pool.

Sixth Day: Cross the Fraser at Agassiz and follow backroads along sloughs to Chilliwack. Visit the spectacular Bridal Veil Falls Provincial Park. Cycle carefree through the flat, rich Fraser delta farmland to Sumas. Spend the evening and camp overnight at Whatcom County's Silver Lake Park.

Seventh Day: Miles of Whatcom County's rolling farms and forest lead to Lake Whatcom's north shore and Bellingham's Whatcom Falls Park. A short detour around Bellingham is followed by a climb up Chuckanut Drive, with views of Puget Sound, to Larrabee State Park for the overnight camp.

Eighth Day: After a pleasant traverse of the flat Skagit delta, the route goes on to Fidalgo Island, Deception Pass, Oak Harbor, historic Coupeville, Ebey's Landing and cemetery, and Fort Casey.

Ninth Day: Follow side roads down Whidbey Island to a bowl of delicious clam chowder at Freeland Cafe, on to Langley, Clinton, and the Mukilteo ferry. A short ride along Olympic View Drive completes the tour at Edmonds, the starting point.

MILEAGE LOG

FIRST DAY

- **0.0** Edmonds Ferry Terminal. Take ferry to Kingston. Follow **State Route 104 West** to Port Gamble.
- **4.2** Turn right with S.R. 104 at traffic light as State Route 307 (Bond Road) continues on to Poulsbo.
- **8.0** Port Gamble. Restored old-time shops, attractive park, cemetery. Proceed on across Hood Canal Bridge.
- **11.7** Turn right on **Paradise Bay Road**. Follow main thoroughfare as it charges up and down several hills.
- **17.3** Turn left on **Oak Bay Road** as Paradise Bay Road ends.
- **18.6** Turn right on **Beaver Valley Road (State Route 19)** toward Chimacum and Port Townsend as Oak Bay Road ends.

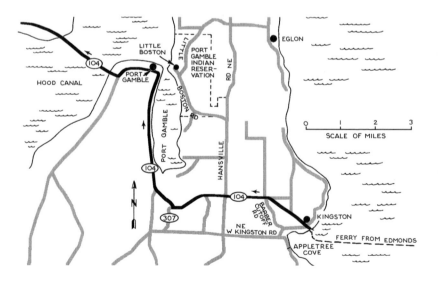

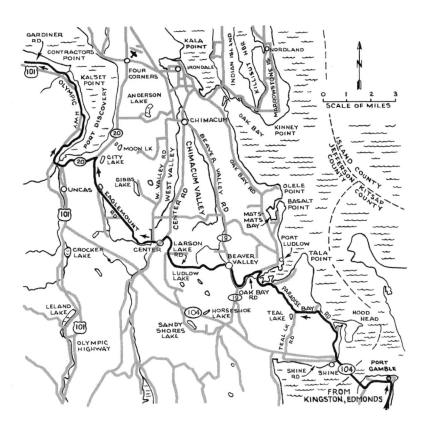

19.6 Turn left on **Larson Lake Road** toward Center and Quilcene by grocery. Head uphill. Running water from spout on right at 20.4.

23.5 Turn left on **Center Road** toward Port Angeles.

23.8 Turn right at wye on **Eaglemount Road**.

29.1 Turn left on **State Route 20** as Eaglemount Road ends.

30.9 Turn right on **U.S. 101**. Cafe on left, grocery 0.2 mile farther.

31.8 Turn right on **Gardiner Road**. Lodge and restaurant on right at 32.9.

33.6 Turn right on **U.S. 101** and continue on wide shoulder.

35.2 Turn right on side road as highway bends left. No name signs here, but road is later marked **Gardiner Road**.

37.8 Rejoin highway and immediately bear right on old roadway again.

39.1 Rejoin highway. This time stay on it, going downhill.

40.4 Turn right on **Old Blynn Road** toward East Sequim Bay Road.

43.3 Rejoin **U.S. 101**. Delicatessen on right at 44.1.

44.2 Turn right into Sequim Bay State Park; overnight camping, group camp. Park ranger telephone: (360) 683-4235. Motels and B&B nearby in Sequim.

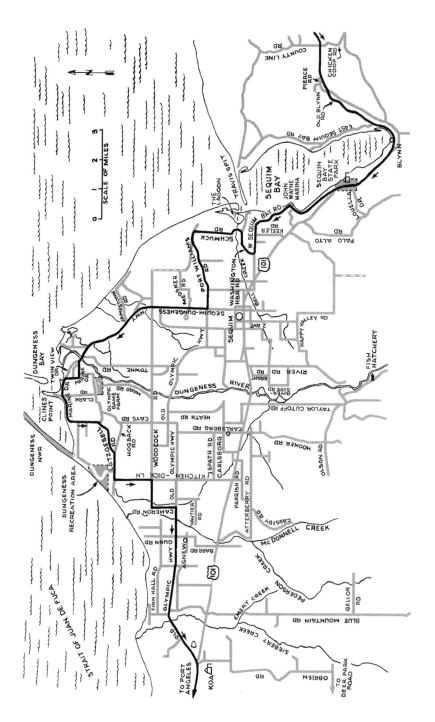

SECOND DAY

0.0 Leave state park, turn right on **U.S. 101**.

0.6 Turn right on **West Sequim Bay Road**. John Wayne Marina on right at mile 1.7, B&B on right at mile 2.4.

3.9 Turn right on **Washington Harbor Road**.

4.7 Turn left on **Schmuck Road** toward Public Boat Launch as Washington Harbor Road is marked dead end.

6.0 Turn left at yield sign as sign points right to Public Boat Launch. Road eventually is named **Port Williams Road**.

8.1 Turn right at stop sign on **Sequim-Dungeness Highway** toward Olympic Game Farm. Sign points left to Olympic Game Farm at 8.6. Road changes name to **Marine Drive** by old schoolhouse at 11.9. Sign points left to game farm at 12.1.

15.8 Turn right at stop sign on **Lotzgesell Road** toward Port Angeles and Dungeness Recreation Area. Dungeness Recreation Area and Dungeness National Wildlife Refuge on right at mile 16.4; picnic tables, pit toilets, campsites. Road bends left and is renamed **Kitchen-Dick Lane**.

17.6 Turn right on **Woodcock Road**, which bends left and is renamed **Cameron Road**.

19.1 Turn right on **Old Olympic Highway**.

23.4 Turn right on **U.S. 101** toward Port Angeles. KOA campground on opposite side of highway. Keep right around weighing station. Scenic viewpoint turnout at 25.6. Enter Port Angeles at mile 28.0.

30.4 Turn right on **Lincoln Street**, then left on **Railroad** to Blackball Ferry Terminal. Cafes, restaurants. If you have time, the 8.2-mile round trip to Ediz Hook is worthwhile. Take ferry to Victoria. Stay in one of Victoria's many hotels or continue on next day's tour to campground.

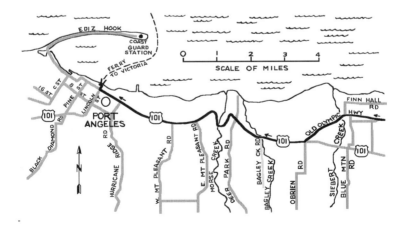

THIRD DAY

0.0 Starting from the Blackball Ferry Terminal on **Belleville Street**, continue right along water on main thoroughfare. As it rounds the peninsula the road is named **Dallas Road**. Sign on left at 1.8 marks mile zero of Trans-Canada Highway. Proceed through Beacon Park. Road changes name to **Hollywood Crescent** at 3.5, then to **Robertson Street**.

4.0 Turn half right on **Ross Street**, which is immediately renamed **Crescent Road**.

4.4 Bear left on **King George Terrace**.

5.0 Turn right with Scenic Drive on **Beach Drive**. Sealand Aquarium and coffee shop on right at 6.8. Continue on **Cadboro Bay Road** as it joins from the left at 9.8. Road turns left at 10.4 and is renamed **Telegraph Bay Road**.

10.8 Turn left on **Arbutus Road** with Marine Scenic Drive. Bear right at mile 11.9 as Finnerty Road joins from the left.

12.5 Turn right on **Gordon Head Road** as Arbutus ends. The thoroughfare is successively renamed **Ferndale Road** at 12.7, **Grandview Drive** at mile 13.4, and **Ash Road** at mile 13.6. Enter Mt. Douglas Park.

14.4 Turn right on **Cordova Bay Road** as Ash Road ends at stop sign.

15.6 Turn right with Cordova Bay Road as Royal Oak Drive goes left. Grocery and cafe at mile 17.0, Fable Cottage at mile 17.3.

18.0 Bear right on **Fowler Road** with Scenic Drive No. 3 as Cordova Bay Road goes left. Fowler is shortly renamed **Sayward Road**.

18.9 Cross Patricia Bay Highway (B.C. 17) and turn left at T intersection on **Hamsterly Road**.

19.0 Turn right on **Brookleigh Road** toward Gazebo Tea Garden. Donut House on left.

20.4 Turn left on **Oldfield Road** as Brookleigh ends, then right on **Brookhaven Road**.

20.8 Turn right on **Old West Saanich Road** as Brookhaven ends.

22.6 Bear right on **West Saanich Road** (**B.C. 17A**) as Old West Saanich Road ends. Benvenuto Avenue goes left 1.2 miles to Butchart Gardens at 23.0. Bakery, grocery, coffee shop, bicycle shop at 23.8. Additional grocery stores at 28.0 and 32.1. *Note: McTavish Road goes right at mile 28.2 to Sidney; ferry to Anacortes and Deception Pass via San Juan Islands. See tours 39, 40, 41, and 72.* Continue on West Saanich Road at mile 32.0 as B.C. 17A turns right on Wain Road.

33.3 Turn right on **Landsend Road**.

35.8 Turn left on **Patricia Bay Highway** (**B.C. 17**).

36.3 Swartz Bay Ferry Terminal. Snack bar. Buy ferry ticket to Tsawwassen and proceed directly to numbered slip as directed by ticket agent. Coffee shop and restaurant on ferry. Get off at Tsawwassen terminal and proceed east on causeway.

39.3 Turn right on **52 Street** and crank uphill.

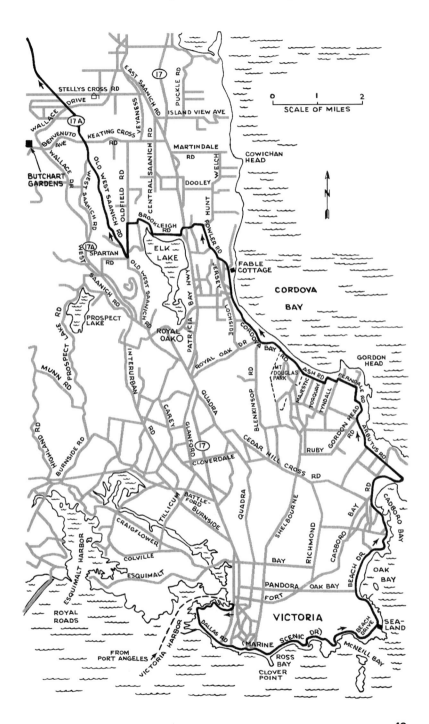

40.2 Turn right on **12th Avenue**. *Note: To visit the Tsawwassen motels, cafes, and shops, turn left on 12th Avenue 0.5 mile.*

40.7 Turn left on **English Bluff Road** as 12th Avenue ends.

42.0 Turn left on **1st Avenue** as English Bluff Road is marked No Exit.

43.0 Turn right on **56 Street** as 1st Avenue ends. Cross border, check in at U.S. Customs, and continue south on **Tyee Drive**. Department store on left at mile 44.6 is the last source of supplies before Lighthouse Marine Park.

44.6 Turn right on **Gulf Road**.

47.3 Turn left on **Marine Drive** as Gulf Road ends by tavern.

46.3 Turn right into Whatcom County's Lighthouse Marine Park. Telephone: (360) 945-4911. Restaurant next door.

FOURTH DAY

0.0 Leave Lighthouse Marine Park and turn right on **Marine Drive**, which bends left and becomes **Edwards Drive**. Road turns left at mile 0.6 by marina.

1.3 Turn right on **APA Road** from Tyee Drive. *Note: Route may be shortened 2.6 miles by continuing straight on Tyee Drive through customs to Tsawwassen.*

3.1 Turn left on **Boundary Bay Road**. Rural cycling through country lanes, peaceful wooded roadsides with occasional houses. Coast down around a bend and into Boundary Bay.

4.4 Bear right on **Elm Street**.

4.5 Turn left on **Bayview Drive** and cycle along the water. Road bends left along border at 4.4. Proceed west along the border on **Roosevelt Road** to the border crossing.

6.2 Turn right on **Tyee Drive** through customs and continue on **56 Street** through Tsawwassen. Cafe and bakery on the right at 7.8.

9.2 Bear right on **B.C. 17** through open delta country.

10.2 Turn right on **28th Avenue** just before B.C. 17 rises on a bridge over the railroad tracks.

10.7 Turn left on **64th Street** as 28 Avenue ends. At 11.1 cross railroad tracks. The 90-car, double-header unit trains run these tracks daily. That many hopper cars loaded with coal are not about to stop for you, so keep out of their way.

11.7 Turn right on **36 Avenue**, crossing railroad tracks again at 12.2.

12.7 Turn left on **72 Street**. Cross railroad tracks at 13.7.

14.2 Turn right on **Ladner Trunk Road (B.C. 10)**, a busy road with narrow, 30-inch shoulder. Endure it for three miles.

17.0 Turn right on **Hornby Drive** at traffic light as Ladner Trunk Road swings left across B.C. 99 on an overpass. Cafe on other side of freeway. Go under railroad trestle at 18.9.

19.4 Turn left on **112th Street** as Hornby Drive ends. Cross freeway on an overpass, then cross railroad tracks.

20.0 Turn right on **Ladner Trunk Road (B.C. 10)** and cross railroad tracks at mile 20.4. Continue uphill at mile 20.9.

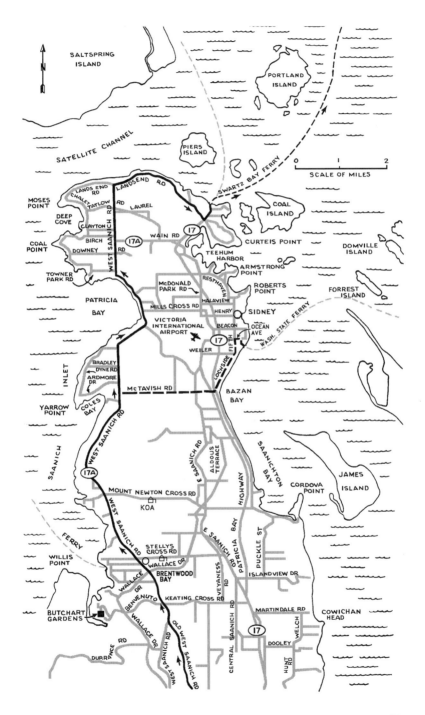

21.4 Turn right on **120 Street** at top of hill. Road bends left at 21.8 and becomes **New McLellan Road**. At 23.0 road is renamed **56 Avenue**.

23.2 Turn left on **132 Street**. Stop and cross B.C. 10 at mile 23.4.

23.7 Turn right on **60 Avenue**. Cross King George Highway (B.C. 99A) at 24.5.

25.2 Turn left on **144 Street**. Go downhill, across the valley, and up on the other side. Cross 72 Avenue at 26.8.

28.0 Turn right on **82A Avenue** by grocery.

28.3 Turn left on **146 Street** as 82A Avenue ends. Road turns right and becomes **84 Avenue**.

30.4 Turn left on **160 Street** and cross the Fraser Highway with traffic light.

31.0 Turn right on **88 Avenue**.

34.4 Turn half left on **Harvie Road** at stop sign in Port Kells. Cross Trans-Canada Highway on an overpass and cross 96 Avenue. Cafe.

35.8 Cross railroad tracks and turn right on **98A Avenue**. Follow roadway through industrial district as follows: Left on **197 Street**, right on **101 Avenue**, right on **199B Street**, and left on **100A Avenue**.

37.2 Turn left on **201 Street**. Road turns right at 37.5 and is renamed **102B Avenue**.

38.4 Turn left on **208 Street** as 102B Avenue ends.

39.0 Turn right on **Allard Crescent**. Derby Reach Provincial Park with camping along river on left at 40.4. A triangular, prismatic granite monument, guarded by chain link fence, on the left at 41.7 marks the site of the first permanent settlement in the lower Fraser Valley, the original Fort Langley.

42.9 Turn left on unmarked road as Allard Crescent ends. Road eventually marked **McKinnon Road**.

43.2 Turn left at wye and continue on **96 Avenue**.

44.1 Turn left on **Glover Road** in Fort Langley. Groceries, restaurants, bakery, motel, B&B.

44.7 Turn right on **Mavis Avenue** toward Fort Langley Historical Park.

"I have had all the fun I can stand. I want a motel tonight!"

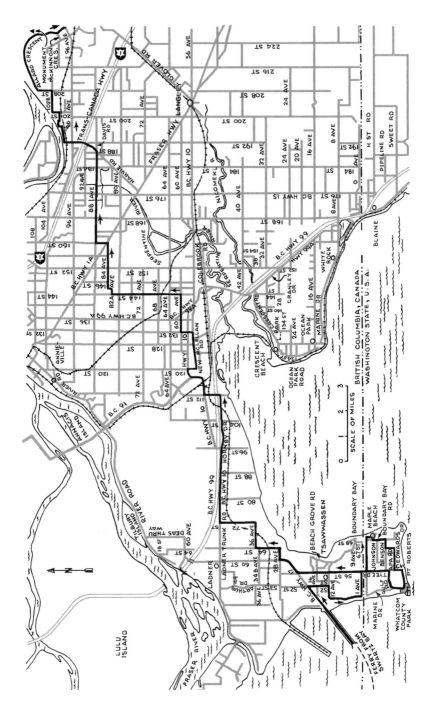

44.9   Fort Langley Historical Park. Visit park, return to Glover. *Note: If not equipped for camping, see fourth day alternate route to Mission, below.*

45.2   Turn right on **Glover Street** toward ferry.

46.0   Albion Ferry. Cross river and turn right toward Lougheed Highway. Cross B.C 7 and continue uphill on **240 Street**. Grocery.

46.7   Turn right on **102 Avenue**.

47.4   Bear right and uphill on **Jackson Road** as 102 Avenue ends. Road bends left at 48.1 and becomes **100 Avenue**.

50.4   Follow thoroughfare right as road changes name from **100 Avenue** to **268 Street**. Immediately turn left again on **100 Avenue** and plunge downhill.

51.1   Turn left on **272 Street** as 100 Avenue ends. Grocery on right at mile 52.3. Continue uphill.

53.9   Turn right on **Dewdney Trunk Road** as 272 Street ends. Iron Mountain Service Station and Grocery at 55.2; the last food supply before Rolley Lake.

57.2   Turn left on **Rolley Lake Street**.

57.7   Turn right on **Berg Avenue** as Rolley Lake Street is marked No Exit.

58.2   Turn left on **Bell Street** as Berg Avenue ends.

59.1   Turn left into Rolley Lake Provincial Park.

59.3   Turn right into camping area. Water tap here.

59.7   Campsites with toilet and shower facilities. Picnic area and swimming beach along lake.

FOURTH DAY ALTERNATE ROUTE

45.1   Fort Langley Historical Park. Head out park drive, then make a sharp right turn onto **River Road**. Bicycle along the Fraser River, pass below the fort, and emerge into open farmland. Road name changes to **88 Avenue.**

49.9   Turn left with River Road as 268 Street goes right. Cross main-line railroad tracks at mile 50.2.

51.2   Turn right on **Le Feuvre Road**. Railroad crossing at mile 51.5. Climb hill. Road is renamed **Graham Crescent** near top of hill as Marsh-McCormick Road goes right.

54.2   Turn left on **McTavish Road** as Graham Crescent ends.

55.2   Turn right on **Satchell Street** as McTavish is marked No Exit. Road bends left at mile 56.2 and is renamed **Taylor Road**.

56.8   Turn right on **Mt Lehman Road** as Taylor is marked No Exit.

57.8   Turn left on **Harris Road**. Railroad crossing at mile 59.4.

61.9   Turn left on **Riverside Street** at stop sign in Matsqui.

62.9   Go under highway overpass and turn left up entrance ramp to **B.C. 11**. Go through yellow-painted notch in curbing and use sidewalk on bridge over the Fraser River. Watch for broken glass.

64.0   Go through notch in curbing to the shoulder of the roadway and coast down into Mission City.

64.7   Turn left on **Horne Street** toward B.C. 7 and City Centre.

64.8   Turn right up and over railroad overpass. Very steep approach.

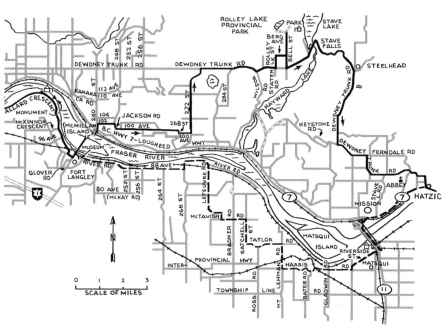

65.0   Turn right on **B.C. 7 (Lougheed Highway)**. Information Centre on left with public washrooms at mile 65.8; motel at mile 66.7.

67.4   Hatzic Store on left; continue at Fifth Day, mile 14.7, below.

FIFTH DAY

0.0   Leave Rolley Lake camping area and turn left on park entrance road.

0.6   Turn right on **Bell Street**.

2.1   Turn left on **Dewdney Trunk Road**. Grocery at mile 2.4.Pass Stave Falls at mile 3.1 and Silver Creek Park at 8.1; day park by lake.

10.0   Turn left with Dewdney Trunk Road as Keystone Road goes right.

10.5   Bear left past Cedar Valley Centre with Dewdney Trunk Road.

11.1   Turn right with Dewdney Trunk Road as Ferndale Road goes on.

11.9   Turn left with Dewdney Trunk Road as Cade-Barr Road goes on. Westminster Abbey on right at 12.8. Start downhill at mile 13.3.

13.4   Turn left with Dewdney Trunk Road as Manson Street goes right.

14.4   Turn right with Dewdney Trunk Road as Draper Street goes left.

14.7   Turn left on **Lougheed Highway** (**B.C. 7**). Hatzic Store here. General store and cafe at 17.7.

19.2   Turn right on **Nicomen Island Trunk Road**.

21.1   Turn right at small wye as Waring Road comes in from the left. No street sign.

22.0   Keep left as Howell Road forks right.

25.2   Turn right on **B.C. 7** as Nicomen Island Trunk Road ends. At 26.1 cross railroad tracks, then turn corner with the highway at DeRoche (grocery) and head east again, passing Lake Errock. Cross Harrison

49

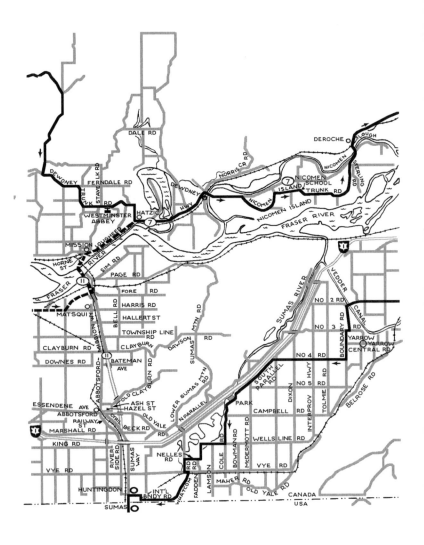

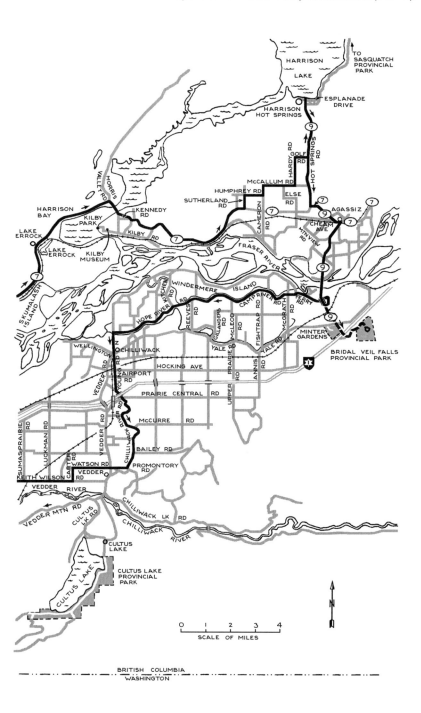

River at 34.6. Kilby Museum (free admission) 1.2 miles on right. At 36.0 start up long hill. Water runs from a commercialized spring at 38.0. Scenic overlook with tables at 38.1. Continue down steep hill.

41.4 Turn left on **Sutherland Road**.

41.9 Turn right on **Humphrey Road** as Sutherland Road ends.

42.2 Turn left on **Cameron Road**. Road bends right at 43.0 and becomes **McCallum Road**.

43.5 Turn left on **Hardy Road**, which bends right and is renamed **Golf Road**.

45.0 Turn left on **B.C. 9** (**Hot Springs Road**). Camping facilities on both sides of road after one mile.

47.1 Hot Springs Road ends at Esplanade Drive along the shore of Harrison Lake. Harrison Hotel is to left with the hot springs one mile beyond. Public swimming pool at this corner. Sasquatch Provincial Park is to the right and four miles around the lake. Campgrounds at Deer Lake seven miles above the day park area.

SIXTH DAY

0.0 Starting from the shore of Harrison Lake in the town of Harrison Hot Springs, head south out of town on **Hot Springs Road** (**B.C. 9**)

4.0 Turn left with **B.C. 9** and **B.C. 7** toward Agassiz. Continue through Agassiz on the combined highways.

5.0 Turn right with B.C. 9 as B.C. 7 continues on. Cross railroad tracks.

6.4 Bear right with B.C. 9 as B.C. 7 access road goes left. Cross the Fraser River.

8.2 Get into left-turn lane and turn left on **Rosedale Ferry Road**. *Note: For a visit to Bridal Veil Falls Provincial Park, continue straight through blinking light on B.C. 9 past Minter Gardens. Cross Trans-Canada Highway on an overpass and continue around cloverleaf to left on **Bridal Falls Road** to park entrance and then right and uphill on **Page Road**. Grocery and cafe. Return to Rosedale Ferry Road after visit.* Continue with **Ferry Road** as it turns under B.C. 9.

9.9 Road name changes to **Camp River Road** as McGrath Road goes left. Proceed along a slough among trees. Road is narrow, winding, and scenic with almost no traffic. A made-to-order "bicycle path." Hop farm on left at 11.4.

15.0 Turn left on **Hope River Road** as Camp River Road ends and Kitchen Road goes right. Country homes give way to a residential district.

17.6 Turn left on **Young Road North** at a small wye as Hope River Road ends. Ride through center of Chilliwack; Park, B&B, bakeries and bicycle shop. At 20.1 go under Trans-Canada Highway and continue on **Chilliwack River Road**.

23.7 Turn right with **Promontory Road** as Chilliwack River Road ends.

24.3 Cross busy Vedder Road and continue on **Watson Road**.

25.5 Turn left on **Carter Road**.

26.0 Turn right on **Keith Wilson Road** as Carter ends.

30.4 Cross Vedder Canal and turn left on **Boundary Road**. Jog right on

No. 3 Road at mile 31.3, then left again on **Boundary Road**. *Note: Yarrow Central Road goes left 1.2 miles to Yarrow at mile 31.8; city park, deli, grocery, cafe.* Enter the 33,000 acres of fertile farmland reclaimed from Sumas Lake.

32.3 Turn right on **No. 4 Road**.

35.4 Road bends left and becomes **South Parallel Road**.

37.2 Bear left on **Cole Road** as a freeway access goes right by a highway rest park.

37.6 Bear right into Hougen Park. Picnic tables, washrooms. Swimming in Sumas River for those who do not mind the algae-colored water.

38.0 Pedal out of park in same direction. Continue on **Cole Road**.

39.2 Turn right on **Wells Line Road**, following as it bends left at 40.2. Road bends right at 40.8 and is renamed **Nelles Road**. *Note: Dairy farm with great ice cream at this corner.*

41.2 Turn left on **Whatcom Road**.

41.8 Turn left on **Vye Road**, then right again on **Whatcom Road**. Road bends right and is renamed **International Boundary Road**. International Boundary Monument #33 at mile 42.2 commemorating Treaty of 1846. Monument #32 at 43.1. Road bends right, then left and is renamed **Second Street**.

45.0 Turn left on **C Street**, cross border through customs and ride through Sumas. Grocery, cafe.

45.9 Turn left on **Front Street** toward Mt. Baker as State Route 9 goes right.

46.6 Turn right with **Sumas Road** toward Mt. Baker.

47.0 Turn left on **Reese Hill Road** as Sumas Road dead ends.

47.7 Turn right with Reese Hill Road toward Mt. Baker.

51.5 Bear right with **Kendall Road** as Reese Hill Road goes straight.

52.6 Turn left on **South Pass Road** toward Whatcom County Silver Lake Park. Road bends right at mile 57.5 and is renamed **Silver Lake Road**.

60.2 Main entrance to Silver Lake Park on left. Group camp entrance is 0.3 mile farther.

60.5 Group camp entrance, unmarked road left. Large enclosed kitchen shelter, pit toilets. Nearest food concession is in Maple Falls, 3.2 miles farther. Park manager telephone: (360) 599-2776.

SEVENTH DAY

0.0 Silver Lake group camp entrance. Head south on **Silver Lake Road**.

3.2 Turn right on **State Route 542 (Mt. Baker Highway)** as Silver Lake Road ends. Cafe, grocery, B&B.

6.2 Turn left with S.R. 542. Grocery store, cafe. Another cafe at 13.4.

14.4 Continue straight on S.R. 542 as S.R. 9 joins from the left.

15.0 Turn left on **Deming Road** as Marshall Hill Road (gravel) comes in from right. Pass Mt. Baker High School on the right at mile 15.6.

18.6 Turn left on **State Route 542** from Deming Road and go past Nugent's Corner; grocery, cafe, and bakery.

19.6 Cross Nooksack River and turn right on **Cedarville Road**. Road bends left by the logging rodeo grounds and is renamed **Goshen Road**.

21.8 Turn left on **Sand Road**.

24.6 Turn right on **Mt. Baker Highway (State Route 542)**.

25.4 Cross Squalicum Creek and turn left on **Squalicum Lake Road**.

28.1 Turn right on **Jensen Road** as Squalicum Lake Road ends. Road rounds a corner and becomes **Agate Bay Lane**.

29.8 Turn right on **North Shore Drive** and follow around Lake Whatcom. Grocery at 34.8, park on left at 35.5. Road is renamed **Electric Avenue**.

36.2 Turn right on **Arbor Street** into Whatcom Falls Park. Bear right and continue on **Sunset Lane**. Stop below at falls for walk down to view bridge. Continue on road out of park.

37.1 Turn right on **Lakeway Drive**. Busy traffic.

38.5 Turn left on **Lincoln Street** at traffic light by Fred Meyer Center.

39.4 Turn right on **Byron Avenue** as Lincoln ends, then left as Byron ends.

39.6 Turn right and cross freeway on overpass.

39.8 Turn sharp left at first traffic light after crossing over the freeway. Continue past a shopping center. Bakery and ice cream parlor.

40.0 Turn right on **Fielding Street** as road goes on to freeway entrance. Fielding Street turns corner and becomes **32 Street** at 40.2.

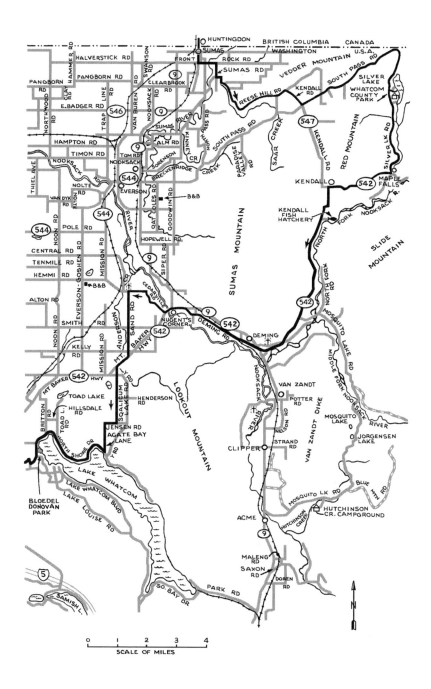

41.0 Turn right on **Donovan Avenue**.

42.1 Turn right on **Old Fairhaven Parkway (State Route 11)**.

42.3 Turn left on **12 Street (S.R. 11, Chuckanut Drive)** toward Larrabee State Park. *Note: Thriftway store is two blocks to the right on 12 Street. Fairhaven Bicycle Shop is two blocks beyond Thriftway.* Fairhaven Park and rose garden on left at 42.5 and last diminutive grocery store before campground at 43.6.

47.4 Turn right into Larrabee State Park.

EIGHTH DAY

0.0 Leave Larrabee State Park south exit and head right (south) on **Chuckanut Drive (State Route 11)**.

7.5 Turn right on **Edison Road (State Route 237)**. Cafe, grocery.

8.5 Follow S.R. 237 through Edison. Cafe. Continue south on S.R. 237.

9.0 Turn right on **Bay View–Edison Road** toward Bay View State Park.

10.7 Turn left toward Bay View State Park as Samish Island Road goes on. B&B and Bay View State Park on left at 15.4; restrooms. *Note: Padilla Bay Shore Trail goes right at mile 16.2; scenic side route, returning to road at mile 18.2.*

19.1 Turn right on wide shoulder of **State Route 20**. Cafe across highway. Cross Swinomish Channel. Alternative through La Conner is nine miles longer.

21.9 After crossing bridge, turn right on **South March's Point Road**, then immediately left at T junction with main thoroughfare. *Note: March's Point Road at 22.7 goes right around point; interesting five-mile side loop.*

24.4 Turn left at stop sign on **March's Point Road** and cross State Route 20. Continue on **Christiansen Road** along edge of a golf course. Grocery and cafe.

24.6 Bear right with Christiansen Road as Summit Park Road goes left.

25.5 Turn right on **Satterlee Road** as Christiansen Road ends. Go along beach, then up a steep hill.

25.8 Turn left on **Gibralter Road** at top of hill as Satterlee ends.

28.3 Turn left on **Deception Road** as Gibralter Road ends. Bear right and uphill with Deception Road at 28.9.

29.1 Turn left on **State Route 20** as Deception Road ends. Cafe.

29.6 Bear left with S.R. 20 and cross Deception Pass bridge. Deception Pass State Park entrance on right at 31.6. Drive-in and grocery farther on left.

33.1 Turn left on **Ducken Road**.

33.4 Turn right on **Monkey Hill Road**.

35.9 Turn left on **Henni Road** at wye.

37.2 Turn sharp right on **Jones Road**.

37.4 Turn left at bottom of hill on **Dugualla Dyke Road** as Dugualla Bay Road goes on. Ride along top of dike.

38.1 Turn left as Dugualla Dyke Road ends and crank uphill. Keep right around curve on **Taylor Road**.

40.3 Bear right, then left with Taylor Road as Fakkema Road goes on.

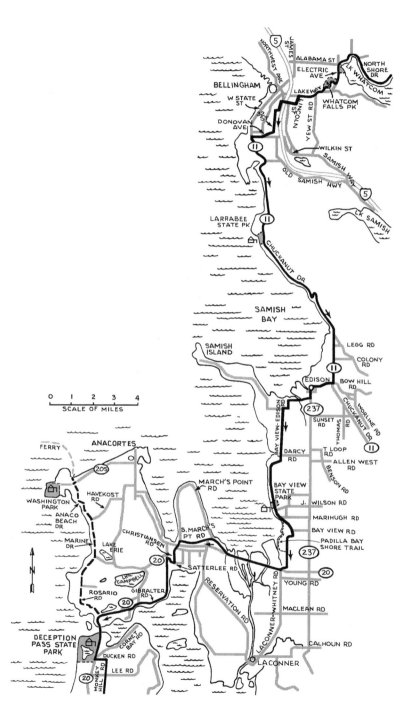

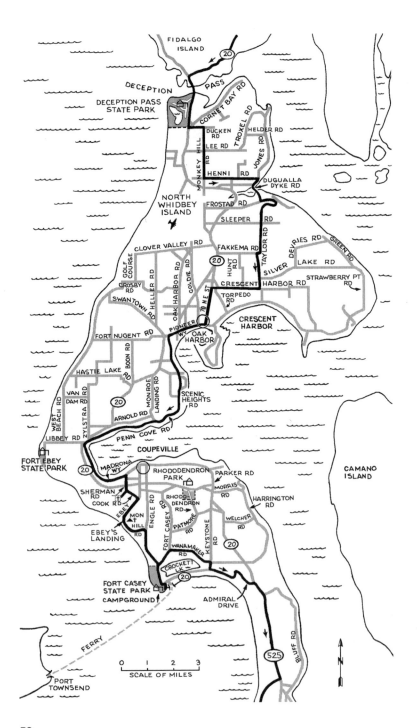

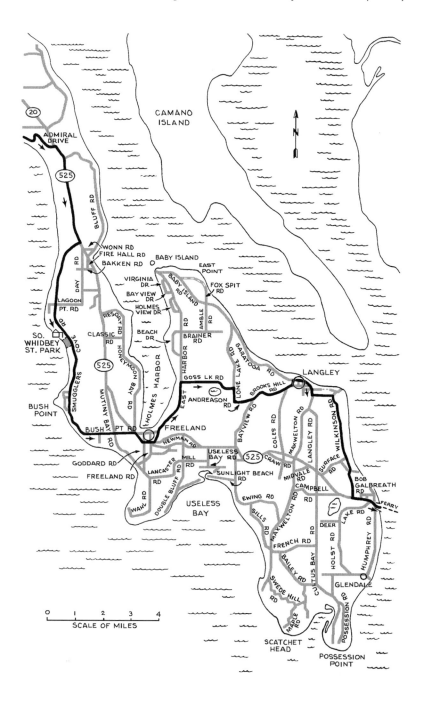

41.8 Turn right on **Crescent Harbor Road**.

43.5 Bear left at wye on **70 N.E. Street** as Crescent Harbor Road ends.

44.9 Turn right on **East Pioneer Way** in Oak Harbor, joining **State Route 20** at 46.0. Beware of Right Turn Only lane. Grocery, cafes, bakery, bicycle shop.

46.4 Turn left on **Scenic Heights Road**. Eventually changes name to **Penn Cove Road**. Follow it.

52.5 Turn left on **State Route 20**.

53.2 Turn left on **Madrona Way**.

55.6 Turn right on **Sherman Road**. For groceries or food service continue on Madrona Way one mile to Coupeville. Coupeville also has old blockhouse, museum, Indian dugout canoes. Return to this intersection and head south on Sherman Road.

56.2 Proceed straight as Cook Road goes left; continue 0.3 mile to old cemetery. James Davis Blockhouse here. Return to **Cook Road** and turn right (east).

57.0 Turn right on **Ebey Road** to Ebey's Landing at mile 58.0. Continue uphill.

59.1 Turn right on **Engle Road**.

59.8 Turn right into Fort Casey State Park campground by Keystone Ferry Terminal.

NINTH DAY

0.0 Leave campground, turn left, then right on **Fort Casey Road**, past Crockett Blockhouse on the right at mile 0.4.

0.8 Turn right on **Wanamaker Road**.

2.4 Turn right on **State Route 20**.

2.8 Continue straight as S.R. 20 goes right. Ride along beach residential area. Follow around hairpin turn and continue uphill at mile 3.9.

4.3 Turn right on **Admiral Drive**.

5.0 Turn right on **State Route 525** and bicycle along shoulder.

9.1 Turn right on **Smugglers Cove Road** and follow it. South Whidbey State Park at 13.6; restrooms, water. Continue on. Road changes name to **Bush Point Road** as it rounds corner.

18.2 Turn right on **State Route 525**.

18.9 Turn left toward Freeland.

19.1 Turn left on **East Harbor Road**. Freeland Cafe near this corner.

21.6 Turn right on **Goss Lake Road** and crank uphill.

23.9 Turn right on **Lone Lake Road**.

24.5 Turn left on **Andreason Road** with thoroughfare.

25.1 Turn left on **Bayview Road**, which goes over a hill and becomes **Brooks Hill Road**. Enter Langley on **Third Street**.

27.1 Turn left with scenic drive on **Saratoga Avenue** one block before stop sign.

27.3 Bend right with **First Street**.

27.6 Continue uphill out of town on **Cascade Avenue**.

27.9 Bear left with thoroughfare on scenic drive.

28.3 Turn left on **Sandy Point Road** with scenic drive. Island County Fairgrounds on right.
29.3 Turn right with scenic drive on **Wilkinson Road**.
31.5 Bear left with Wilkinson Road as Bob Galbreath Road goes right.
32.4 Turn left on **Bob Galbreath Road**.
33.3 Turn left on **State Route 525**.
34.0 Board Mukilteo ferry. Leave ferry and head uphill on S.R. 525.
38.9 Turn right on **Beverly Park–Edmonds Road**. Road bends and is renamed **52nd Avenue West**.
41.8 Turn right on **168 Street S.W.** at blinking red light.
42.5 Bear left on **Olympic View Drive**.
47.1 Turn right onto **Puget Drive**.
47.3 Follow thoroughfare left with **9 Avenue North**.
47.5 Follow thoroughfare right on **Caspers Street**.
47.8 Go straight on Caspers Street as ferry traffic goes left on Third Street.
48.0 Turn left on **Sunset Avenue** along the waterfront.
48.4 Back to ferry terminal on **Main Street**. Tour completed. Hope you had an enjoyable ride.

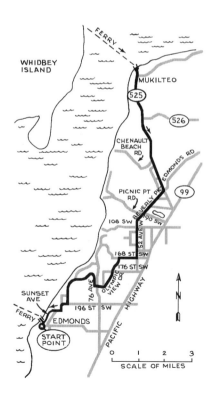

WHATCOM COUNTY

Whatcom County, the northernmost portion of western Washington, is virtually unspoiled by big-city sprawl. Whatcom's largest city, Bellingham, lies near one corner, leaving the rest of the county to agriculture and forest. As though this were not already ideal for bicycling, Whatcom County has provided a series of parks unmatched by any other county. The cities and towns also are intensively park oriented. Add to this the native stands of western paper birch covering much of this county, the backdrop of Mt. Baker and the North Cascades, and the scenic wanderings of the Nooksack River, and one has the potential of many beautiful bicycle routes. Three state parks are situated along Puget Sound: Larrabee, Birch Bay, and Peace Arch. These northern parks host a predominantly Canadian clientele from Vancouver, just across the border. Large Canadian investments in Whatcom County real estate have also been reported, but this has not changed the delightful rural scenery nor cluttered the backroads with heavy traffic. Although a long drive from Washington State's major population centers, the rides here offer ample reward for the effort.

60 BIRCH BAY–PEACE ARCH

STARTING POINT: Picnic area parking lot, Birch Bay State Park, Whatcom County. Take exit 266 from I-5 (State Route 548, Grandview Road). Proceed west on Grandview Road to Jackson Road. Turn right and then left on Helwig Road into Birch Bay State Park. Hostel accommodations available on Alderson Road 0.5 mile from Birch Bay.

DISTANCE: 36 miles.
TERRAIN: Mostly level, with a few hills.
TOTAL CUMULATIVE ELEVATION GAIN: 900 feet.
RECOMMENDED TIME OF YEAR: All seasons.
RECOMMENDED STARTING TIME: 9:30 to 10:00 A.M.
ALLOW: 5 hours.
POINTS OF INTEREST
Peace Arch State Park, Blaine
Resort town of Birch Bay
Drayton Harbor seascapes

Although this is classed as a Whatcom County ride, it directs the cyclist briefly across the border into British Columbia and requires a return to the United States through customs. The precautions regarding border crossings should therefore be reviewed (see the International section preamble) before starting this ride.

The International Peace Arch was erected in 1914 on the parkway median of the Pacific Highway (U.S. and B.C. 99) on the 49th parallel between Washington State and British Columbia. As a symbol of friendship and open border between the countries of Canada and the United States, it has two iron gates, one hinged to the U.S. side, the other to the Canadian side. To bar the portal, both countries must close their gates.

The roadside custody of the Peace Arch has since been assumed by I-5, barring the use of the roadway to bicyclists. The monument stands in the midst of a large green island between lanes of the freeway. Customs houses at either end of the island slow the traffic for reasonably safe pedestrian crossing. Surrounding this island is a beautifully landscaped international park with green lawns, trees and flowers of all seasons, restrooms, heated kitchen-picnic shelters, and playground equipment. Visitors to the park wander at will on foot across an unmarked international boundary line. In viewing the arch and the gardens, the U.S. visitor inevitably wanders to the Canadian side, but strict adherence to U.S. Customs rules requires that the boundary-crossing visitor report to a customs house before reentering the United States. This ride, accordingly, is routed along the border in Canada to the nearest nonfreeway U.S. Customs house before returning to U.S. territory.

Other than Peace Arch Park and Birch Bay's bustling resort area, this ride is mostly rural; cleared pasture and hayfields alternate with forest through-

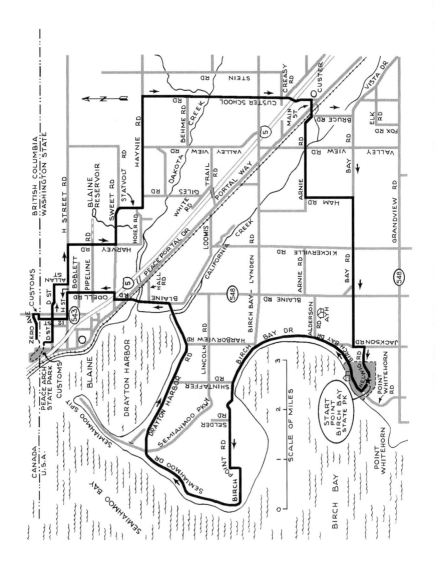

out. Depending upon the tide, sparkling waterscapes or miles of mud flat greet the rider along Drayton Harbor. The western paper birch, abundant in the eastern portions of Whatcom County, is almost eradicated in the Birch Bay area, so that the name now hardly applies.

MILEAGE LOG

0.0 Leave the picnic area parking lot and continue toward the beach area. Turn right along **Birch Bay Drive** and enjoy the view of Birch Bay. Continue on through the resort town of Birch Bay as Jackson Road comes in from the right at mile 1.3. Speed limit ten miles per hour on busy holiday weekends. Several food concessions here for those who like to camp in state parks the easy way. Cross creek and turn left with Birch Bay Drive at mile 1.7 as Alderson Road continues 0.5 mile to AYH Birch Bay Hostel.

2.8 Bear left with Birch Bay Drive as Birch Bay–Lynden Road forks right to I-5.

3.7 Keep left as Shintaffer Road goes right. Speed limit shortly increases to 40 miles per hour as the road leaves Birch Bay. Now on **Birch Point Road**. Road bends right at 6.4 and is renamed **Semiahmoo Drive**. Oceanspray and elderberry decorate the roadside.

9.3 Cross Semiahmoo Parkway and continue on **Drayton Harbor Road**. *Note: Semiahmoo Parkway goes left 2.0 miles along Semiahmoo Spit to Semiahmoo Resort; cafe, grocery, marina, park, shelters, boat rentals.* Elderberries, nettles, and deadly nightshade glimmer green from the roadside.

11.8 Bear left with Drayton Harbor Road as Harborview Road enters from the right.

12.7 Cross the estuarial channel of California Creek and turn left on **Blaine Road** as Drayton Harbor Road ends; pie shop, grocery.

13.4 Cross Dakota Creek's tidal channel and enter Blaine city limits. Continue across railroad tracks and Peace Portal Drive on **Bell Road**.

14.0 Turn right on **Sweet Road** as Bell Road ends and cross I-5 on an overpass.

14.2 Pass a side road on the left, then turn left on **Odell Road**.

15.2 Turn left on **H Street** as Odell ends. At 15.5 pass Blaine's Lincoln Park and the U.S. Border Patrol building.

15.7 Cross State Route 543 and turn right on **12 Street**.

16.0 Turn left on **D Street**.

16.7 Turn right by Denny's Restaurant toward Peace Arch Park, just before D Street goes under freeway. This is **2nd Street**.

16.9 Parking lot, Peace Arch State Park. Taking your bicycle with you, walk through the park with its lawns, gardens, and historic monuments. Picnic tables make this an inviting lunch stop. Northeast of the Peace Arch is a spectacular array of rockeries and flower beds. After observing these, walk bicycles north and east around them to **Peace Park Drive**. Mount bicycles and proceed to right.

17.5   Road swings left and becomes **Zero Avenue (0 Ave.)**. Bicycle past eastern portion of the park and along the international border.

18.5   Turn right on **176 Street (B.C. 15)** and report to U.S. Customs. After leaving customs house, bear right at 12 Street Exit Only sign and proceed up **12 Street**.

18.7   Turn left on **D Street**, cross State Route 543, and crank up a steep hill. D Street turns right at 19.4 and is renamed **Allan Street**.

19.5   Turn left on **H Street** as Allan Street ends.

20.5   Pass Blaine Cemetery, turn right on **Harvey Road**, and enjoy recovering all that uphill energy in an exhilarating downhill run.

21.6   Turn left on **Sweet Road**.

22.4   Bear right with thoroughfare on **Statvolt Road**. Road bends left at 22.9 and is renamed **Haynie Road**.

24.9   Turn right on **Custer School Road** past green pasturage, dairy farms, and fields of corn and potatoes. Cross I-5 on a long, arching bridge at 28.4.

28.9   Turn right on **Main Street** in Custer (grocery). Cross Portal Way and railroad tracks, continuing west.

29.2   Turn right on **Bruce Road**, which bends left along the railroad tracks and is renamed **Arnie Road**.

30.7   Turn left on **Ham Road** as a bend appears ahead on Arnie Road.

31.7   Ride up a sharp rise and turn right on **Bay Road** Open pastures and hayfields on all sides have margins decorated by fir, maple, mountain ash, cherry, and occasional birch trees. Spiraea and blackberry vines also add their decorations. Savannah sparrows fizzle from the meadows, and swallows swoop ahead of the bicycles just inches from the pavement. Cross Kickerville Road at mile 32.7.

33.7   Continue straight on Bay Road as main thoroughfare bends right on Blaine Road.

34.7   Turn left on **Jackson Road** as Bay Road turns to gravel.

35.0   Turn right on **Helwig Road** into Birch Bay State Park.

36.1   Parking lot, picnic area, Birch Bay State Park. End of ride.

"Your first try at wheel building?"

61   BIRCH BAY–HOVANDER HOMESTEAD PARK

STARTING POINT: Picnic area parking lot, Birch Bay State Park, Whatcom County. Take exit 266 from I-5 (State Route 548, Grandview Road). Proceed west on Grandview Road to Jackson Road. Turn right, then left on Helwig Road into Birch Bay State Park.

DISTANCE: 36 miles.
TERRAIN: Moderate; some flat, some hills.
TOTAL CUMULATIVE ELEVATION GAIN: 1100 feet.
RECOMMENDED TIME OF YEAR: All seasons.
RECOMMENDED STARTING TIME: 9 A.M.
ALLOW: 6 hours.
POINTS OF INTEREST
ARCO and Tosco refineries
Intalco Aluminum Company plant
Lake Terrell Wildlife Recreation Area
Hovander Homestead Park

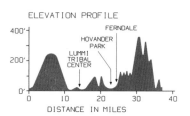

Back at the turn of the century, Håkan Hovander, an architect from Sweden, emigrated to the United States and constructed an elegant homestead on the banks of an accretion bend along the Nooksack River in Whatcom County, Washington, near Ferndale. The county purchased this property from Mr. Hovander's son Otis in 1969 and has developed it into a fascinating day-use-only park. Managed by the Ferndale Senior Citizens, the house is open 10 A.M. to 6 P.M. Wednesday through Sunday, Memorial Day to Labor Day. The lower floor of the big house has been restored with antique furnishings in every room. The large, roomy kitchen is filled with early-day cooking utensils and other culinary equipment.

Farm implements of yesteryear, housed in a big red barn, include both powered and horse-drawn machinery. Tools, ropes, and harnesses fill a toolshed while a cream separator, large milk cans, butter churn, butter press, and hand-crank ice cream freezer complete the picture of a prosperous dairy farm at the beginning of the twentieth century. Goats, rabbits, chickens, pigs, ducks, sheep, and cows greet visitors from fenced yards near the barn.

Colorful flowers and shrubs behind a white picket fence set the house apart from the huge expanse of green lawn. Other flower beds located around the grounds make this a beautiful setting indeed. A small vegetable garden thrives in the deep, sandy loam soil. Sweet corn, grown in the farm garden, is available for a nominal fee to the summer picnicker. Varnished picnic tables dot the acres of lawn. A kitchen shelter boasts electric range tops and sinks. Several fireplaces offer barbecue possibilities. An old water tower, converted to a lookout tower with stairs inside, gives one a sweeping

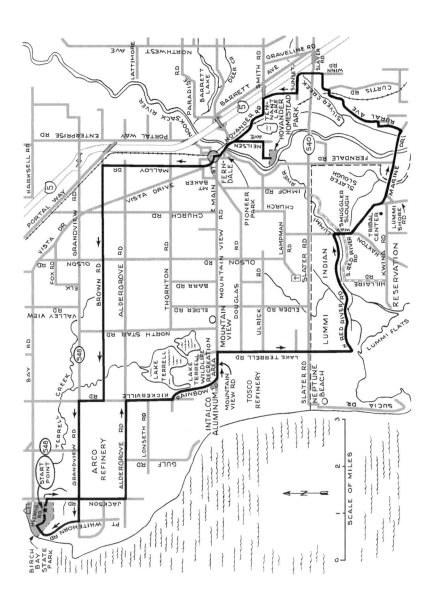

view of this most attractive and unusual park. Our bicycle tour stops here for lunch and a touch of nostalgia.

Views of the ARCO refinery, the Intalco aluminum plant, and the Tosco refinery reflect the modern technologies of petrochemistry, metal refining, and electrical energy. Peas, corn, and beans flourish in the flat valley land of the Lummi Indian Reservation, while green, rolling, upland pastures complete this rural ride as the bicyclist returns to Birch Bay State Park.

MILEAGE LOG

0.0 Picnic area parking lot at Birch Bay State Park. Proceed easterly through the park on **Helwig Road**.

1.0 Turn right on **Jackson Road** as Helwig ends. Towers and tanks of the ARCO refinery appear among hayfields and pastures where dairy cattle graze contentedly.

2.7 Turn left on **Aldergrove Road** as Jackson is marked Dead End. A big pipeline from the refinery runs under the road on the left and heads downhill toward the oil tanker terminal on Cherry Point.

4.7 Turn right on **Kickerville Road**.

5.7 Bear left (east) on **Rainbow Road** as Kickerville Road is marked Dead End. The Lake Terrell Wildlife Recreation Area appears on the left as the road again swings south.

6.9 Bear left with **Mountain View Road** at stop sign and blinking red light as Intalco Road goes hard right into the aluminum plant. Networks of power lines funnel into the surrealistic installation.

7.4 Turn right on **Lake Terrell Road** and proceed downhill past the Tosco refinery. Entrance to Lake Terrell Wildlife Recreation Area is to the north on Lake Terrell Road. At 9.4 cross Slater Road (S.R. 540) and continue downhill toward the Lummi Indian Reservation. At 10.5 the road bends left (east) past trailer homes and platted lots. Views of Lummi Bay tide flats. At 11.5, now on **N. Red River Road**. Ducks and herons frequent the sluggish, slowly moving slough. Peas, beans, and hay are harvested from the fields on the north side of the road; wild rosebushes line the other side along the river.

13.1 Turn right on **Haxton Way** and cross the Lummi River.

13.4 Bear left on **Lummi Shore Road**.

14.4 Bear left and downhill at wye by Tribal Center. Bear left again at stop sign. Now on **Marine Drive**. Bulrushes and cattails grow along the marshy roadsides. Cross Ferndale Road at mile 15.3 and leave the Lummi Indian Reservation. Cross Nooksack River at mile 15.6.

16.0 Cross a creek, turn left onto **Rural Avenue**, and follow its twists and turns.

17.9 Turn right, cross tracks with Rural Avenue, then turn left on other side of tracks as Curtis Road comes in from right.

18.6 Cross Slater Road at stop sign and continue on **La Bounty Road**. As it bends left and right the road is renamed **Sunset Avenue** and **La Bounty Drive**.

20.3 Turn left on **W. Smith Road** at stop sign. Road bends right at mile 20.6 and becomes **Hovander Road**.

21.4 Turn left on **Neilsen Avenue**.

22.1 Turn right into Hovander Homestead Park.

22.6 Tour Hovander Homestead Park, enjoy a picnic lunch, then return to Neilsen Avenue and turn left (north) toward Ferndale. *Note: Tennant Lake Park, with Interpretive Center, boardwalk, fragrance garden, and wildlife observation tower, is 0.2 mile right from this intersection.*

23.8 Turn left on **Hovander Road**.

24.0 Stop, then turn left on **East Main Street**, cross the Nooksack River, and enter Ferndale.

24.2 Turn right on **3rd Avenue** at third traffic light. Bakery on right.

24.3 Turn left on **Vista Drive** as 3rd Avenue ends.

24.6 Bear right on **Malloy Drive** as Shuksan Street crosses. Head up the first of several low, rolling hills.

26.9 Turn left on **Brown Road** as Malloy ends and proceed uphill and across Vista Drive at mile 27.8.

31.9 Turn right on **Kickerville Road** as Brown Road ends.

32.3 Turn left on **Grandview Road**, past main entrance to Atlantic Richfield Company Cherry Point Refinery at mile 33.7 and across Jackson Road at 34.4.

35.3 Turn right on **Point Whitehorn Road**, which bends right at 36.0 and enters Birch Bay State Park.

36.2 Turn right over small bridge toward overnight camping area.

36.3 End of ride at picnic area parking lot.

"...is steep and goes straight down to the water."

62 LUMMI ISLAND

STARTING POINT: (A) 32 miles: Pioneer Park in Ferndale. Take exit 262 (Ferndale, Axton Road) from I-5. Head west toward Ferndale on Main Street, cross the Nooksack River, and turn left on First Avenue at the first traffic light. Pioneer Park is at the end of First Avenue. Park in the picnic area parking lot.
(B) 51 miles: Birch Bay State Park. Take exit 266 from I-5 (Custer, Grandview Road). Proceed west on Grandview Road. Turn right on Jackson Road and then left on Helwig Road into Birch Bay State Park. Park in the picnic area parking lot.

DISTANCE: 32 or 51 miles.
TERRAIN: Moderate.
TOTAL CUMULATIVE ELEVATION GAIN: 32-mile tour, 630 feet; 51-mile tour, 1100 feet.
RECOMMENDED TIME OF YEAR: July through September.

RECOMMENDED STARTING TIME: 32-mile tour, 9:30 to 10:00 A.M.; 51-mile tour, 8:30 to 9:00 A.M.
ALLOW: 32-mile tour, 5 hours; 51-mile tour, 7 hours or overnight.
NOTE: Toll ferry.
POINTS OF INTEREST
Reef-net boats and boatyard

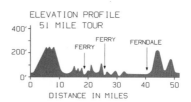

The Lummi Peninsula is encompassed by the Lummi Indian Reservation, as illustrated by the Tribal Center at the northern end of the peninsula with school, church, and other community structures. Lummi Island, however, is outside the reservation, and it is in this island's Legoe Bay that the reef-net boats are anchored in fall to harvest the annual sockeye run. An extensive boatyard with rail-mounted launching dollies houses the wooden boats at other times of the year, providing "dry-land" storage and convenient maintenance areas.

But culture is not the only attraction on this ride. Miles of seascape stretch to the west, south, and east. The rocky cove between Migley Point and Village Point invites closer investigation on foot. For the hiker-biker, trails lead to the summit of Lummi Mountain from Sunrise Cove. A gravel bar stretches across The Portage at low tide to Point Francis and Neontawanta Beach. Automobiles drive this bar, although occasionally one gets stuck in the middle of the bar with an incoming tide. An enterprising local resident maintains a large farm tractor just for towing stranded vehicles up out of the salt water.

M.V. Whatcom Chief, Whatcom County's only ferry, plies the waters between Gooseberry Point and Lummi Island hourly near midday. The ferry is not large and can accept only a dozen or so bicycles without preempting one or more of the automobile spaces. The crossing is short, however, and when a waiting line occurs, additional crossings are made until the line is emptied.

Traffic on Haxton Way may be heavy at times. On Saturday morning, autos will be heading toward summer homes on Lummi Island, returning by the same route on Sunday afternoon. The mileage log is written for the recommended route on a Sunday. For the least traffic on a Saturday ride, bicycle south on Lummi Shore Road and return via Haxton Way.

MILEAGE LOG—32 Miles

0.0 Pioneer Park in Ferndale. Head south on road through park.

0.2 Turn right on **Ferndale Road** at back entrance of Pioneer Park. Cross State Route 540 at mile 2.0. Noisemakers and stuffed owls on poles help to protect blueberry fields from birds. Potatoes and table beets compete for root space in the fertile soil of the Nooksack delta.

3.9 Turn right on **Marine Drive** and cross Smuggler Slough. Tall bulrushes and cattails grow in the marsh.

4.8 Bear left, then right, then left again around a wye by the Lummi Tribal Center. Continue west on **Kwina Road**. A sign denotes U.S. Naval Security Group Activity Center.

5.7 Turn left on **Haxton Way** and continue up and down rolling hills. Trees prohibit views of water.

10.5 Turn right by marina, cafe, and tavern to ferry landing. Upon leaving ferry on Lummi Island turn right on **N. Nugent Road**. *Note: Well-stocked grocery 0.1 mile left from ferry landing is the only one on the island.* Road undulates along the shore, becoming quite narrow in places and occasionally swinging inland. The road rounds Migley Point at 13.1 and is renamed **West Shore Drive**. Orcas Island comes into view. As the route rounds Village Point at 15.6 the road name changes to **Legoe Bay Road**. Lighthouse, gravel beach. Portions of the beach are posted private property. Views of Mt. Baker, Orcas Island, Lummi Peak. Clark Island and Barnes Island form a rocky foreground to Mt. Constitution on Orcas. Reef-net boats anchor here in Legoe Bay. Reef-net boat storage and launching facilities at mile 16.3. Cross several sets of launching-tram rails and pass Lummi Island Congregational Church and cemetery on the right at mile 16.6 as the road bends inland and starts uphill.

17.3 Turn left on **S. Nugent Road** toward ferry landing.

18.0 Ferry landing. Upon landing at Gooseberry Point, turn right on **Lummi View Drive** past Whatcom County's Lummi Marine Park at mile 19.0. The road rounds a corner by The Portage at 19.8. Continue along **Lummi Shore Road** as it undulates along the top of a cliff. Cow parsnips and wild roses grow along the road.

26.1 Keep left on Lummi Shore Road as Marine Drive goes right. The Tribal Center here boasts totem poles, a health center, and the Lummi branch Whatcom County Boys' Club.

27.2 Bear right on **Haxton Way**. At 28.2 cross Slater Road (S.R. 540) and continue north.

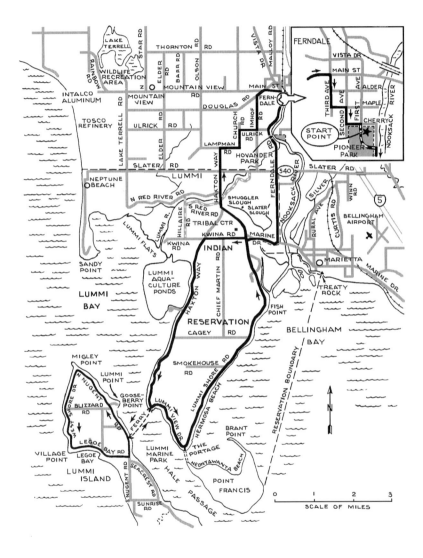

28.7 Turn right on **Lampman Road** as Haxton Way ends. The road bends left at 29.2 and is renamed **Church Road**.

29.7 Turn right on **Ulrick Road**.

30.2 Turn left on **Imhof Road**.

31.0 Turn right on **Douglas Road**.

31.2 Turn right on **Main Street** as Douglas ends.

31.7 Turn right on **Third Avenue** at traffic light in Ferndale. Bakery is to the left on Third Avenue. Turn left on **Maple Street**, right on **Second Avenue**, left on **Cherry Street**, then turn right into Pioneer Park.

32.1 Back at starting point in Pioneer Park.

MILEAGE LOG—51 Miles

0.0 Picnic area parking lot in Birch Bay State Park. Head east out of park on **Helwig Road**.

1.0 Turn right on **Jackson Road**. Pass the towers and tanks of the ARCO refinery as cows graze peacefully in the foreground.

2.7 Turn left on **Aldergrove Road** as Jackson is marked Dead End.

4.7 Turn right on **Kickerville Road**. Multiple sets of power lines appear, all heading south toward the Intalco aluminum plant.

5.7 Bear left on **Rainbow Road** as Kickerville goes on to a dead end. At 6.3 power lines focus into Intalco plant on the right as Lake Terrell and Mt. Baker appear to the east. Abandoned orchard trees in the Lake Terrell Wildlife Recreation Area still bloom and bear fruit.

6.9 Bear left on **Mountain View Road** at stop sign and blinking red light.

7.4 Turn right on **Lake Terrell Road**. Proceed over top of hill and start the long descent past the Tosco refinery toward Lummi Bay. Miles of mud flats or waterscape, depending on the tide. At mile 10.5 the road rounds a sharp bend, becoming **North Red River Road**, and makes the final descent to the Nooksack delta.

13.1 Turn right on **Haxton Way**. Continue right on Haxton Way as Lummi Shore Road goes left at 13.5.

19.0 Gooseberry Point ferry landing by marina and tavern. Pay the fee and cross on the ferry. Turn right on Lummi Island on **N. Nugent Road**. *Note: Well-stocked grocery is 0.1 mile left from the ferry landing .* At 21.5 round Migley Point as the road is renamed **West Shore Drive**, and at 24.0 round Village Point; reef-net boats, view of Orcas Island.

25.7 Turn left on **S. Nugent Road**.

26.4 Turn right toward ferry landing just past grocery store. Cross on ferry and turn right on **Lummi View Drive**.

28.2 Road bends left by The Portage and becomes **Lummi Shore Road**.

34.5 Keep left by Lummi Tribal Center as Marine Drive goes right.

35.6 Bear right on **Haxton Way**. At 36.6 stop and cross S.R. 540 (Slater Road).

37.1 Turn right on **Lampman Road**.

37.6 Road bends left and is renamed **Church Road**.

38.1 Turn right on **Ulrick Road**.

38.9 Turn left on **Ferndale Road** as Ulrick ends.

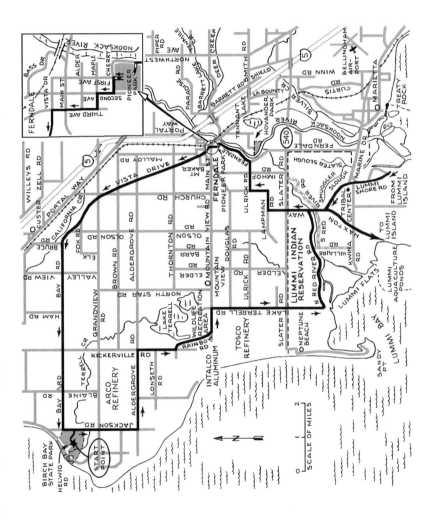

39.6 Turn left into back entrance of Pioneer Park and ride through the park.

39.8 Turn left on **Cherry Street** at main entrance to park. Proceed right on **Second Avenue**, left on **Maple Street**, right on **Third Avenue**. Cross Main Street at traffic light; Ferndale bakery.

40.2 Turn left on **Vista Drive** and start up long, moderate grade. The name of the road changes to **Bay Road** as Bruce Road goes right at mile 44.8. Cross Kickerville Road at mile 47.6.

48.6 Continue straight on Bay Road as thoroughfare bends right on Blaine Road.

49.6 Turn left on **Jackson Road**.

49.9 Turn right on **Helwig Road** into Birch Bay State Park.

51.0 Back at starting point.

"I think I'll get this smoked."

63   FERNDALE–EVERSON
(Nooksack Netherlands)

STARTING POINT: Pioneer Park in Ferndale, Whatcom County. Take exit 262 from I-5 and head west. Cross Nooksack River, then turn left at first traffic light on First Avenue. Pioneer Park is at the end of the street. Park in parking lot.

DISTANCE: 38 miles.
TERRAIN: Mostly flat, several short hills.
TOTAL CUMULATIVE ELEVATION GAIN: 550 feet.
RECOMMENDED TIME OF YEAR: Any season.
RECOMMENDED STARTING TIME: 9:30 A.M. *Note: Shops closed on Sunday in Everson and Lynden.*
ALLOW: 5½ hours.
POINT OF INTEREST
Nooksack Valley scenery

ELEVATION PROFILE

200′   EVERSON LYNDEN

0′

0   10   20   30   40
DISTANCE IN MILES

The fertile Nooksack River bottom land, ideally suited to the industrious immigrant Dutch farmers, has been given careful and expert care for four generations. Fields of corn and potatoes spread across many acres, and hundreds of dairy cattle graze the lush, green pasturelands. Raspberries and blueberries also occupy an important place in the agricultural picture.

This Nooksack Netherlands bicycle ride follows the flood plain of the Nooksack Valley between Ferndale and Everson. Only a few glimpses of the river are afforded, however, as extensive use of dikes and levees has been necessary to keep the river under control during the flood season. A fine network of backroads gives the bicyclist an opportunity to see farms and their animals close at hand. Names on the mailboxes show the large percentage of residents of Dutch ancestry in the valley. Views of snow-capped Mt. Baker to the east belie the otherwise complete picture of the flat Netherlands.

The attractive small town of Lynden exudes a feeling of pride in the community, exemplified by neatly tended gardens in the yards along immaculate streets. All shops close on Sunday, including the bakeries.

MILEAGE LOG

0.0   Leave Pioneer Park on **First Avenue**. Head out to the traffic light.
0.2   Turn right on **Main Street**. Cross the Nooksack River, go under a railroad trestle, and cross over I-5.
1.0   Turn left on **Barrett Avenue**. Bicycle through open farmland. Road bends right at mile 1.4 and becomes **Paradise Road**. Pass Woodland Cemetery at mile 3.0.
3.2   Turn left on **Northwest Drive**. Pass under major power line. Road bends right at 6.1 and becomes **West Wiser Lake Road**. Snowberries grow along the fences. Cross Guide Meridian Road at 8.7 as

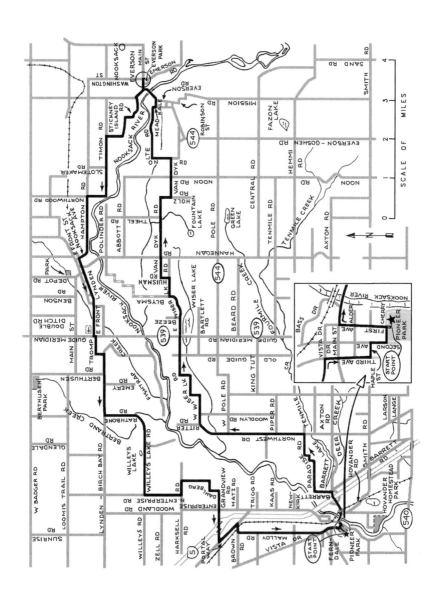

road is renamed **East Wiser Lake Road**. Public fishing access to the lake appears on the right.

9.8   Turn right with Wiser Lake Road as Blysma road goes on.

10.3   Turn left on **Huisman Road**. Road turns right at mile 10.6 and is renamed **Van Dyk Road**. Cross Hannegan Road at mile 11. 2.

13.8   Turn left on **Nolte Road** as Van Dyk Road turns right. Road bends right and changes name to **Mead Avenue** at mile 15.8.

15.7   Turn left on **Kale Street** and join **State Route 544**. Join **Everson Road** as it comes in from the right and cross the Nooksack River.

16.5   Turn right on **Main Street** with S.R. 544 into Everson; cafe.

16.7   Turn right on **S. Washington Street** and right again into Everson Park; shelter, tables, restrooms. After lunch return to Main Street.

16.9   Turn left on **Main Street** and continue straight as S.R. 544 goes left. Road bends right at mile 17.2 and is renamed **Park Drive**.

17.5   Bear left on **Stickney Island Road**. Blueberry farm.

19.2   Turn left on **Timon Road** as Stickney Island Road ends. Road turns right at 20.8 and becomes **Northwood Road**.

21.2   Turn left on **Hampton Road** at stop sign. As it enters Lynden the road climbs a hill and is renamed **Nooksack Avenue**.

22.9   Turn left on **East Front Street**. Shopping center, bakeries, ice cream parlor, and groceries at mile 24.3. Northwest Washington Fairgrounds on the left at mile 24.6; fair is held in mid-August.

25.0   Turn left on **State Route 539** as Front Street ends and then immediately right again on **Tromp Road** by a drive-in. Road soon bends left.

25.7   Bear right on **Lynden–Birch Bay Road** as Tromp Road ends. Notice the many birch trees.

27.3   Turn left on **Rathbone Road**, which crosses a creek at 28.2, bends right, and is renamed **Willeys Lake Road**.

30.2   Turn left on **North Enterprise Road** as Willeys Lake Road ends.

31.2   Turn left on **Harksell Road** as thoroughfare swings right.

31.6   Turn right on **Dahlberg Road** as Harksell is marked Dead End. Turn several corners with Dahlberg Road. Road bends right at 32.8 and becomes **Grandview Road**, crosses Enterprise Road at mile 33.3, and I-5 on an overpass at mile 33.9.

34.2   Turn left on **Portal Way** (**Old 99**).

34.9   Turn right on **Brown Road**.

35.1   Turn left on **Malloy Road**. Proceed over several short hills.

37.4   Bear left on **Vista Drive** at stop sign.

37.7   Turn right on **Third Avenue** past bakery in Ferndale. Turn left on **Maple Street** from Third Avenue, then right on **Second**, left on **Cherry**, and right into Pioneer Park; end of ride at mile 38.0.

64 BELLINGHAM–LYNDEN (Bloedel–Berthusen)

STARTING POINT: Bloedel-Donovan Park in Bellingham, Whatcom County. Take exit 253 from I-5 in Bellingham. Turn right on King Street, then left on Lakeway Drive 1.6 miles. Bear left on Electric Avenue as the road forks. Bloedel-Donovan Park is on the right, surrounded by a chain link fence, 0.9 miles farther. Ample parking lot. Park open 8 A.M. to 8 P.M.

DISTANCE: 44 to 52 miles.
TERRAIN: Half hilly, half flat. Strenuous.
TOTAL CUMULATIVE ELEVATION GAIN: 1900 feet.
RECOMMENDED TIME OF YEAR: Avoid snow, otherwise year around.
RECOMMENDED STARTING TIME: 9 A.M., spring through summer; 8 A.M., fall and winter. *Note: Shops closed on Sunday in Lynden and Everson.*
ALLOW: 7 hours.
POINTS OF INTEREST
Berthusen Memorial Park (closed September 30 to April 15)
Wayside chapel

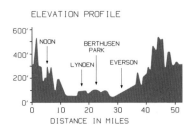

The road winds through the hills, following a small creek. Corn and wheat cover the lower hillsides. Small farmhouses appear occasionally, nestled in the valleys. Groves of birch trees rustle in the breeze. A bit of New England? No, this is Whatcom County in western Washington.

The cultural surroundings change unexpectedly as this tour leaves Bellingham's lakeside suburb and threads its way north to the Nooksack Valley. The New England scenario is encountered early in the ride, followed by the predominantly Dutch names on mailboxes and road signs in the broad, flat Nooksack Valley near Lynden. Dutch pastries in the bakery windows in Lynden are difficult to ignore. On Sundays, however, shops are closed and these treats are not available.

Berthusen Park is worth seeing for its own sake. The 237-acre homestead was donated to the city of Lynden to be maintained as a perpetual park. Much of the land is leased to neighboring farmers for grazing and crops, providing revenue to operate and maintain the public park areas. The yard around the farmhouse is lavishly landscaped, requiring much of the caretaker's time for maintenance. The Berthusens' privy, fashioned from an old cedar stump, now is a quaint showpiece. The main barn has been taken over by the Puget Sound Antique Tractor and Machinery Association to house their equipment, which they display at an annual threshing bee in August. Behind the house and barn, Bertrand Creek rushes under a bridge leading to the picnic areas. A grove of magnificent old fir and cedar trees provides shade for secluded park benches, tables, fire circles, playground

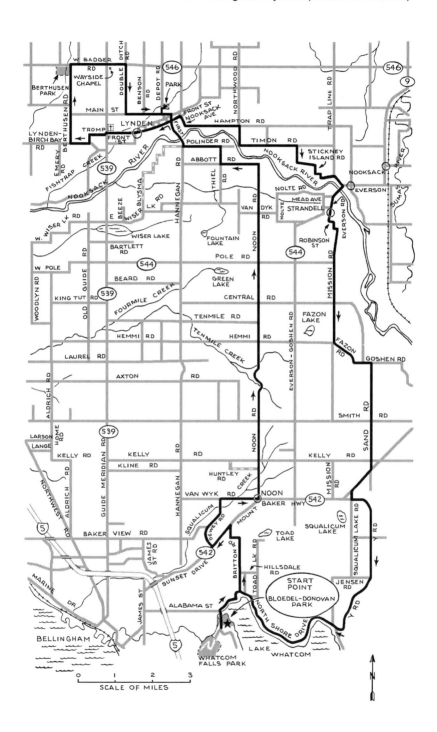

equipment, and picnic shelters with fireplaces. Two roomy, enclosed cooking-dining shelters boast gas stoves, sinks with hot water, varnished tables, and benches with backs. What a wonderful place for a group cook-out!

As the route returns to Lynden, a small wayside chapel attracts attention. Diminutive pews face a small altar. Muted music fills the chapel in response to commands from a push button.

Lynden's City Park on Fishtrap Creek offers another opportunity for rest and recreation. Paths through the forest and a footbridge over Fishtrap Creek invite the visitor to stay.

On the return to Lake Whatcom the hills begin again, building to a climax at the pass between Squalicum and Lookout mountains. After a long, two-mile descent from the pass, one last series of short hills bars the way along North Shore Drive before the route returns to its starting point.

MILEAGE LOG

0.0 Parking lot, Bloedel-Donovan Park in Bellingham. Leave the park and turn right on **Electric Avenue**. Bear right as various roads join from the left and the road changes name to **North Shore Drive**. Bear left at 0.7 as animated arrows warn of a sharp turn.

0.9 Turn right with North Shore Drive at the base of a small hill, then left and uphill on **Britton Road**.

2.9 Turn left on **Mt. Baker Highway (State Route 542)** and ride along the right-hand shoulder.

3.6 Go past Chance Road, then turn right on **Dewey Road** and descend to the floor of Squalicum Creek Valley.

4.1 Turn right with Dewey Road as Baker View Road goes left . Ride past a power substation along fences decorated with Scotch broom.

5.0 Turn right on **Van Wyk Road** as Dewey Road climbs up to meet it and ends. Descend to the valley again, cross Squalicum Creek, and climb the hill to the community of Noon by the Mt. Baker Highway.

6.0 Turn left on **Noon Road**. Descend to the valley again and recross Squalicum Creek for the last time. Ascend a hill on the other side; top a summit at mile 7.3.

9.0 Descend to Tenmile Creek, wind around base of hill, and ascend hill on the other side. The road bends left at 14.7 and is renamed **Abbott Road**. A short distance farther, a turnout from the roadway on the right affords access to the bank of the Nooksack River. At low water, miles of gravel bars are exposed.

15.8 Turn right on **Thiel Road**. At mile 16.2 follow the thoroughfare left as it is renamed **Polinder Road**.

17.3 Turn right on busy **Hannegan Road** and cross the Nooksack River into Lynden.

18.0 Turn left on **Front Street** as First Street goes on. *Note: To shorten this ride by eight miles, turn right on Third Street from Front Street, cross Main Street, and stop for lunch at Lynden's City Park on Fishtrap Creek. Return to Main Street and continue at log mileage 26.9.* Oak trees line Front Street as it passes through the shopping district. A Dutch bakery on the left has a strong attraction for bicyclists. At Seventeenth Street, a shopping center on the right offers the double attraction of a second bakery and an ice cream parlor. All are closed on Sunday. Bicycle racks are provided in the parking lot. Continue on Front Street past Northwest Washington Fairgrounds.

19.8 Pass colorful Monumenta Cemetery, turn left on **Guide Meridian Road (State Route 539)**, and immediately turn right on **Tromp Road**, which soon bends left and heads downhill.

20.5 Turn right on **Birch Bay–Lynden Road** as Tromp Road ends.

21.0 Turn right on **Berthusen Road**. Strawberry fields and green pastures line the way. At 21.8 continue as the thoroughfare on Main Street joins from the right. At 22.0 stay on Berthusen Road as the thoroughfare turns left on Loomis Trail Road. At 22.8, Berthusen Memorial Park on the left is the nominal lunch stop. For inquiries about group facility reservations, write the caretaker at 8837 Berthusen Road, Lynden, WA 98264, or call (360) 354-2424.

23.1 Turn right on **West Badger Road**. Roadside sign here for Berthusen Park.

24.1 Cross State Route 539 and continue on **State Route 546 (East Badger Road)**. Little wayside chapel on the right, open sunrise to sunset.

24.6 Turn right on **Double Ditch Road**. Deep ditches appear on both sides of the road. Farm ducks dabble in a ditch as though it were made just for them.

25.8 Turn left on **Main Street**. Lynden schools appear to the left and right. At 26.9 cross Third Street (Depot Road); Lynden's City Park is to the left 0.3 mile.

27.0 Turn right on **First Street** as Main Street ends.

27.1 Turn left on **Front Street** at traffic signal; do not continue downhill on First Street.

27.4 Turn right on **Nooksack Avenue**. This descends a hill and is renamed **Hampton Road**.

29.2 Turn right on **Northwood Road**. Road bends left at 29.6 and is renamed **Timon Road**.

31.2 Turn right on **Stickney Island Road**. Road name changes to **Park Drive** as Trap Line Road goes left at 32.9. Road bends left by Everson Riverside Park at 33.1 and is renamed **West Main Street**.

33.3 Turn right on **Everson Road (State Route 544)** at stop sign. Cross the Nooksack River.

33.7 Bear left with Everson Road as Kale Street (S.R. 544) goes right.

34.2 Turn left on **Robinson Street** in Strandell and cross abandoned railroad grade. The road turns right and is renamed **Mission Road**.

37.5 Turn left on **Fazon Road** as Hemmi Road goes right. Bear left with the thoroughfare as it acquires the name **Goshen Road**.

38.8 Turn right on **Sand Road**. *Note: To visit Deming Logging Fairground, continue on Goshen Road 1.5 miles.*

41.4 Turn right on **Mt. Baker Highway (State Route 542)**.

42.2 Cross Squalicum Creek and turn left on **Squalicum Lake Road**.

42.4 Turn left on **Y Road**. Continue on Y Road over the pass and down through the forest to Lake Whatcom.

46.7 Bear right on **North Shore Drive** at the bottom of the hill and follow around the north end of the lake.

51.6 End of tour at Bloedel-Donovan Park.

*"Would you believe **all** the jelly doughnuts?"*

65   DEMING–SILVER LAKE

STARTING POINT: Parking lot of Mt. Baker Senior High School in Deming. Take exit 255 from I-5 in Bellingham. Head east on Mt. Baker Highway (State Route 542) 15 miles to Deming. Turn right on First Street by cafe and grocery, then right again on Deming Road to starting point.

DISTANCE: 41 miles.
TERRAIN: Hilly.
TOTAL CUMULATIVE ELEVATION GAIN: 1300 feet.
RECOMMENDED TIME OF YEAR: March through November.
RECOMMENDED STARTING TIME: 9 to 10 A.M.
ALLOW: 6 hours.
POINTS OF INTEREST
Whatcom County's Silver Lake Park
Thousand-year-old cedar log by Deming Post Office

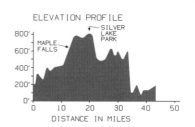

Silver Lake Park, part of Whatcom County's fabulous park system, lies hidden and sequestered in the upland foothills of the Mt. Baker National Forest. Green lawns paved with gravel paths carpet the picnic area along the shores of the lake, while hiking trails lead into the quiet, secluded forest. Overnight accommodations range from campsites nestled back among the trees to rustic cabins for rent by the day or week. A separate group camp offers protective shelter to its occupants. Outhouses of unique A-frame design typify the imaginative wood frame and log architecture of service buildings, lodge, and limited food concession.

Our bicycle ride stops at Silver Lake Park for lunch. The route to this Valhalla of parks begins in Deming and, crank by crank, slowly journeys up into the ethereal world of the forest primeval. Fog and mist accompany the ascending parties, casting a spell only to be broken by occasional shafts of sunlight.

A swift descent through dense forest precedes the dash along the Canadian border. South Pass Road heads up steeply but soon gentles out through clearings in the forest. Streams trickle down the hillside through large stands of western paper birch, as three minor summits precede another precipitous drop to the Sumas River Valley. Rural valley roads, interrupted by the communities of Lawrence and Nugent's Corner, complete the tour back to Deming.

MILEAGE LOG

0.0   Parking area of Mt. Baker Senior High School in Deming. Head east along **Deming Road** past post office. Slice of large cedar log on display on right.

0.6   Turn left, cross the highway, and head up **Marshall Hill Road**. The gravel surface is usually in good, firm condition. At mile 2.0 a waterfall cascades from spring on the left.

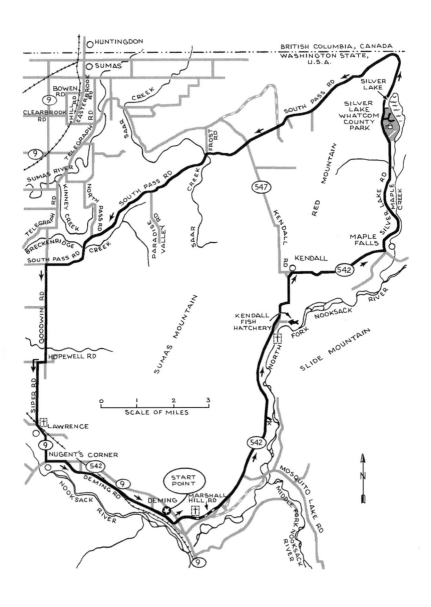

2.1 Turn left on **State Route 542**. Grocery store and coin laundry at mile 3.1. Cross Bell Creek at mile 3.9. An unmarked side road goes right at mile 4.8 to the bank of the North Fork Nooksack River. A roadside park here with fireplaces, grass, trees, trash bins, and chemical toilets. Cross Kendall Creek at mile 8.3.

9.1 Bear right with S.R. 542 at a wye as State Route 547 (Kendall Road) goes left. Grocery and cafe.

12.2 Turn left on **Silver Lake Road** by grocery and post office. The route follows Maple Creek north past cattle grazing the green pastures; pleasant valley scenery. Proceed gradually uphill, passing southern boundary of Whatcom County's Silver Lake Park at mile 15.2; driveway on right at mile 15.4 goes to ranger's residence and the group camp area.

15.7 Turn right into Silver Lake Park, a superbly designed and maintained Whatcom County park.

16.2 Main lodge, food concession, and picnic area by lake. After lunch, head back out of park.

16.7 Leave the park, turn right, and continue heading over a summit past Black Lake Scout Camp on right at mile 17.9. Road bends left by the U.S.–Canadian border and is renamed **South Pass Road**. Continue down through a valley, across State Route 547, up over a pass, and down into the next valley.

31.5 Turn left on **Goodwin Road**. On the left, an old schoolhouse, complete with bell, is now the home of Glen Echo Community club. A lumber mill is on the right.

34.0 Bear right with thorougfare on **Hopewell Road** as Goodwin Road is marked Dead End.

34.3 Turn left with thoroughfare on **Siper Road**.

36.1 Cross railroad tracks and turn left at stop sign on **State Route 9** as Lin Road goes on to a dead end.

37.2 Turn left on **State Route 542** in Nugent's Corner. Cafe, bakery, grocery.

37.5 Turn right on **Deming Road**. Railway grade crossing at mile 39.7.

40.8 End of ride back at Mt. Baker Senior High School.

"Trying out cleats."

66 DEMING–MOSQUITO LAKE

STARTING POINT: Parking lot of Mt. Baker Senior High School in Deming. Take exit 255 from I-5 in Bellingham. Head east on Mt. Baker Highway (State Route 542) for 15 miles to Deming. Turn right on First Street by cafe and grocery, then right again on Deming Road to starting point.

DISTANCE: 28 to 38 miles.
TERRAIN: Hilly.
TOTAL CUMULATIVE ELEVATION GAIN: 740 feet.
RECOMMENDED TIME OF YEAR: Spring through summer. Avoid hunting season.
RECOMMENDED STARTING TIME: 9 to 10 A.M.
ALLOW: 4 to 5 hours.
POINTS OF INTEREST None outstanding, just interesting rural scenery.

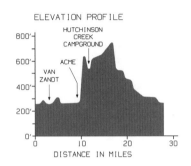

Mosquito Lake, the apparent namesake for this ride, is an insignificant, marsh-edged puddle that few people other than an occasional desperate sport fishing enthusiast or hunter ever visit. The lake is not a major feature of the tour. The name of this ride comes rather from Mosquito Lake Road, which winds through spectacular back-country scenery. Mt. Baker, although close by, is eclipsed by the steep foothills, but this lack is more than made up for in other ways. This is basically a short ride, but it offers challenging hills and can be extended by incorporation of short side trips.

The old concrete highway east of Deming, once the main highway, cuts through a picturesque, rocky prominence above the Nooksack River. Deadly nightshade vines line the roadside ditch, decorating it with dark blue flowers and bright red berries. Everybody's Store at the Van Zandt junction is a fascinating place. Home-cooked meals, Bavarian sausages, Greek cheeses, organic-grown staple foods in bulk, and noodles of all types excite the culinary imagination. But don't load the bicycle too heavily: the first hill up Mosquito Lake Road is a dandy.

Hutchinson Creek Campground (Washington State Department of Natural Resources) furnishes picnic tables along a rushing stream. Great old fir and cedar stumps display the springboard notches of yesteryear's logging techniques. Second-growth timber now has reached considerable size, making this an attractive campground. The creek, however, is the only apparent water supply. Hiking trails lead off along the creek. As the route continues, Douglas fir plantings in various stages of growth illustrate the DNR forestry methods. Soon the road dives down steep switchbacks to the Middle Fork Nooksack, where small farms line the valley and extend up the steep hillsides. An old schoolhouse, converted into a senior citizens' center, informs the passerby that this is Welcome Valley. If you like backwoods rides, this is a good one.

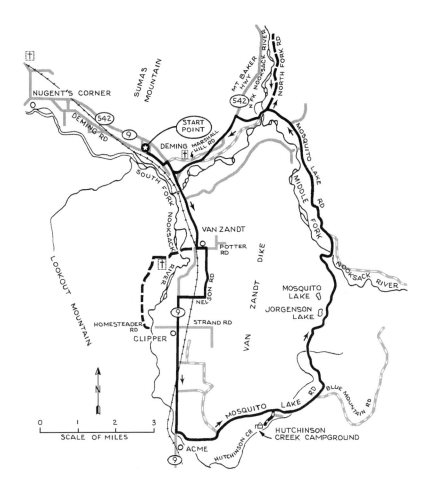

MILEAGE LOG

0.0 Parking lot of Mt. Baker Senior High School in Deming. Head east on **Deming Road**.

0.5 Turn right on **State Route 542 (Mt. Baker Highway)**.

1.0 Turn right on **State Route 9**. At mile 2.2 an old cemetery on the left is built up above the surrounding terrain to ensure against flood erosion.

3.2 Continue straight as S.R. 9 bends right at Van Zandt junction and turn left on **Potter Road**; Everybody's Store on the right. *Note: For an interesting side trip, follow Potter Road 3.3 miles up the valley to the right by the grocery. The bridge is out near Clipper, however, so unless venturesome wading is contemplated, retrace route.*

3.5 Turn right on **Nelson Road** as Potter Road is marked Dead End.

5.4 Cross railroad tracks and turn left on **State Route 9**. Acute-angled railway crossing at mile 7.4.

8.9 Turn left on **Mosquito Lake Road** just before S.R. 9 crosses the South Fork Nooksack River to Acme (grocery, cafe closed Mondays). At 9.3 a gravel turnout provides access to the riverbank as the road swings away from the river. Climb steep hill.

11.5 Turn right on a gravel road toward Hutchinson Creek Campground. Bear right shortly thereafter as a side road forks left. Picnic tables, pit toilets, trails. Nominal lunch stop.

12.6 Return to **Mosquito Lake Road** and turn right. The road parallels Hutchinson Creek as forest closes in on both sides, primarily alder, maple, and cedar; the alder bark is white, almost like birch. Flora include foxglove, buttercup, salmonberry, elderberry, and thimbleberry. Sword ferns decorate the road and creek banks, and maidenhair ferns spread their lacy fronds from under overhangs. Cross Hutchinson Creek at 13.7 and again, for the last time, at 15.0. Glimpses of Mosquito Lake on the left at 17.4.

18.6 Start a steep downhill run to the Middle Fork Nooksack. Cross the river and continue down the valley. At 20.5 the road performs a zigzag maneuver past poultry farms. Deep green pastures show the results of fertilizer spreading. Number 41 Welcome schoolhouse at mile 22.2, dated 1918, has been converted to the Welcome Valley Senior Center with attractive landscaping; open midday Thursdays only. North Fork Road goes right at 23.6. *Note: This is another interesting side trip of 8.6 miles round trip to Racehorse Creek, where the road heads steeply uphill. Good views of the river for the first 2.4 miles, after which the road heads away from the river and becomes unpaved. Must return to this junction.* Cross the North Fork Nooksack River at 23.9.

24.6 Turn left on **Mt. Baker Highway** (**State Route 542**) as Mosquito Lake Road ends. Cafe on the left at 25.9.

26.9 Continue on S.R. 542 as S.R. 9 joins from the left. A small lily pond on the right nestles between rock cliffs. The Nooksack River appears on the left.

27.4 Bear left on **Deming Road** as Marshall Hill Road goes right.

28.0 Back at starting point.

67   BELLINGHAM HARBOR–LAKE WHATCOM

STARTING POINT: Boulevard Park in Bellingham. Take exit 250 from I-5 (State Route 11 South, Chuckanut Drive). Turn left at exit on State Route 11 (Old Fairhaven Parkway). Turn right at traffic light on 12th Street and continue on thoroughfare as it is renamed Finnegan Way and 11th Street. At junction with S. State Street, turn left on Bayview Drive into Boulevard Park.

DISTANCE: 42 miles.
TERRAIN: Hilly.
TOTAL CUMULATIVE ELEVATION GAIN: 1900 feet.
RECOMMENDED TIME OF YEAR: Any season.
RECOMMENDED STARTING TIME: 9 A.M.
ALLOW: 5 hours.
POINTS OF INTEREST
Boulevard Park
Bloedel-Donovan Park
Whatcom Falls Park
Cornwall Park
Old City Hall

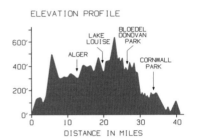

Bellingham's Boulevard Park, a recent addition to that city's park system, offers the unusual attractions of a covered pedestrian railroad overpass and stairway, a gazebo overlooking Bellingham Harbor, and a pedestrian cause-way bridging a portion of that harbor. Green lawns and ocean breezes bring out numbers of kite fliers on sunny days. Inviting as it may be, it is only the first of several parks along this tour route.

Soon after leaving Boulevard Park, the route joins the Interurban Park Trail, using the grade of an old electrified railway that joined Bellingham and Mt. Vernon with passenger and local freight service from 1912 to 1930. A long-missing trestle forces travelers down a circuitous path to Arroyo Park, where the county road system is rejoined. The route then makes its way through parklike scenery with forested hillsides and several sparkling lakes.

Whatcom County's Samish Lake Park, a short side trip, offers facilities for swimming, picnicking, boating, or just the chance to relax among the trees. Shelters and a summer food concession add to the atmosphere of the park.

As the route winds its way up the hill from Lake Whatcom, the Sudden Valley Campground invites passersby to stop for an overnight sojourn. A few hills later, Whatcom Falls Park and Bloedel-Donovan Park compete for attention and the opportunity to host a picnic lunch. In addition to the falls, Whatcom Falls Park exhibits the rearing ponds of a fish hatchery, while Bloedel-Donovan Park, built on the site of a former sawmill, proudly displays an old steam logging railroad locomotive alongside green lawns and lake-front beaches.

The wooded trails of Cornwall Park present yet another diversion from the automotive road system. The many trail branches pose decision problems, but a simple key is found to unravel the maze: just keep right. Monuments tell of the early history of the western Masonic Lodge and of a trail built along the route of an ambitiously planned intercontinental telegraph system to Siberia via the Bering Strait. The telegraph line was the brainchild of Perry McDonough Collins, who promoted the idea to the Western Union Telegraph Company, and construction was pursued vigorously by the company after the failure of the first transatlantic cable in 1865. Several thousand miles of line had been completed when, in 1867, the second Atlantic cable was successfully completed and the first cable repaired and put into service. This put an end to the ambitious British Columbia–Alaska–Siberia route. Portions of this "Telegraph Trail" are traversed also in Tour 56. At the exit from the park, the route continues on a parkway along Squalicum Creek. Marinas and other harbor scenery follow the end of the parkway.

Although not truly a park, the Old City Hall museum has its own attractions, with many interesting free exhibits. From here it is only a short ride along the waterfront back to Boulevard Park.

MILEAGE LOG

0.0 Parking lot of Boulevard Park in Bellingham. Go out entrance on **Bayview Drive**.

0.2 Turn half right on **11th Street** as Bayview Drive ends. Continue through Fairhaven on thoroughfare as its name changes to **Finnegan Way** and **12th Street**. Cafes, grocery.

1.0 Turn left at traffic light on **Old Fairhaven Parkway (State Route 11)**. Wide asphalt walkway alongside road.

1.7 Turn right on gravel-surfaced path shortly before 24th Street crosses. A sign by the path prohibits motorized vehicles. Continue on **Interurban Park Trail**.

2.5 Bear left and downhill on a side trail as a barricade appears ahead. Dismount and walk bicycles down steep trail with stepped erosion stops.

2.6 Turn left on **Old Samish Road (Lake Samish Road)** as trail ends. Arroyo Park appears alongside as the road climbs a moderate grade up the creek valley. The traffic of I-5 roars by on the left as the clearings of suburban farms punctuate the forested valley. A hiking trail to Pine and Cedar lakes goes right at mile 4.5.

7.1 Turn right as Old Samish Road ends. Grocery on right. Descend steep hill.

8.0 Bear left as road forks near base of hill and continue on **East Lake Samish Drive**. *Note: Samish Lake Whatcom County Park is 0.9-mile side trip on right road fork.* Public fishing access with chemical toilets on right at 9.1.

10.5 Turn left on **Nulle Road** and continue under I-5. Continue with thoroughfare as it bends right at 10.8 and is renamed **Pacific Highway** and finally **Old Highway 99 N**.

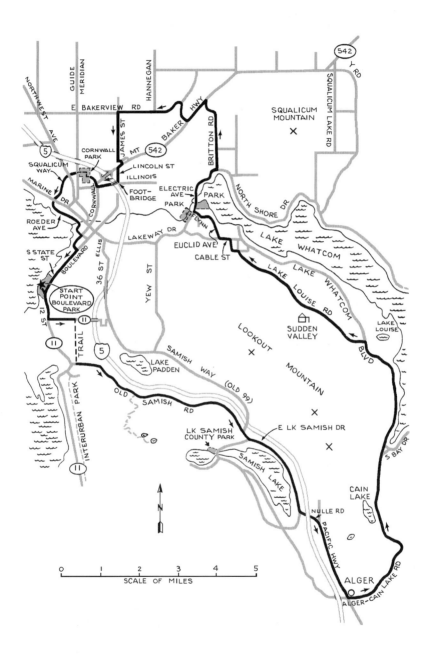

13.1 Turn left on **Alger–Cain Lake Road** by Alger Bar and Grill as Lake Samish Road goes right. Grocery on left at 16.7.

17.7 Bear left on **Lake Whatcom Boulevard** as N.E. Cain Lake Road goes right to South Bay Drive. Road bottoms out near south end of Lake Whatcom, then climbs to contour along the cliffs on the west side of the lake.

21.0 Turn left uphill on **Lake Louise Road** as Lake Louise and Sudden Valley recreational facilities appear on right. Road climbs in stages past Sudden Valley residential areas. Sudden Valley Campground on left at 23.3, open to public for camping from Memorial Day to Labor Day. Enter Bellingham at 25.0.

25.2 Turn left at stop sign on **Fremont Street** and continue uphill past suburban homes.

25.5 Turn right on **Lakeview** as Fremont ends.

25.7 Turn left on busy **Cable Street** as Lakeview ends. Climb over a short rise and descend around a curve.

25.9 Go past Lakeway Street and turn right on **Euclid Avenue**; follow thoroughfare as it is renamed **Lakeside Avenue** and **Flynn Street**. Views of Lake Whatcom.

27.2 Turn right on **Electric Avenue** as Flynn Street ends. *Note: To visit Whatcom Falls Park turn left on Electric Avenue 0.4 mile.*

27.5 Turn right into Bloedel-Donovan Park for lunch stop. Restrooms, green lawns, picnic and swimming facilities, food concession open during summer months. After lunch continue north on **Electric Avenue** as it crosses the exit arm of the lake and is renamed **North Shore Drive**. Grocery on left as road makes a sharp left turn at 28.2.

28.5 Turn left on **Britton Road** and continue on marked bikeway.

30.3 Turn left on **Mt. Baker Highway (State Route 542)** as Britton Road ends. Continue on wide paved shoulder.

31.0 Turn right on **Dewey Road** and descend to valley of Squalicum Creek.

31.5 Turn left on **E. Bakerview Road** as Dewey Road goes right.

33.3 Turn left on **James Street Road**. Cross Squalicum Creek again.

34.5 Turn left with thoroughfare in shopping center, immediately turn right on side road, turn right on **E. Sunset Drive**, and immediately turn left on **Lincoln Street**

35.0   Turn right on pedestrian overpass and cross I-5 as Lincoln bends left and is renamed E. Illinois Street. Continue on **W. Illinois Street** on other side of freeway.

35.8   Turn right on **Cornwall Avenue** at traffic light.

35.9   Turn left into Cornwall Park entrance as Cornwall Avenue is marked Dead End.

36.1   Go past restrooms and bear right on asphalt-surfaced trail. At each opportunity thereafter, bear right on right fork of paved road or trail. At 36.6 cross Squalicum Creek on wooden footbridge. Monument on other side tells of Collins Telegraph Trail. Pass picnic shelter and continue out of park.

36.8   Cross Meridian Street at traffic light and continue on marked bikeway on **Squalicum Way** alongside Squalicum Creek.

38.3   Turn left on **Roeder Avenue** as Squalicum Way ends. Continue past a marina and into Bellingham's port district.

39.6   Cross Whatcom Creek inlet and turn right on **Central Avenue** as Roeder ends. *Note: Old City Hall, now a well-appointed museum, appears on the left up Central Avenue.* Central turns left along Bellingham Harbor, is renamed **Chestnut Street**, and begins to climb.

40.0   Turn right on **Cornwall Avenue** at traffic light. Road descends to port district again.

40.6   Turn left on **W. Pine Street**, cross railroad tracks, and angle left up hill on **Wharf Street**.

40.9   Turn right on **Boulevard** as Wharf Street ends. Continue with thoroughfare as it is renamed **S. State Street**. Upper Boulevard Park area begins at 41.8; scenic trail through trees along top of bluff. Historic information sign at 41.9. *Note: Trail continues across pedestrian bridge over railroad to tall stair tower to lower park; difficult to negotiate with bicycles even when carried.* Return to State Street and continue south.

42.3   Turn right on **Bayview Drive** into Boulevard Park.

42.5   End of tour in parking lot of Boulevard Park.

68 SAMISH VALLEY

STARTING POINT: Fishing access on south shore of Lake Whatcom. Take exit 240 from I-5 (Alger). Head east toward Alger. Cross Old Highway 99 North and continue on Alger–Cain Lake Road, bearing right on N.E. Cain Lake Road as road forks on downhill run. Turn right on South Bay Drive 0.3 mile to fire hall/fishing access start point, posted "Conservation License Required", but parking is allowed along road.

DISTANCE: 29 miles.
TERRAIN: Easy to moderate.
TOTAL CUMULATIVE ELEVATION GAIN: 760 feet.
RECOMMENDED TIME OF YEAR: Anytime.
RECOMMENDED STARTING TIME: 9:30 A.M.
ALLOW: 5 hours.
POINTS OF INTEREST
Lake Whatcom Steam Railroad
Samish Salmon Hatchery

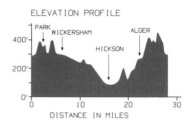

The Samish River, a small, slowly moving stream originating in the Nooksack River Valley between the Whatcom County towns of Acme and Wickersham, flows southward through a narrow gap between Anderson Mountain and a long, steep ridge of 4000-foot peaks. Its shallow drainage is emphasized by the vast, swampy areas that line its banks. Several smaller creeks empty into it as it turns westward and winds its way through a broad valley, eventually emptying through a tidal estuary into Samish Bay near Edison. In periods of heavy rainfall the river occasionally rises over its banks to flood many miles of its valley.

Our bicycle tour enters the valley of the river Samish after skirting the southern end of Lake Whatcom and negotiating the low pass between Stewart Mountain and Anderson Mountain. Summer rides will be accompanied by the nostalgic sound of a steam train huffing and puffing its way up this grade to enter the valley at Wickersham. Blasts of the steam whistle echo for miles. Foxglove dots the dry banks along highway cuts, and salmonberries thrive in the moist soil of the swales. Carefully cultivated cornfields and new berry vines parading in neat rows contrast with old, neglected orchards. Alder forest closes in, then gives way to a broader open valley where pastures support horses and cattle. Numerous small creeks, their beds dug deep and lined with stones, meander throughout the valley. Dairy farms occupy many acres near Old Highway 99, providing nesting sites for the several varieties of swallows that call the valley home from early spring to early fall.

Upon encountering the old highway, our tour leaves the Samish Valley and follows the narrow course of Friday Creek north past two Skagit County parks and a fish hatchery. One of the oldest in the state, the salmon hatchery has been in continuous operation since 1895. Nearby Pomona Grange Park offers picnic tables, shelter, and an informative nature trail.

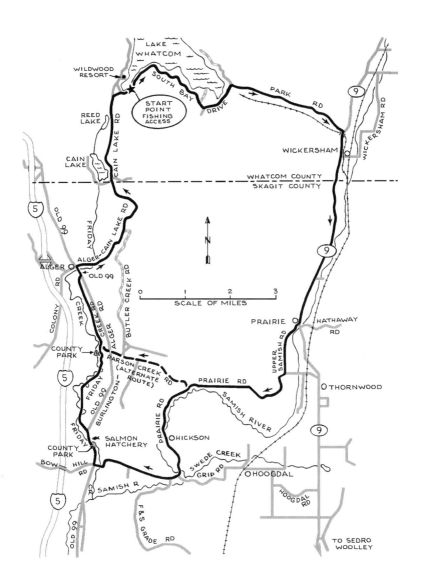

Cain Lake appears on the left just as the route heads back into Whatcom County. Glen Haven Grocery provides a welcome snack stop. Platted residential acreage rolls over the gently sloping hillside, accompanying an exhilarating downhill run to Lake Whatcom at South Bay, the end of this ride.

MILEAGE LOG

0.0 Fishing access on south shore of Lake Whatcom. Head east on **South Bay Drive** through second-growth forest.

3.3 Community of Park. Cross railroad tracks and turn right on **Park Road**. At 5.7 pass small Mirror Lake.

6.1 Turn right on **State Route 9** at stop sign and pass over the tracks of the Lake Whatcom Railway below in a narrow cut. Community of Wickersham at 6.8. At 7.2 enter Skagit County, leave Whatcom County. Cross under power lines at mile 8.8 as valley begins to broaden out. Samish River winds down the eastern edge of the valley to the left.

10.4 Turn right on **Upper Samish Road**. Pedal through forest past abandoned houses and neglected orchard trees with gnarled branches. Beef cattle graze the pastures.

11.7 Turn right at stop sign onto **Prairie Road** as Upper Samish Road ends.

14.3 Keep left, still following Samish River as it winds through the valley; Parson Creek Road goes right. *Note: As an alternative, Parson Creek Road can be followed to Donovan Park to shorten this ride by 3.5 miles.* Road nudges up alongside the river and crosses it at 15.4, passes Hickson Community Hall and Fire Station at 15.8. Again cross Samish River on concrete bridge. Keep right with Prairie Road as Grip Road goes left. Horizons retreat as the valley broadens at 16.8. Stay with Prairie Road as F & S Grade Road crosses valley to the left. Cross Friday Creek at 18.5.

18.7 Turn right onto **Old 99 North** as Bow Hill Road goes on and uphill. Skagit County's Pomona Grange Park and Samish Salmon Hatchery at 19.1.

19.5 Turn left on **Friday Creek Road**. Diversion dam at mile 19.8 on Friday Creek supplies water through pipeline to fish hatchery. Road crisscrosses the creek several times. Donovan County Park (Skagit County) on the left at mile 21.7; picnicking, swimming, fishing. Crank uphill and emerge into pastureland. Friday Creek parallels below on the left.

23.4 Turn left on **Old 99 North** for a short distance. Cross Silver Creek.

23.5 Turn right on **Alger–Cain Lake Road**. Tavern/cafe (good food) at this corner. At 26.3 enter Whatcom County, leave Skagit County. Cain Lake on the left. Glen Haven grocery on left at 27.0.

28.0 Bear right on **N.E. Cain Lake Road**.

28.3 Turn right on **South Bay Drive** at stop sign at bottom of hill.

28.6 Back at starting point.

SKAGIT COUNTY

In recent years, Skagit County has been known to the bicyclist for the League of American Wheelmen's annual Mt. Vernon Century Run each September. The delightfully flat delta regions of the Skagit and Samish rivers, rich in agricultural, aquatic, and forest scenery, are but a sample of the available touring. The middle and upper reaches of these rivers and their tributaries, although generally not as flat, offer many more miles of rewarding low-traffic routes. Fidalgo Island, at the western extremity, provides extensive waterscapes. The wide distribution of state and city parks throughout the county provides welcome rest, picnic lunch, and camping facilities for bicycle touring and compensates for the general lack of county parks. The natural features and the low-traffic byways of this region, rather than highly developed recreational facilities, are the principal attractions for bicycle touring. Come see for yourself what Skagit County has to offer.

"Did you get a good look?"

69 BAY VIEW–BELLINGHAM (Chuckanut–Samish)

STARTING POINT: Bay View State Park. Take exit 231 from I-5 just north of Burlington. Follow signs for Edison and Bow. Turn left on Wilson Road toward Bay View and Bay View State Park. Turn right to the state park in Bay View as Wilson Road ends. Park in the Joe Hamel Beach parking lot.

DISTANCE: 48 miles.
TERRAIN: Hilly with moderate grades.
TOTAL CUMULATIVE ELEVATION GAIN: 1300 feet.
RECOMMENDED TIME OF YEAR: Spring through fall.
RECOMMENDED STARTING TIME: 8:30 A.M.
ALLOW: 6 hours.
POINT OF INTEREST
Chuckanut Drive

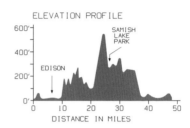

ELEVATION PROFILE

Chuckanut Drive has long been a favorite scenic drive for motorists, offering far-reaching views of Samish and Chuckanut bays. This road also is great for scenic bicycle touring. The roadway twists and turns almost continuously, forcing automotive traffic to go at a slow pace. The grade for the old Tacoma–Bellingham Interurban Railway, which winds along the hillside above the highway, has been acquired by Whatcom County for recreational use. Although largely unimproved, it provides an interesting alternative to the less scenic portions of the highway.

The route from Bay View State Park through Edison is shared with several other rides in this vicinity, but the constantly changing agricultural activities always make it interesting. As the turn is made onto Chuckanut Drive, two miles of straight highway appear, but a wide shoulder eases traffic concerns. This is past in a matter of minutes, and the slow, winding, up-and-down hills can be enjoyed. Several turnouts occur along the way, offering viewpoints over the water. Gulls wheel about the cliffs while ducks and loons probe the shores. A bald eagle often perches in the treetops, watching for a meal opportunity. Larrabee State Park, at the summit of Chuckanut Drive, offers picnicking and hiking opportunities but comes too early in the ride for a lunch stop. Instead, the route proceeds to the bottom of the hill, then ascends gradually along Chuckanut Creek, and eventually joins with Old Highway 99 for a plunge to Samish Lake. Samish Lake Park, one of Whatcom County's many extraordinary recreational facilities, offers swimming and picnicking opportunities. A food concession is open from Memorial Day to Labor Day. After lunch the route follows scenic backroads around the Samish River Valley. A short meander along Joe Leary Slough leads to Bay View–Edison Road and the return to Bay View State Park.

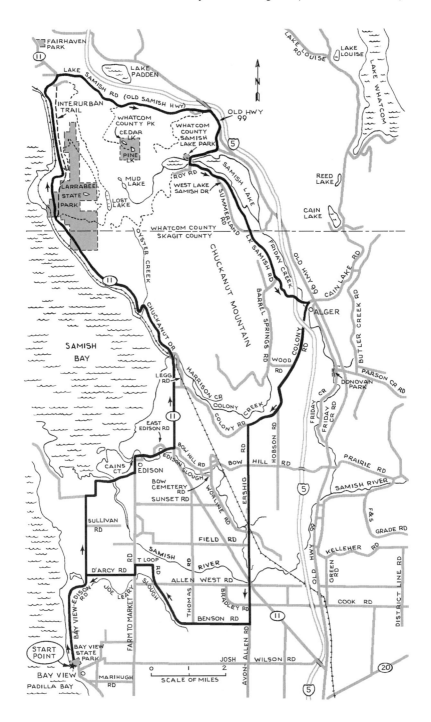

MILEAGE LOG

0.0 Beach parking lot of Bay View State Park. Leave the park and turn right (north) toward Edison on **Bay View–Edison Road**.

4.7 Turn right with Bay View–Edison Road. At 5.8 cross the Samish River, at this point an estuary with high dikes.

6.3 Turn left at stop sign at T junction as Bay View–Edison Road ends.

6.6 Bear left on **Cains Court** in Edison, right on **Gilmore Avenue**, then left and continue out of town on **West Bow Hill Road**.

7.8 Turn left on **State Route 11 (Chuckanut Drive)**. At 10.0 the road rises on a bridge over the railroad tracks and Colony Creek and continues uphill. Bigleaf maples color the hillside in fall. Cross Oyster Creek as the road dips around a horseshoe bend at 11.7. Rest areas on the left at 12.4 and 13.4 with good views of Puget Sound. South entrance to Larrabee State Park at 15.5; picnic areas. Interurban Trail heads uphill to the right; alternative bike route. North entrance to Larrabee State Park and campground at 15.8. A trail goes up Chuckanut Mountain on the right to a viewpoint and Fragrance Lake. The road starts down, undulating as it descends.

19.6 Turn right on **Lake Samish Road** at the bottom of the hill and start up again on a moderate grade. Mailboxes along the road bear street names of **Old Samish Road** and **Old Samish Highway**. At 21.6 continue on the road as a trailhead appears on the right for Whatcom County's Pine Lake and Cedar Lake parks. These are hike-in day parks; trail not recommended for bicycles.

24.3 Turn right on **Old Highway 99** as it comes in from the left on an overpass of I-5. This is the summit of the ride. A grocery store on the right is the last one before the lunch stop.

25.1 Bear right near the bottom of the hill as the road forks. This is easy to miss on a fast downhill run.

26.0 Turn right into Whatcom County's Samish Lake Park. Food is not allowed along the beach, but several beautifully varnished picnic tables are secluded along trails among the trees farther up the hillside. A food concession in the main lodge is open afternoons from Memorial Day to Labor Day. After lunch, leave the park and continue across a bridge over an arm of Samish Lake.

26.1 Turn left on **West Lake Samish Drive** as Roy Road continues on to a dead end.

26.9 Turn left with West Lake Samish Drive as Summerland Road continues and starts uphill.

28.7 Continue on **Lake Samish Road** as Summerland Road goes right and Nulle Road goes left. Continue straight toward Alger at 30.2 as Barrel Springs Road angles right; cross I-5 on an overpass at 30.6.

31.0 Turn right on **Colony Road**. At 31.7 pass under I-5 and continue gradually uphill past swampy ponds with water lilies and vine maple. Emerge shortly among cleared pastures.

34.9 Turn left on **Ershig Road**. After a level stretch, the road starts downhill. Cross railroad tracks at the bottom of the hill.

38.9 Bear left on **State Route 11 (Chuckanut Drive)**, cross the Samish

River, and bear right on **Sam Bell Road**. At 39.0 cross Allen West Road and continue on **Avon-Allen Road**. Grocery immediately to the left on Chuckanut Drive.

39.9 Go past intersection of Bradley and Cook roads, then turn right on **Benson Road**.

43.1 Cross Allen West Road and continue on **T Loop Road** by tavern.

44.1 Turn left on **Farm To Market Road** as T Loop Road ends.

44.3 Turn right on **D'Arcy Road**.

45.5 Turn left on **Bay View–Edison Road** and crank uphill.

48.1 Turn left into Bay View State Park.

48.2 Back at starting point.

*"So **that's** what it says!"*

70 BAY VIEW–SEDRO WOOLLEY

STARTING POINT: Bay View State Park. Take exit 231 from I-5 just north of Burlington. Follow signs for Edison and Bow. Turn left on Wilson Road toward Bay View and Bay View State Park. Turn right to the state park in Bay View. Park in the Joe Hamel Beach parking lot.

DISTANCE: 40 miles.
TERRAIN: Periodic hills interspersed with flat.
TOTAL CUMULATIVE ELEVATION GAIN: 1000 feet.
RECOMMENDED TIME OF YEAR: All seasons.
RECOMMENDED STARTING TIME: 9 A.M.
ALLOW: 5½ hours.
POINTS OF INTEREST
Trumpeter swan wintering area

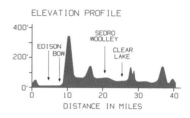

Although this tour has several hills, it also offers many miles of quiet roads along the level valley floors of the Samish and Skagit rivers. Observed from the hilltops, acres of wheat, corn, peas, and cole crops turn the valley into giant checkerboard patterns.

For most of the year, the Skagit and Samish rivers are well behaved, flowing placidly at levels far below the tops of their diked banks. Under conditions of heavy fall or spring rains, however, the waters rise to threaten inundation of the countryside. The high dikes surrounding the Skagit, with the help of dams on that river's upper reaches, do a good job of containment. The Samish River, although of much lesser volume, occasionally overflows its banks and takes over the countryside. In any case, it is always discomforting to peek over a dike and observe the water behind it several feet above the level of the roadway.

In addition to the major rivers, many creeks, sloughs, and ditches drain the valleys. Ducks and great blue herons fly suddenly from these watercourses as the startlingly unusual two-wheeled vehicles roll by. Red-winged blackbirds tinkle their songs from cattail clumps. In winter, flocks of tundra and trumpeter swans swim placidly in the Nookachamps Creek basin or graze the fields in the Skagit Valley where, with financial support from the Washington State Department of Wildlife, farmers plant winter grain crops to provide forage for the swans.

MILEAGE LOG

0.0 Joe Hamel Beach parking lot, Bay View State Park. Leave the park and turn right (north) toward Edison on **Bay View–Edison Road**. The road climbs a bit, allowing several views of Padilla Bay, then descends to the Samish Valley.
4.7 Turn right with Bay View–Edison Road toward Edison. The left fork of this road goes four miles to Samish Island and a large filbert nut farm.

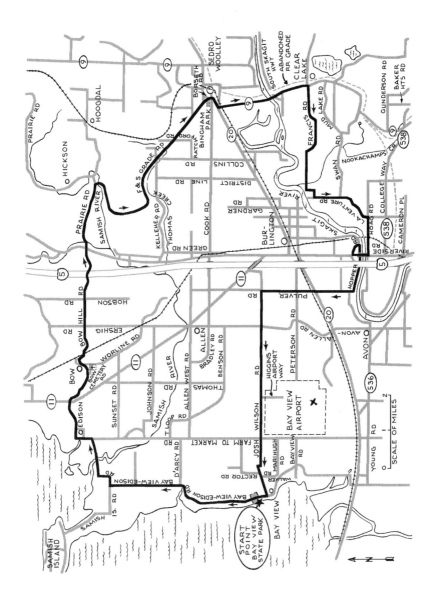

Moored boats line the dikes at the Samish River crossing.

6.3 Turn left at stop sign as Bay View–Edison Road ends. Take either fork of the road through Edison as they rejoin at the other side of town.

7.8 Cross State Route 11 (Chuckanut Drive) and continue on **Bow Hill Road** past a dairy farm with cheese store, a blueberry farm, through the community of Bow at mile 8.7, across the railroad tracks, and up Bow Hill. This is a fairly long, steep pitch.

11.1 Go over the summit of Bow Hill, sail down the other side, and cross I-5 on an overpass.

12.4 Cross Old 99 No. road and continue on **Prairie Road**. Cross Friday Creek.

14.3 Turn right on **F & S Grade Road**. Descend to the Samish River bridge, cross, and climb the shoulder of Butler Hill on an easy grade. Sword ferns grow among the trees. Occasional gaps in the forest allow interesting views of the valley. Descend to the Skagit Valley and follow F & S Grade Road into Sedro Woolley.

19.9 Turn right at junction with **Borseth Road (State Routes 9** and **20)**, then immediately right again into Bingham Park for lunch. Bingham Park is not heavily endowed with recreational facilities, but the picnic tables, shelter, trees, and lawn make this a good bicycle lunch stop. After lunch, follow State Routes 20 and 9 south to the Route 9 junction. Cafes in Sedro Woolley city center.

20.6 Turn left with **State Route 9**. Ride along the causeway shoulder, being careful to watch for broken glass. Cross the Skagit River and continue toward Clear Lake. Fast, heavy traffic through here.

23.2 Turn right on **Francis Road** as Old Day Creek Road goes left. The road proceeds by several oxbow lakes, makes several bends, climbs a hill, and is renamed **La Venture Road**.

28.5 Turn right on **Hoag Road**, freewheel downhill, then attack another short, steep hill.

29.5 Turn right on **Riverside Road (Old Highway 99)** and cross the Skagit River. A sidewalk is available, but look out for broken glass.

29.7 Turn right on **Whitmarsh Road**, follow it down to **Hopper Road**, and turn right again. Proceed west under the bridge and along the Skagit River on Hopper. The road turns right (north) at 31.0 and becomes **Pulver Road**. Follow Pulver Road past cultivated fields. Cross State Route 20.

33.6 Turn left on **Josh Wilson Road**, cross the valley, and head up a steep grade on Bay View Ridge.

39.2 Turn right on **Bay View–Edison Road** toward Bay View State Park.

39.6 Turn right into Bay View State Park, then left down to the beach parking lot. End of ride.

71 BAY VIEW–MT. VERNON

STARTING POINT: Bay View State Park, Skagit County. Take exit 231 from I-5 north of Burlington. Follow signs for Edison and Bow. Turn left on Wilson Road to Bay View and Bay View State Park. Turn right toward state park on Bay View Road in Bay View as Wilson Road ends. Park in the Joe Hamel Beach parking lot.

DISTANCE: 41 miles.
TERRAIN: Mostly flat.
TOTAL CUMULATIVE ELEVATION GAIN: 190 feet.
RECOMMENDED TIME OF YEAR: Any season.
RECOMMENDED STARTING TIME: 9 A.M.
ALLOW: 5 hours.
POINTS OF INTEREST
Anacortes Water Treatment Plant
Flowering bulb fields in season

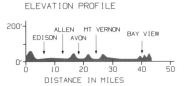

Certainly this is a ride for all seasons. Farming is at its best in this fertile, flat land north and west of Mt. Vernon. Fields of brilliant yellow daffodil, scarlet tulip, and blue Dutch iris dazzle the eyes from March into June. Gladioli display a rainbow of colors. Fall crocus covers the land with a blanket of lavender. In addition to floral crops, the deep, rich soil produces quantities of winter wheat, corn, and peas. A carefully tended blueberry farm near Bow encompasses many acres as it expands its operation, while nearby strawberries and raspberries flourish in the loamy earth. Eggs and chickens are raised on a large ranch along Riverbend Road. Carrots, broccoli, and cabbage compete for the remaining acreage. Homes and buildings, neat and clean, enhance the picture of industrious, hard-working, and successful farmers.

Magnificent views of snowy, 11,000-foot Mt. Baker close by to the north-east add to the pleasures of this bicycle ride, while the Olympics parade along the southwestern horizon. Mt. Constitution on Orcas Island projects its silhouette against the northwestern sky. Across Padilla Bay from the state park, oil refinery towers on March Point send up plumes of steam, while flames shoot out of waste stacks.

This ride is recommended for the bird watcher. In winter, shallow Padilla Bay hosts rafts of waterfowl, such as mallards, baldpates, pintails, buffle-heads, red-breasted mergansers, and scaups, to name a few. Black cormo-rants, necks extended, fly swiftly by, barely skimming the surface of the water. A great blue heron, its long neck folded into an S shape, slowly flaps its huge wings as it disappears in the distance after being flushed from a tidal slough or marshy place. A large-headed bird flying slowly and silently over the fields and marshes will be the short-eared owl, who enjoys being out in the daytime. Flocks of robins descend on holly trees in the winter to devour the red berries. In summer, swallows surround every farmhouse.

The high point of the tour for the machinery buff is the Anacortes Water Treatment Plant, which withdraws water from the Skagit River. Completed in 1972, it is a modern plant with many interesting features. A glance into the "clear well" at the plant entrance provides a convincing demonstration that Anacortes has a sparkling, clean water supply. Tours of this facility are welcomed. Just let the supervisor know a day in advance by writing to 2809 Riverbend Road, Mt. Vernon, WA 98273, or telephone (360) 424-8085 or 293-2151. The facility is open from 8 A.M. to 5 P.M. daily. Allow one hour for the full tour.

Mt. Vernon is the logical stop for lunch on this ride. The Lions Park along the Skagit River just before the route enters the city center is a good picnic spot. For a winter ride, restaurants in Mt. Vernon offer the added attraction of indoor warmth.

MILEAGE LOG

0.0 Bay View State Park, parking lot by the beach. Leave park and turn right (north) toward Edison on **Bay View–Edison Road** (no street signs here). Bay View Cemetery to the right at mile 1.0. Mt. Baker juts up over the horizon as route enters the Samish Valley.

4.8 Turn right toward Edison at a T junction as Samish Island Road goes left. At 6.0 cross Samish River. Tugs, a sailing ketch, and gill-net boats moor along the riverbank downstream from the bridge.

6.6 Turn left at stop sign as Bay View–Edison Road ends.

6.9 In Edison follow the main thoroughfare through town on **Cains Court** and **McTaggart Avenue**. Bear left as Main Avenue intersects from the right by cafe. The road plays tag with Edison Slough as it meanders through farm fields. Cross State Route 11 at 8.1 as the road is renamed **Bow Hill Road**.

9.1 Turn right on **Bow Cemetery Road**. Mallard ducks nest along the marshy swales, parading strings of ducklings in spring.

9.4 Turn right on **Worline Road** as Bow Cemetery Road ends. Bow Cemetery at this corner dates back many decades. Some of the older headstones lean at odd angles.

11.4 Turn right with **Ershig Road**. Dairy milking shed on the left at 12.2.

12.7 Bear left on **State Route 11**, cross Samish River, and immediately bear right on **Sam Bell Road**. Cross Allen West Road and continue on **Avon-Allen Road**. Cross Wilson Road at 14.9 and Peterson Road at 16.1 as Avon-Allen Road circumnavigates base of hill. Peterson leads uphill to the airport on the right. At 17.3 cross railroad tracks and State Route 20. Light planes circle with sailplanes in tow.

18.2 Turn left on **Avon Road** by white church. Cornerstone proudly displays date of 1884.

18.4 Turn left on **Bennett Road** as Avon Road ends.

19.3 Turn right on **Hopper Road** at a stop sign as Bennett ends and Pulver Road goes left. Hopper turns left and runs along base of dike at mile 19.5. At mile 20.2 go under I-5.

20.5 Bear left and up to Old 99 bridge. Turn right over bridge. Sidewalk is often littered with glass and undesirable to ride on. If traffic is heavy, push bicycles carefully along sidewalk. Turn right on **Stewart Road** upon leaving the bridge. Go under freeway at 21.0 and continue

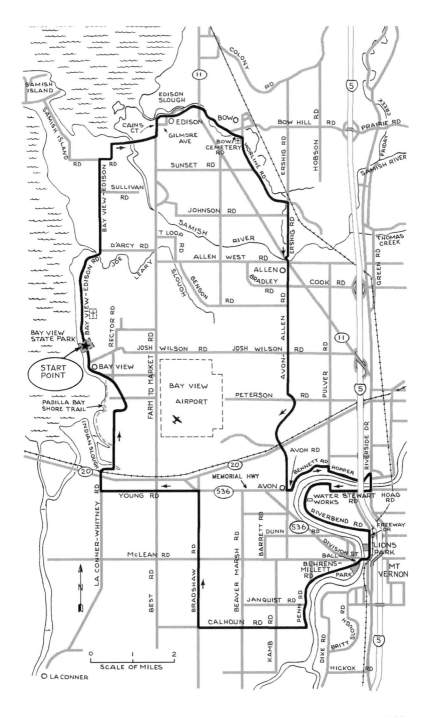

toward **Riverbend Road**. *Note: Buffet and fast-food restaurants are left on Freeway Drive.* Road bends right, then left along the river dike.

23.3 Turn left into City of Anacortes Water Treatment Plant; interesting tour available. After visit, continue along Riverbend Road.

25.0 Turn right on **Freeway Drive** as Riverbend Road ends. Enter Mt. Vernon. Lions Park on right at 25.3; tables, shelters, restrooms, playground. Fence along river protects the unwary from tumbling down the steep bank. Continue along wide concrete sidewalk as it bends right along a Wrong Way street.

25.6 Turn right on **Division Street** at traffic light in Mt. Vernon. Cross Skagit River and immediately turn left on **Ball Street**. (If you overshoot you can turn left on next street, which is Baker.) Edgewater Park on left at 26.1. Road runs along top of dike and gives excellent view of Skagit River, eventually descending from dike and joining **Penn Road**. Road turns right at a potato storage house at 28.3 and becomes **Calhoun Road**. Cross Kamb Road at mile 29.1 and Beaver Marsh Road at mile 29.9.

31.0 Turn right on **Bradshaw Road**. Cross McLean Road at 32.5.

34.0 Turn left at junction with State Route 536. Stay on left shoulder of road and bear left with **Young Road**.

36.4 Turn right on **LaConner-Whitney Road** as Young Road ends.

36.8 Cross State Route 20 by cafe and cross railroad tracks. This is Whitney. Bear right (east) toward Bay View. Cross South Fork Indian Slough at 37.3; tidal dam east of road. Cross North Fork Indian Slough at 37.7; dam on left. *Note: Padilla Bay Shore Trail, marked* Bike Route, *goes left here; interesting two-mile diversion from highway.* Continue straight at crest of short hill at 39.0 as Bay View Road intersects from right. Good views to the west of fertile delta farms, Padilla Bay, and March Point with its oil refineries. Enter Bay View at 40.0; continue toward Bay View Park as Wilson Road goes right to Burlington and I-5.

40.5 Turn right into Bay View State Park.

40.7 Back to parking lot by the beach.

72   FIDALGO ISLAND

STARTING POINT: Fishing access at the south end of Pass Lake, just north of Deception Pass. Take exit 230 (State Route 20) from I-5 and proceed west toward Anacortes. After crossing the Swinomish Channel bridge, follow signs for Oak Harbor and Deception Pass. The fishing access is on the right just as the highway swings south toward the Deception Pass Bridge in Deception Pass State Park.

DISTANCE: 34 miles.
TERRAIN: Hilly with steep grades.
TOTAL CUMULATIVE ELEVATION GAIN: 2100 feet.
RECOMMENDED TIME OF YEAR: All seasons.
RECOMMENDED STARTING TIME: 9 A.M.
ALLOW: 6 hours.
POINTS OF INTEREST
Oil refineries on March Point
Washington Park

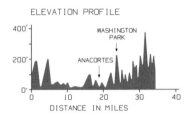

Fidalgo Island, separated from the mainland by the Swinomish Channel, is seldom recognized by the casual traveler as being an island. To most motorists, it is merely a portion of the highway to Deception Pass or the Anacortes ferry terminal. Close investigation, however, reveals this island to have more miles of backroad seascape than any of the other Puget Sound islands. In addition to the water views, this tour offers the bicyclist the chance to examine oil refineries and an unusual city park. Side trips to Guemes Island and LaConner are available, but although this trip is relatively short in miles, it is long on hills. The basic 34-mile loop is enough to satisfy all but the true masochist.

MILEAGE LOG

0.0 Fishing access, south end of Pass Lake. Turn left on **Rosario Road** and merge left with **State Route 20**. A wide, smooth, paved shoulder eases the stress of highway riding.
1.3 Turn right on **Deception Road** by a cafe and plunge downhill.
1.5 Bear left at a wye near the bottom of the hill and turn left at a stop sign with Deception Road. Continue along the water.
2.1 Turn right on **Gibralter Road**. Continue on Gibralter Road as it winds up a hill and past Fidalgo Elementary School at mile 4.5.
4.9 Turn right on **Satterlee Road** and plunge downhill. Pass by Similk Bay Golf Course and start uphill again.
6.5 Turn right on **Summit Park Road** at a stop sign. A forest of oil refinery towers appears to the north.
6.8 Turn right on **Thompson Road**, then left again on **Stevenson Road**.
7.5 Bear left on **Reservation Road** as it merges from the right.
7.8 Cross State Route 20 and turn right on **South March's Point Road**.

111

8.3 Turn left on **March's Point Road**. Depending upon the tide, the scenery here may be shimmering water or miles of mud flats in Padilla Bay. This is a favorite habitat for herons, ducks, grebes, and loons. The road undulates along the water, with many grand viewpoints. Cows graze contentedly alongside the refineries. Large, windblown fir trees lean over the water, and old orchard remnants still bear crops of apples. Immense petroleum tanks with protective safety dikes terrace the hillside above the road. At 11.2 the road goes under a causeway with pipeline from a deep-water tanker terminal to the north, and Anacortes appears across Fidalgo Bay. At 13.1 railroad tracks cross the road and shallow Fidalgo Bay on pilings. This is another waterfowl haven, typically inhabited by cormorants, goldeneyes, loons, buffleheads, pintails, grebes, and scaups. Deer graze contentedly in the fenced green pastures by the refineries.

14.0 Bear right on **State Route 20** and continue on a wide, smooth shoulder.

14.8 Bear right on **Fidalgo Bay Road**. Mt. Baker makes a striking backdrop to green and white refinery tanks and towers. Madrona and dogwood trees line the road. At 16.0 rock screens cover the bank above the highway on the left. The highway's elevation overhead mutes the roar of traffic, allowing bicyclists to enjoy a placid ride along the water. Railroad tracks march across Fidalgo Bay on pilings and pull alongside the road.

16.9 Turn right with thoroughfare on first side road, which bends left again by a power substation. Take the next right turn on **T Avenue**, which parallels the waterfront.

17.9 Cross railroad tracks and turn right on **RQ Avenue**, which shortly is renamed **R Avenue**. A grocery and several fast-food concessions appear between 13th and 11th streets, offering an opportunity to stock the panniers or the stomach with lunch materials.

18.9 Turn left on **4th Street** at a stop sign. As streets dead end, meander along the waterfront and continue on **6th Street**. The Guemes Island ferry terminal, right on **I Avenue**, offers restrooms and a closer look at Guemes Channel. *Note: A side trip to Guemes Island (approximately five miles of roads) is available at this point.* Return to **6th Street** and meander along the water up to **9th Street** and **E Avenue**. Continue south and west along the water to 12th Street.

20.6 Turn right on **12th Street (State Route 20 Spur)**, which is shortly renamed **Oakes Avenue**. At 21.5 a turnout offers picnic tables and a view of the water.

22.7 Continue straight on **Sunset Avenue** toward Washington Park as S.R. 20 Spur swings right to the Anacortes ferry terminal.

23.5 Continue into Washington Park as Beach Road road forks right to beach access. Picnic areas, beach, boat launching, and limited camping facilities are offered here. Continue right, then left on the park loop road. At 23.9 a picturesque wind-blown fir tree leans out over the water. The road goes up the hill on switchbacks with occasional turnouts for viewpoint trails.

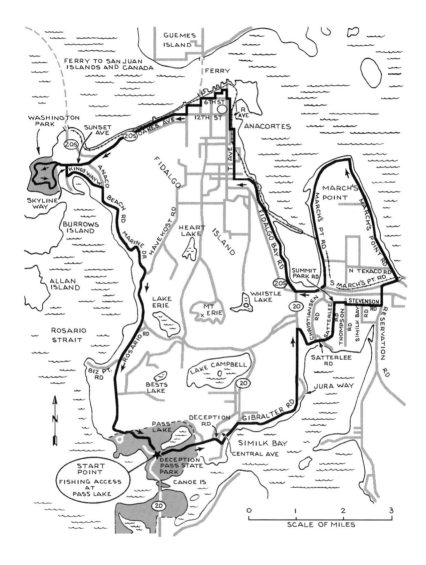

25.3   The road reaches a summit on a rocky promontory. Gnarled juniper, madrona, and fir trees grow from crevices in the moss-covered rocks. In early spring the rocky soil is covered with a carpet of diminutive wildflowers, including the rare calypso orchid, shooting star, yellow buckwheat, white cerastium, pink armeria, and various lilies. Expansive views of Puget Sound and nearby small islands are gained by a short walk along the rock. A few yards down the road from this promontory, a trail leads right to Havekost Monument, a large granite sphere and pedestal. A legend on the monument relates that T. H. Havekost, a pioneer settler, presented this land as Havekost Park to the City of Anacortes. This property was combined with other land donations and named Sunset Park, later changed to Washington Park. Pass the park caretaker's house at mile 25.9. Tame deer roam the clearings here. Bear right and out the park gate past hedges of wild roses.

26.2   Turn right on **Skyline Way**.

26.4   Turn left on **Kingsway West**, which courses around Flounder Bay, then climbs the hillside. Grocery /delicatessen at this corner.

27.4   Turn right on **Anaco Beach Road** and start downhill. Several hills and valleys challenge the leg muscles here. Road is eventually renamed **Marine Drive**.

29.5   Continue on Marine Drive as Havekost Road goes left. More hills.

30.5   Bear right on **Rosario Road** as Marine Drive ends. A tremendous sand bank on the left has been bared by road building. Follow this road as it undulates along the rocky coastline. Skagit County's Sharpe Park invites a short rest stop on the right at the top of a rise at mile 32.3. Rosario Beach Road goes right down to Rosario Beach Park and Walla Walla College Marine Station at mile 32.8.

33.9   Junction with State Route 20 at the south end of Pass Lake. Turn left into the fishing access parking lot. End of ride.

"Look what we found!"

73 BIG LAKE–MT. VERNON (Nookachamps)

STARTING POINT: Big Lake School parking lot (nonschool days only). Take exit 227 (State Route 538, East College Way) from I-5. Turn right (south) on State Route 9 as S.R. 538 ends, 2.2 miles to Big Lake School.

DISTANCE: 38 miles.
TERRAIN: Hilly.
TOTAL CUMULATIVE ELEVATION GAIN: 1100 feet.
RECOMMENDED TIME OF YEAR: Spring through summer. Avoid opening week of lakes and streams fishing season.
RECOMMENDED STARTING TIME: 9 A.M.
ALLOW: 6 hours.
POINT OF INTEREST
High valley and mountain scenery

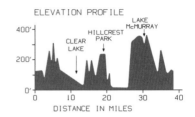

Bicycles whisper along the road, slowly descending through upland pastures and forest. A magnificent buck deer suddenly raises his head, stares for a few brief seconds, then goes bounding off into the forest as though mounted on pogo sticks.

Although the cast for this scene is not always complete, the setting never ceases to be appropriate. The valley of Nookachamps Creek, from the marshy margins of Lake McMurray and Big Lake to the gurgling forest streams of the upper east fork and the swan refuges of the main channel, presents a pastoral scene of unusual variety and beauty. The admission fee is levied in the form of hills to climb.

Flora and fauna are abundant along this ride. Our experience with the deer was, of course, a rare occurence, but for the bird watcher and listener, performances are staged daily in summer by Swainson's thrushes, chickadees, goldfinches, western tanagers, and red-tailed hawks. Tundra and trumpeter swans inhabit the refuges near Clear Lake in winter.

Wild syringa and spiraea blossoms perfume the roadsides. Wild roses provide decoration all year with their pink blossoms and red hips. Fields of corn, bright yellow mustard flowers, and peas head the list of cultivated crops. Apple trees hang over fences.

MILEAGE LOG

0.0 Leave the parking lot by Big Lake School and head north on **State Route 9**.

2.0 Turn right and downhill on **Knapp Road** just after passing a junction sign for State Route 538. Cross the West Fork Nookachamps Creek and start uphill. At the top of the hill, the road emerges into an upland basin with wide-ranging views.

2.6 Turn left on **Baker Heights Road** as Knapp Road ends.

3.4 Turn right on **Gunderson Road** as Baker Heights Road ends. Wide, rolling vistas of pastureland and mountains. At 6.5 the road bends and parallels the East Fork Nookachamps Creek and is renamed **Beaver Lake Road**. Cultus Mountain looms overhead to the east. A massive rock formation at 8.1 juts up out of the flat valley floor, a pillar with near-vertical sides. Cornfields and cow pastures surround this massif. A public fishing access appears by Beaver Lake, with pit toilet at 10.1. Pink spiraea and white oceanspray bushes line the road.

11.2 Turn right on **South Front Street** in Clear Lake. The Sedro Woolley Municipal Beach here is an attractive park but seems to be seldom open.

11.5 Cross State Route 9 and turn right on **Fir Street**.

11.6 Turn left on **Mud Lake Road** and cycle past Mud Lake. A large dairy farm on the left has several large steel silos. Cornfields in the valley to the right provide filler material.

13.3 Turn right on **Swan Road** as Babcock Road goes on, cross Nookachamps Creek at mile 13.6, and crank uphill.

15.2 Turn left on **Francis Road**.

16.2 Now on **Laventure Road** as Hoag Road goes right. Continue on Laventure as road signs are undecided whether to call it Laventure or **La Venture Road**. Pass Skagit Valley Community College and La Venture School.

18.2 Turn right on **East Section Street** as La Venture ends.

18.5 Turn left on **South 18 Street**.

18.9 Turn right on **Blackburn Road** as 18 Street ends. At this corner is Little Mountain Grocery Store, last food supply before lunch stop.

19.2 Turn right on **South 13th Street**.

19.3 Turn left into Hillcrest Park. Extensive, imaginative playground equipment. Rest rooms, cooking shelters with wood stoves, firewood, sinks, water, and electricity invite group cookouts. Sheltered picnic tables are welcome in the rain. This is the recommended lunch stop.

19.7 Head north and west out of the park on **South 11th Street,** then turn left on **Fowler**.

19.8 Follow Fowler around a bend where it becomes **South 10th Street** and finally **Blodgett Road**.

20.0 Cross Blackburn Road and immediately turn left on Blodgett Road as Cedarvale Road continues down the hill. *Note: For cafe lunch, turn right on Anderson Road at 20.5, cross I-5, and turn left 0.5 mile as Anderson ends.*

21.7 Turn right on **Hickox Road** as Blodgett ends.

21.8 Turn left on **Burkland Road**.

23.8 Turn right on **Johnson Road** as Burkland Road ends.

24.3 Turn left on highway frontage road (**Cedarvale Road**) as traffic roars by on I-5.

25.5 Turn left on **State Route 534 (Lake McMurray Road)**. At 25.9 the road crosses a marshy creek and starts ascending to the pass between Devil's Mountain and Conway Hill. This is a fairly strenuous climb. Continue uphill as Lake 16 Road goes left to public fishing at mile 27.3. Teasel plants grow along the roadside, and acres of skunk

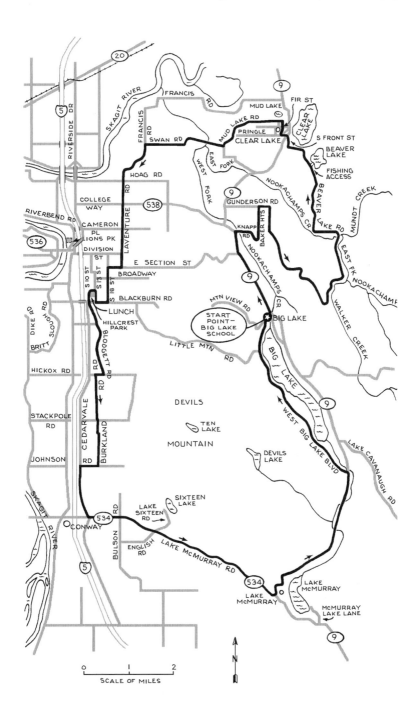

cabbage perfume the air in spring. At 29.8 the road summits and starts down into the Nookachamps Valley.

30.4 Turn left at stop sign on **State Route 9**. A grocery is 100 yards to the right on S.R. 9. Continue around Lake McMurray as the road winds up and down the hillside.

34.0 Turn left on **West Big Lake Boulevard** as granite cliffs appear on the left. Public fishing access at mile 36.4 on the right on Big Lake.

38.3 Back at Big Lake School. End of ride.

74   SEDRO WOOLLEY–CONCRETE

STARTING POINT: Parking lot by Sedro Woolley High School. Take exit 230 from I-5 and follow State Route 20 east to Sedro Woolley. Turn right on State Route 9, left on West State Street, and right on Third Street to Nelson. Park in front of school building on Nelson.

DISTANCE: 52 to 55 miles.
TERRAIN: Mostly flat, a few moderate grades.
TOTAL CUMULATIVE ELEVATION GAIN: 540 feet.
RECOMMENDED TIME OF YEAR: All seasons.
RECOMMENDED STARTING TIME: 9 A.M. summer, 8 A.M. winter.
ALLOW: 7 hours.
POINTS OF INTEREST
Nut Acres filbert farm
Remains of Superior Portland
    Cement plant in Concrete

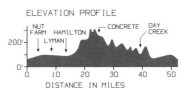

To the casual motorist, State Route 20 appears to be the only road between Sedro Woolley and Concrete. It therefore comes as a delightful surprise to most bicyclists that one can ride this course on enjoyable backroads, spending less than two miles on the highway. The old, bumpy concrete roadway has been paved over with blacktop, making smooth riding through the old town of Lyman. Lyman is now bypassed by Highway 20, and its beautiful old homes and magnificent trees enjoy a drowsy atmosphere along the river.

Closer to Sedro Woolley, the Nut Acres filbert farm provides a special bonus to the nut fancier, offering its nuts at low prices on a U-pick basis during late September and early October.

For many years the Superior Portland cement plant at Concrete supplied materials for construction of the Seattle City Light dams on the Skagit River. With the completion of these projects, the plant was shut down and demolished, and little but the office building remains. A safety award plaque stands in front of this building, proclaiming years of meritorious operation.

The most prominent feature of this ride is the Skagit River itself. Changing vistas of the rushing waters follow one another along the route on both sides of the river. Traffic is very light, making the riding carefree. Miles of agricultural and forest land refresh the eye to make this a relaxing ride.

MILEAGE LOG

0.0 Head south on **Third Street** from parking area in front of Sedro Woolley High School.
0.2 Turn left on **Jameson**.
0.9 Bear left on **Railroad Avenue** as Jameson goes on to a dead end.
1.4 Turn right on **Hoehn Road** as Minkler Road goes on. An old schoolhouse on the right at mile 3.3 has been converted to an attractive

119

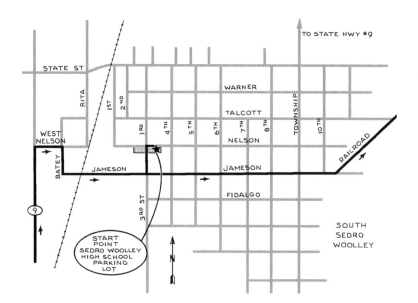

residence. Nut Acres filbert farm is on the right at mile 3.8, just past Duffy Road.

6.2   Turn right on **Minkler Road**.

7.1   Turn right on **State Route 20** and continue on eight-foot oiled shoulder. Pilings from a long-abandoned railroad trestle march across marshy Minkler Lake.

7.8   Turn right on **Lyman-Hamilton Road**.

9.4   Enter Lyman on **Main Street**. A small park on the right shows signs of years of use but still offers water and shelter.

9.9   South Main Street goes right to impressive old houses and yards along the Skagit River. Continue on **West Main Street**. As it enters Hamilton, the road is named **Maple Street**.

13.4   Turn right between two taverns across from market in Hamilton. A street name sign one block later identifies this as **Cumberland Street**. The road turns, is renamed **Water Street,** and continues as a narrow road with trees and shrubbery forming an arch overhead. At 14.0 a public fishing access provides a chemical toilet. Signs proclaim the Shangri-la real estate development as mailboxes rename the road **Shangrila Drive**.

14.9   Turn right at a stop sign on an unmarked road as Shangrila Drive ends and continue along the Skagit River. Cornfields decorate the landscape to the left. Road is eventually marked **Cape Horn Road**.

19.7   Turn right with Cape Horn Road as Wilde Road continues on. *Note: B&B 0.5 mile farther on Wilde Road.* Ride around a bend and crank uphill. Kinnikinnick spreads its trailing vines and red berries along the roadside banks.

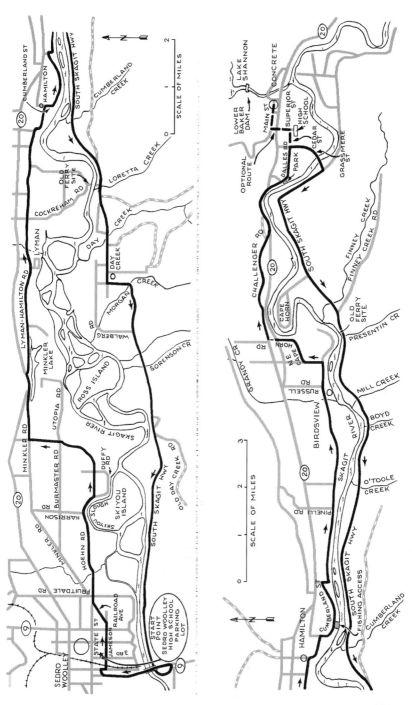

121

21.0 Cross State Route 20 and continue on dirt trail across old railroad grade. Turn right on **Challenger Road** as Gallagher Road continues on. Old log railings appear along the road as it climbs the hillside, descends, and climbs twice again.

23.8 Rejoin **State Route 20** and continue eastward (left). Challenger Road continues on, unpaved and quite rough.

24.0 Turn right on **Dalles Road** and ride along the Skagit River. Trees form a canopy overhead.

25.5 Turn right on **Concrete–Sauk Valley Road** at stop sign as Cedar Street continues on. *Note: For a 2.4-mile side trip past the old cement plant site to cafes in Concrete, continue on Cedar Street, left on Superior Street across State Route 20, then right on Main Street. Return to Concrete–Sauk Valley Road and continue toward the river.* Mt. Baker appears above the nearby forested hills, giving a treat of alpine scenery. This scene is replaced shortly by a view of the Skagit River gorge from the Dalles Bridge.

26.4 Turn right toward Day Creek and Sedro Woolley on **South Skagit Highway**. Public fishing access on right with chemical toilets appears at 30.4.

40.8 Turn left with the main thoroughfare. Day Creek Store appears on the left, stocked with refreshing treats.

50.0 Cross underneath, then turn left (north) on **State Route 9**. Cross the Skagit River and continue along causeway.

51.4 Turn right on **West Nelson** as Goodyear Road goes left.

51.5 Turn right on **Batey** with thoroughfare.

51.6 Turn left with thoroughfare and cross the railroad tracks. Now on **Jameson**. Pass high school athletic field.

52.0 Turn left on **3rd Street**.

52.1 Back at the starting point.

CLALLAM AND JEFFERSON COUNTIES

The tours in these two counties are treated together as the best representatives of the Olympic Peninsula. Although the Olympic Peninsula loop has always been a great attraction for motorists and cyclists alike, the narrow roads, heavy traffic, and logging trucks make much of the route something to be endured. The tours presented here, on the other hand, make the best of the backroads, offering many of the peninsula's most scenic attractions with a minimum of exposure to highway traffic. The rhododendrons of the Quimper and Toandos peninsulas, the great trees and sunny beaches of Kalaloch, and the great sand spits of Dungeness are all strong attractions. Fully seeing, hearing, smelling, and appreciating these attractions from the low-traffic backroads can best be done from a bicycle.

75 SEQUIM BAY–DUNGENESS PARK

STARTING POINT: South parking lot of John Wayne Marina on Sequim Bay. Take State Route 104 east from Kingston to U.S. Highway 101, then north through Discovery Bay and Blynn. Turn right on West Sequim Bay Road 0.5 mile past Sequim Bay State Park 1.2 miles to marina.

Distance: 43 miles; can be shortened to 35 miles.
TERRAIN: Moderate to mountainous.
TOTAL CUMULATIVE ELEVATION GAIN: 1800 feet; short ride 800 feet.
RECOMMENDED TIME OF YEAR: Any season.
RECOMMENDED STARTING TIME: 9 A.M.
ALLOW: 8 hours (6 for short ride).
POINTS OF INTEREST
Olympic Game Farm
Clallam County Dungeness Park
Dungeness Spit

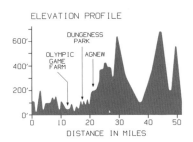

To the casual motorist Sequim is just a wide spot in the road with an annoying stretch of speed limit. To the hiker and sightseer it is the Dungeness Recreation Area and the Olympic Game Farm. To the retiree it is sun country and uncluttered landscapes. To the bicyclist it is all of these and more. Few motorists ever stop to observe the milky glacier water flowing through the braided, gravelly channels of the Dungeness River. Only a hiker or bicycle rider has the repeated opportunity to see and hear the bright willow goldfinch, or "wild canary," as he flits from fence post to fence post. Other avian sights for the self-propelled include turkey vultures and radio-controlled model gliders soaring on the dynamic wind wave over the cliffs by Dungeness. To these attractions are added the striking narrow canyons of rushing creeks and the unusual views from upland meadows.

These are many of the features of this ride. To see them all, however, requires a long day. The route is complicated by the absence of bridges that washed out decades ago and were never replaced. Roads do not go through from the middle to the upper portions of Happy Valley. The upland valley traverse is interrupted by these deficiencies, and the resulting route resembles a crazy waltz step.

MILEAGE LOG

0.0 John Wayne Marina. Leave parking lot and turn right (north) on **West Sequim Bay Road**. The road winds up a moderate grade to a summit at mile 1.7.

1.5 Turn right on **Washington Harbor Road** in the middle of a downhill run.

2.3 Turn left on **Schmuck Road** as Washington Harbor Road is marked Dead End. The road crosses the small valley of Bell Creek, past swamp dogwood, snowberry, wild roses, syringa, ninebark, and

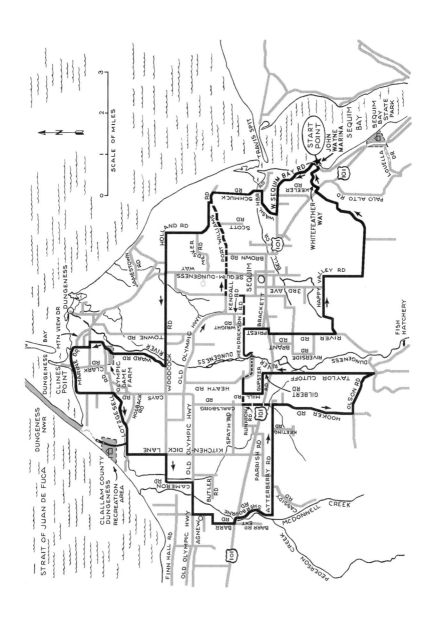

oceanspray and climbs the far valley wall. Fields of alfalfa, wheat, and oats cover the rolling plateau beyond, offering lush foliage to the occasional deer.

3.7 Turn left at T junction on **Port Williams Road**.

4.0 Turn right on **Holland Road**, which dives down a hill, crosses Gierin Creek and emerges by homes surrounding a golf course.

6.6 Cross Sequim-Dungeness Way and continue on **Woodcock Road**.

8.9 Cross the Dungeness River and turn right on **Ward Road** toward Olympic Game Farm. Ride along Dungeness River. Buffalo and elk appear in pasture to the left just before the game farm entrance at mile 10.3. The guided tour (Memorial Day to Labor Day) is well worth the 90 minutes needed to enjoy it. The nominal fee goes to support the farm and its propagation of endangered species. Continue north, cross Matriotti Creek, and crank up short steep hill.

10.6 Bear right at stop sign at top of hill on **Lotzgesell Road**.

11.1 Turn left on **E. Anderson Road** as Lotzgesell ends at a stop sign.

11.2 Turn right on **Marine Drive**. Ride along cliff overlooking Dungeness Spit to viewpoint over Clines Point at 11.8. Rosebushes, oceanspray, and snowberries cling to the bluff, displaying decorative blossoms and berries. Continue past a B&B, a motel, and wind-sculptured fir trees growing along the edge of the cliff. At 12.8 the road bends left, is renamed **Cays Road** and heads toward the towering Olympic Mountains.

13.7 Turn right at stop sign on **Lotzgesell Road**.

15.2 Turn right on **Voice of America Road** into Dungeness Recreation Area Clallam County Park.

15.8 Lunch stop in picnic area along bluff; restrooms, water. The blacktop road continues into the campground area. A dirt trail winds through the forest and down the cliff to the Dungeness National Wildlife Refuge along Dungeness Spit. The round trip to the beach is two miles, with several more miles of beach walk optional. When lunch and hiking are completed, return to park entrance.

16.4 Turn right on **Lotzgesell** at park entrance and stay with it as it turns left (south) after 0.2 mile and is renamed **Kitchen-Dick Lane**.

17.3 Turn right on **Woodcock Road**. Follow Woodcock as it bends left at 18.0 and is renamed **Cameron Road**.

19.0 Turn right on **Old Olympic Highway** as Cameron Road ends. Nice five-foot blacktop shoulder here, narrows to 18 inches after crossing bridge over McDonnell Creek at mile 19.3.

19.8 Turn left on **Barr Road** by church as Gunn Road goes right. At 20.3 the road bends right; note the small irrigation ditches along the side of the road. At 20.6 the road bends left again.

21.3 Cross and turn left on shoulder of **U.S. 101**.

21.5 Turn right on **Sherbourne Road** by gas-grocery. Climb a short, steep rise and emerge into an open valley.

22.3 Follow the thoroughfare as it turns left and is renamed **Atterberry Road**. A slow, steady climb offers rewards of views of the Strait of Juan de Fuca.

25.1 Turn right at stop sign on **Hooker Road** as Brueckner Road continues on to a dead end. *Note: For those interested in the shortened 35-mile ride, turn left across U.S. 101 and follow Runnion Road, Railroad Bridge Trail, Hendrickson Road, Old Olympic Highway, and Port Williams Road back to route from John Wayne Marina; see map.* After two short climbs the road undulates mildly, gradually ascending past woodlots and irrigated upland farms.

27.2 Turn left with thoroughfare on **Olson Road** as Hooker is marked Dead End. Begin a gentle, winding descent through picturesque uplands, crossing an irrigation canal.

28.4 Turn sharp left at a stop sign on **Taylor Cutoff Road** as Lost Mountain Road goes right. Enjoy a long, relaxing, straight downhill run. The Dungeness River appears on the right, then diverges again. Irrigation flumes send rushing water under the road to emerge on the opposite side.

31.0 Cross U.S. 101 and continue on **Gilbert Road**, which soon bends left and is renamed **Gupster Road**.

31.7 Turn right on **Mill Road** as Gupster ends. *Note: Cafe to left on Mill Road.*

32.2 Turn right at stop sign on **East Runnion Road** as Mill Road ends.

32.6 Turn right on **Railroad Bridge Park Trail** as Runnion is marked Dead End. Cross railroad bridge, descend ramp, follow paving-block trail, and turn left at mile 33.2 onto **Hendrickson Road**.

34.0 Turn right on **Priest Road**.

34.6 Turn right on paved shoulder of **W. Washington Avenue (U.S. 101)**.

34.7 Turn left on **River Road** from center left-turn lane and continue on paved shoulder.

36.5 Turn left at a small wye onto **Happy Valley Road** as River Road narrows and enters forest. The road climbs a short hill, then winds through a pleasant rural setting with views of the strait opening up to the north. Wild tiger lilies bloom along the grassy roadside, competing with daisies, oceanspray, yellow monkey flowers, and buttercups for botanical attention.

38.0 Stop for stop sign as 3rd Avenue goes left and continue on as the road bends right, crosses the broad valley, climbs the far slope, and turns left again. The Strait of Juan de Fuca, foreshortened by distance, laps at the base of the mountains on Vancouver Island. As the road begins to descend, the light-colored bluffs of the Miller Peninsula appear to jut out of the sparkling waters of Sequim Bay. Flash down a long, breathless, winding descent to the highway.

42.2 Turn right on **U.S. 101** as Happy Valley Road ends. Turn left almost immediately from center left-turn lane on **Whitefeather Way** toward Port of Port Angeles John Wayne Marina. Continue downhill.

43.0 Turn left at T junction on **West Sequim Bay Road** toward John Wayne Marina.

43.1 Turn right into south parking lot of John Wayne Marina; end of ride.

76   KALALOCH–CLEARWATER

STARTING POINT: Kalaloch Ranger Station Information Center on U.S. 101, 34 miles south of Forks on the Olympic Peninsula.

DISTANCE: 59 miles.
TERRAIN: Flat to hilly with moderate grades.
TOTAL CUMULATIVE ELEVATION GAIN: 2250 feet.
RECOMMENDED TIME OF YEAR: Avoid hunting season, otherwise any nonrainy weekend.
RECOMMENDED STARTING TIME: 8 A.M.
ALLOW: 7 to 8 hours or overnight, camping at Upper Clearwater Campground (DNR).
POINTS OF INTEREST
Beach trails
Views of Mt. Olympus
Destruction Island Overlook
Big Cedar

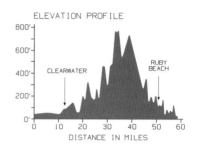

Many bicyclists have yearned to tour Washington State's "coast highway" along the Olympic Peninsula but could not dredge up enough ambition to tackle the whole peninsula loop with its many days of logging truck traffic. Others have longed to travel the rain-forest trails of the Olympic Peninsula, but the thought of a week's backpack trip in the rain held them back. Here is the bicycle tour to satisfy both desires with minor effort and provide the opportunity to walk and sun on the beach as well.

The starting point for this ride, the ranger station by Kalaloch Beach Village, was chosen for its obvious central location on the ride and its overnight lodging facilities. Kalaloch is several hours' driving time from most population centers, and an overnight stay in the vicinity is advocated for a fresh morning start on the ride. In addition to the village lodge and cabins, a park campground and a group camp are available at Kalaloch. Nearby facilities include the South Beach camping area, the Queets River campground, and the Rain Forest Hostel.

The wooden airplanes of a few decades ago depended heavily upon the strong, low-density wood of the Sitka spruce, which grows to great size on the west side of the Olympic Peninsula. This tour winds its way through the Washington State Department of Natural Resources trust lands, a tract of 98,000 acres where occasional stands of virgin timber are still to be seen. Immense stumps and twisted logs peek out from under the young trees in second-growth areas. Much of the timberland is being replanted to Douglas-fir for its greater harvest value, and signs are erected to note the dates of seeding, planting, fertilizing, and thinning. The carefully managed harvesting, adequate cleanup, prompt replanting, care of young trees, and

129

excellent access roads maintain the beauty of the forest setting and are a credit to the management of Washington State's trust lands.

In the coastal section of the Olympic National Park, a fire denuded many of the large cedars a few decades ago, and now the silvery snags perform a skeleton dance along the highway. In the Clearwater Valley, the fragrant smell of cedar permeates the air from one of the last remaining small shingle mills. The great old cedar at the end of Big Cedar Road almost appears as a composite of many trunks, new and old, with roots forming flying buttresses in all directions.

The roar of the ocean surf along the coast road soon diminishes after leaving Clearwater. As the route traverses the DNR trust lands, all is quiet save for the singing of small birds and the occasional low hoot of the blue grouse, unless one has the misfortune to encounter a stream of logging trucks. Bridges span many small creeks, and the road winds over hill and dale, producing ever new vistas to observe. Valleys of the Queets, Clearwater, Snahapish, and Hoh rivers join to make this a virtual "water level" tour, although the steep valley sides present plenty of hills. As the road winds down the Hoh Valley, a brief end-on view of Mt. Tom and the three peaks and snow dome of Mt. Olympus provides a rare treat. Above all, the absence of traffic on this delightful backroad makes this a tour to be remembered. Just be careful to pick good weather for this rain forest tour and pack a good picnic lunch to be enjoyed in one of the many pleasant forest glades.

"... should have turned about six miles back."

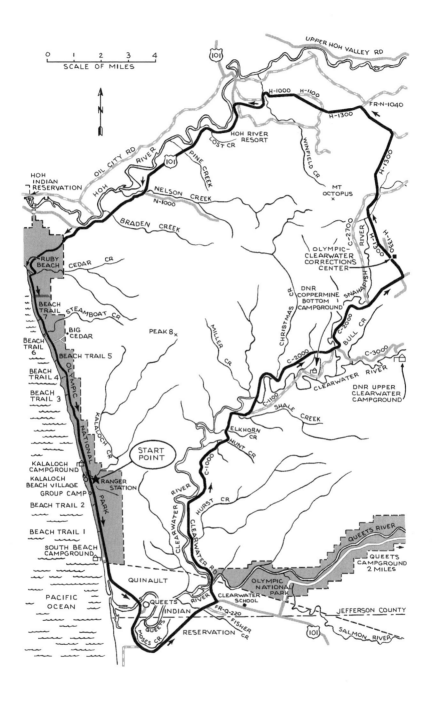

SCALE OF MILES

UPPER HOH VALLEY RD

H-1000 H-1100 FR-N-1040

H-1300

H-1300

HOH RIVER RESORT

WINFIELD CR

MT OCTOPUS

OIL CITY RD

HOH RIVER

LOST CR

PINE CREEK

HOH INDIAN RESERVATION

NELSON CREEK

N-1000

C-2700

CLEARWATER RIVER

BRADEN CREEK

C-1300

H-1330

OLYMPIC-CLEARWATER CORRECTIONS CENTER

SNAHAPISH RIVER

RUBY BEACH

CEDAR CR

CHRISTMAS CR

DNR COPPERMINE BOTTOM CAMPGROUND

BEACH TRAIL 7

STEAMBOAT CR

PEAK 8

MILLER CR

C-2000

C-3000

BULL CR

BIG CEDAR

C-2000

CLEARWATER RIVER

BEACH TRAIL 6

BEACH TRAIL 5

C-1100

DNR UPPER CLEARWATER CAMPGROUND

BEACH TRAIL 4

SHALE CREEK

BEACH TRAIL 3

OLYMPIC NATIONAL PARK

KALALOCH CR

ELKHORN CR

HUNT CR

START POINT

C-1000

KALALOCH CAMPGROUND

RANGER STATION

CLEARWATER RIVER

HURST CR

KALALOCH BEACH VILLAGE GROUP CAMP

BEACH TRAIL 2

CLEARWATER RD

BEACH TRAIL 1

QUEETS RIVER

SOUTH BEACH CAMPGROUND

QUEETS CAMPGROUND 2 MILES

QUINAULT

QUEETS RIVER

OLYMPIC NATIONAL PARK

PACIFIC OCEAN

QUEETS INDIAN

CLEARWATER SCHOOL

MOSES CR

FR-Q-220

FISHER CR

JEFFERSON COUNTY

RESERVATION CR

SALMON RIVER

MILEAGE LOG

0.0 Starting from Kalaloch Ranger Station Information Center, head south on **U.S. 101**. Major points of interest along the way include Kalaloch Beach Trail #2, 0.8; Beach Trail #1, 1.7; Queets River bridge, 4.8.

10.0 Turn left on **Clearwater Road** toward Clearwater and Olympic-Clearwater Corrections Center. Cross the Queets River and continue through Clearwater. Hurst Creek Park at mile 12.6 offers picnic tables by the creek. Follow main thoroughfare on a broad, smooth, blacktop road as it climbs a hill and enters Washington DNR trust lands as road becomes **C-1000**.

19.5 Cross the Clearwater River and continue on road **C-2000**.

23.7 Descend a hill and cross the Snahapish River on a high, one-lane steel and concrete bridge. Bear left as a side road goes right to Upper Clearwater and Yahoo Lake campgrounds.

27.8 Bear left at a wye on **H-1300** toward Olympic-Clearwater Corrections Center as C-2000 turns eastward. H-1300 shortly becomes a wide, smooth, blacktop road. Corrections Center appears on the right 0.5 mile later. Signs discourage loitering in the neighborhood of the prison camp. Mt. Olympus and Mt. Tom rise out of the east end of the valley. At 35.5 continue as the road is renamed **H-1000**. One last view of Olympus emerges as the road dives down a steep hill.

40.0 Turn left on **U.S. 101** as road H-1000 ends. A 30-inch shoulder eases the strain of highway traffic. Ruby Beach trailhead at mile 51.3. Other points of interest along the way include Destruction Island overlook with historical signboard, 52.5; Beach Trail #6, 53.3; Big Cedar Road (a 0.6-mile side trip), 53.7; Beach Trail #4, 55.5; Beach Trail #3, 56.2; Kalaloch Campground, 58.3.

59.0 Kalaloch Ranger Station Information Center. End of ride.

"We finished the improvements right on time."

77   FORT WORDEN–FORT FLAGLER

STARTING POINT: Fort Worden State Park near Port Townsend on the northeast tip of the Olympic Peninsula. Direction signs to the park begin on Kearney Street at the southwest edge of Port Townsend's business district. The signs lead via Walker, Cherry, Redwood, and W streets to the park gate. Park in the space provided in front of the park office building.

DISTANCE: 52 miles; can be shortened to 33 miles.
TERRAIN: Strenuous hills.
TOTAL CUMULATIVE ELEVATION GAIN: 2800 feet; short ride 2000 feet.
RECOMMENDED TIME OF YEAR: Mid-May to mid-June for rhododendron blossoms, otherwise any season. This ride is in partial rain shadow.
RECOMMENDED STARTING TIME: 9 A.M.
ALLOW: 7 to 8 hours (4½ hours for short ride).
POINTS OF INTEREST
Fort Worden State Park
Fort Flagler State Park
Native rhododendrons
Old buildings of Port Townsend

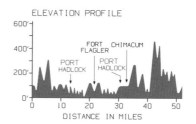

This ride is generously decorated by the native pink rhododendron. Found growing from British Columbia to California, it is named *Rhododendron californicum*, but nowhere is it presented in such profusion to the cyclist as in the Olympic Peninsula area. As if feeling the competition, other botanical species, including pink roses, yellow lupine, yellow broom, orange honeysuckle, white and lavender foxglove, and purple vetch also put on colorful displays. Add to this show two historical state parks and one has the material for a spectacular bicycle tour.

Fort Worden and Fort Flagler, together with Fort Casey on Whidbey Island, were built around the turn of the century to guard the entrance of Puget Sound against intruding foreign warships. The fortifications were extensive, involving thousands of cubic yards of concrete, the most modern "disappearing" rifles with bores up to 12 inches, and even balloon-borne observation posts. All three forts were heavily manned during World War I, but at the close of World War II, the forts were obsolete and ineffective and were abandoned as military posts, never having fired a shot except in practice. Now they serve as picturesque military museums. Powder magazines, mortar and rifle batteries, and observation posts invite hours of exploring. Views of Puget Sound and the Cascade Mountains are spectacular from either park. Other towns with colorful histories along this itinerary include Chimacum, Port Hadlock, and Irondale, which flourished briefly as a West Coast Pittsburgh until the local iron ore ran out. An impressive old

133

building by Discovery Bay was once a popular country inn but is now a private residence adjoining the Chevy Chase Golf Course. These are but a few of the highlights of this ride. The hills are many, some steep and long. The rewards, though, are worth every turn of the crank. Don't miss a great ride.

MILEAGE LOG

0.0 Parking lot by Fort Worden State Park office. Mount bicycles and head west on **Eisenhower Avenue**, then left on **Fort Worden Way** out main gate.

0.2 Turn right on **W Street** at exit from park.

0.3 Turn left on **Redwood Street**. Join **Cherry Street** at mile 0.8.

1.2 Turn right on **F Street** at first stop sign. F Street dips through a valley, ascends a hill, and becomes **Discovery Road**. Rhododendron displays begin.

2.2 Bear right on **19 Street** as it merges from the left. Cross Sheridan Street and continue as the road bends and is renamed **Discovery Road**.

7.4 Continue on Discovery Road as Cape George Road forks right to Beckett Point and Cape George. Note the impressive nineteenth-century architecture of a former country inn. The road rounds a corner and traverses along the top of a bluff overlooking Discovery Bay. At 8.5 cross State Route 20 and continue on **4 Corners Road**.

10.0 Bear right on **Rhody Drive (State Route 19)** toward Chimacum at stop sign as 4 Corners Road ends.

10.1 Turn left on **Irondale Road** toward Irondale and Port Hadlock at first major intersection.

12.0 Turn left at flashing red light in Port Hadlock on **Oak Bay Road (State Route 116)** toward Indian Island, Fort Flagler State Park, and Nordland. A wide, blacktop shoulder begins. *Note: For 33-mile ride, do not turn left to Fort Flagler but continue toward Chimacum on Chimacum Road. Continue with mileage log at mile 31.9.*

12.9 Turn left with S.R. 116 on **Flagler Road** at the top of a hill toward Nordland, Indian Island, and Fort Flagler State Park as Oak Bay Road continues on. Fly down the hill and cross the bridge over Portage Canal. On the other side of the bridge, amidst old orchard trees of a one-time homestead, are picnic tables of Port Hadlock Lions Public Park. As the road continues along the southern edge of Indian Island, a road leads right and down to Jefferson County Park beach access. Syringa, wild roses, and oceanspray bushes put on a floral display.

15.7 Cross the causeway onto Marrowstone Island and turn left at wye with bike route on Flagler Road. Pass Nordland Grocery at 18.1; last grocery before the state park. Ducks and herons search the mud flats of Mystery Bay for tender morsels. Bright yellow butter-and-eggs flowers decorate the edges of pastures. At 20.7 the road enters Fort Flagler State Park. Deer browse placidly along road margins.

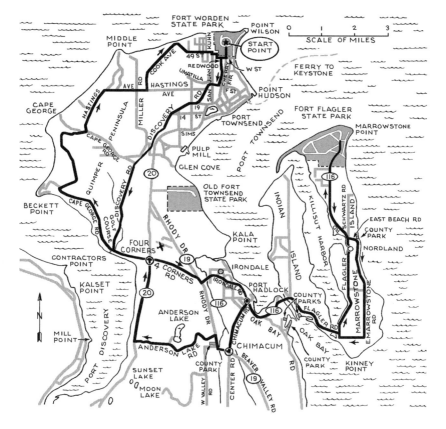

21.3 Crossroads at base of hill in park. Road to left goes to mortar battery, group camp, campground, beach picnic area, food concession. Road to right goes to rifle battery, picnic area, pier. Road ahead goes to park headquarters, AYH hostel, Environmental Learning Center, and main rifle batteries. Take your pick, then return to crossroads and ride out to park entrance. (Log does not include mileage spent beyond crossroads in the park.)

21.9 Leave park entrance, continue toward Nordland on **State Route 116** (**Flagler Road**).

24.1 Turn left on **East Beach Road** toward East Marrowstone and East Beach Park.

24.4 Turn right on **East Marrowstone Road** as a gravel drive continues down to Jefferson County East Beach Park. Pit toilets, shelter with stove, beachcombing, but no obvious drinking water. The backbone of the island is low at this point, and Mystery Bay, with its picturesque wildlife and sailing craft, may be viewed from this road. Sound-View Cemetery, with its ancient headstones, appears on the left.

27.3 Swing right with the thoroughfare as it is renamed **Robbins Road** and climbs a hill.

28.0 Swing right with thoroughfare on **Beach Drive**, then turn left past the island entrance floral wye onto **State Route 116 (Flagler Road)** as it crosses the causeway to Indian Island. Continue across Portage Canal Bridge to mainland.

31.0 Turn right on **Oak Bay Road** toward Port Townsend.

31.9 Turn left on **Chimacum Road** toward Chimacum in Port Hadlock.

33.4 Turn right on **Rhody Drive (State Route 19)** toward Port Townsend as Beaver Valley Road goes left at Chimacum junction. Chimacum Cafe on left at mile 33.2 features homemade pies. Jefferson County Chimacum Park on left at mile 33.9; shelter with stove and water faucet. Pit toilets, campsites, many rhododendrons.

34.4 Turn left on **Anderson Lake Road** toward Discovery Bay and Port Angeles. The road starts out flat, then gets progressively steeper. At 35.3 the road tops a summit and starts down again. At the bottom of the dip Anderson Lake appears, followed at the next summit by signs for Anderson Lake State Park, which has limited public facilities. Another short climb is succeeded by a long, rocketing descent.

37.1 Turn right toward Port Townsend on **State Route 20**.

39.7 Turn left on **S. Discovery Road** by Four Corners Store.

40.9 Turn left on **Cape George Road** toward Beckett Point and Cape George. Ride past the golf course and tackle a long hill with several challenging steep grades. The road finally levels out at 42.5.

43.6 Bear right with Cape George Road toward Cape George as Beckett Point Road goes left to a dead end. Rhododendrons appear.

46.3 Bear left on **Cape George Wye** from the head of a small valley with pastureland. *Note: If cows and horses appear, you have missed the turn.* Bear left again on **Hastings Avenue W.** after a half mile.

49.0 Turn left on **Cook Avenue Extension** toward North Beach. After a short, level stretch the road dives toward the Strait of Juan de Fuca.

50.6 Turn right on **53rd Street** as Cook Avenue is barricaded ahead. The road shortly joins **49th Street**. Jefferson County Fairgrounds on the right at mile 51.6. Stay on 49th Street as it swings right and is renamed **San Juan Avenue**.

51.9 Turn left on **Admiralty Street** as 47th Street goes right. The road swings right, then left, and is renamed **Spruce Street** and **W Street** in quick succession.

52.3 Turn left into Fort Worden State Park on **Fort Worden Way** as Cherry Street goes right.

52.6 Back at starting point.

78   PORT ANGELES–
SOL DUC HOT SPRINGS

STARTING POINT: William R. Fairchild International Airport near Port Angeles. Take U.S. 101 west through Port Angeles, go uphill under viaduct, and turn right on side road toward airport. Turn left at T junction on Lauridsen Boulevard, pass Lincoln Park (camping), turn right on L Street, and then left into airport entrance. Park along entrance roadway in long-term parking area east of terminal.

DISTANCE: Total, 87 miles: first day, 43 miles; second day, 44 miles.
TERRAIN: Strenuous hills.
TOTAL CUMULATIVE ELEVATION GAIN: Total, 4100 feet: first day, 2600 feet; second day, 1500 feet.
RECOMMENDED TIME OF YEAR: May through September.
RECOMMENDED STARTING TIME: 9 A.M.

ALLOW: 2 to 3 days. Plan return on Sunday for least logging truck traffic along Lake Crescent.
POINTS OF INTEREST
Spruce Railroad Trail
Soleduck Valley
Sol Duc Hot Springs
Lake Crescent

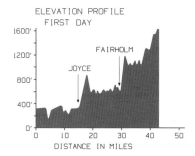

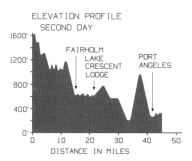

The Olympic Peninsula Loop of U.S. Highway 101 has long been an attraction for automotive and bicycle tourists alike. Both are easily intimidated by the interminable streams of logging trucks that impatiently pound these roads. This tour explores some of the most scenic portions of the northern peninsula with minimum exposure to heavy highway traffic.

The several hills of the first day's portion of the tour, as well as the slow riding of the Spruce Railroad Trail, deserve an early start from the Port Angeles airport. An early ferry from the mainland, or an overnight stay in nearby Lincoln Park or one of the motels in Port Angeles is suggested. The airport cafe serves good food at reasonable prices, and restrooms are available.

From its start at Fairchild Airport, the tour quickly leaves Port Angeles behind and strikes west through level countryside. The Strait of Juan de Fuca to the north and the Olympic Mountains to the south provide a striking backdrop to the rural scenery. Suddenly, the road dives down a hill to a high trestle bridge over the Elwha River and climbs out again to join a secondary state highway.

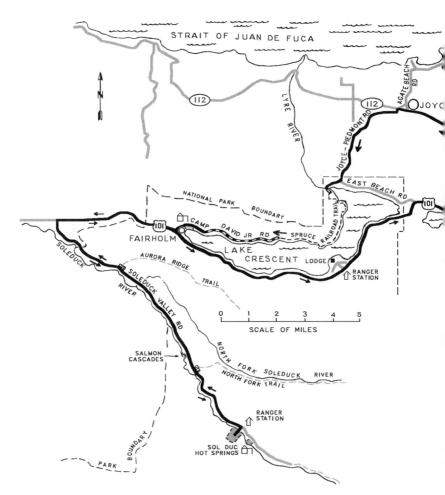

At Joyce, the route turns south by a school and begins a long climb, gentle at first but with steadily increasing authority, to a broad summit. The descent on the other side is steep and winding and is interrupted suddenly by a turn on an obscure side road to the Spruce Railroad Trail trailhead. The first quarter mile of the old railroad grade has been usurped by private property, and the trail is routed over an old truck trail, suddenly diving down a steep, narrow tread to join the railroad grade along Lake Crescent. The old grade is interrupted twice by detours around caved-in tunnels and several times by rockfalls from the adjoining cliffs, but most of the trail is easily ridden with standard touring wheels and tires. The east end of the trail appears suddenly, and a smooth road, unpaved at first, continues along the lake past homes, picnic areas, and the Fairholm Campground to U.S. 101. The 800-foot climb out of the valley is steep and inexorable, and the Soleduck turnoff, just past the summit, is a welcome sight. Here an informa-

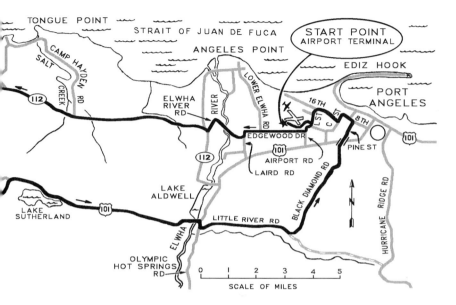

tional display explores the origins of the names of the Soleduck Valley and
Sol Duc Hot Springs and describes flora and fauna to be seen. With this
firmly in mind, bicyclists are suddenly confronted by the Olympic National
Park entrance kiosk, and a demand for entrance tolls. Luckily, the toll for
bicyclists is quite nominal, and the delightfully smooth roadway climbs,
steeply at times, through magnificent old-growth forest along the Soleduck
River to the hot springs resort and park campground.

The resort, with its hot and cold pools, is a popular place for relaxation
and is open from May through October. Reservations for rooms and cabins
are advised; telephone (360) 327-3583. The lodge restaurant offers a wide
variety of food but is not open early for breakfast. For the early riser on the
return trip, Olympic National Park's Lake Crescent Lodge comes at a
convenient point for an enjoyable breakfast. Shortly beyond the lodge
access road, however, bicyclists round a curve on the highway to be
confronted by a long drain grating in the center of the narrow shoulder,
flanked by a scattering of sharp rock fallen from the adjacent cliffs. With
logging trucks and RVs pounding by only a few feet away, this is a danger-
ous situation, so be careful.

Soon the highway shoulder broadens out, climbs over a low divide, and
starts down the long, gentle grade to the Elwha River. Just across the
Elwha, the route turns south, then eastward along the Little River to climb a
strenuously steep backroad to the Black Diamond Divide. Here all the effort
becomes worthwhile as a long, winding plunge rewards bicyclists with an
exhilarating descent. U.S. 101 is crossed on a high bridge, and all that
remains is a few blocks of Port Angeles city streets to the starting point at
the airport.

MILEAGE LOG

FIRST DAY

0.0 Starting from Clallam County's William R. Fairchild International Airport terminal area, head out entrance road.

0.5 Turn right on **L Street** at entrance, then immediately right again on **W. Lauridsen Boulevard** as L Street ends.

0.7 Bear right with thoroughfare on **Edgewood Drive**. Road bends left at 3.2 and is renamed **Laird Road**.

3.5 Turn right on **Elwha River Road**. Pass salmon hatchery and cross Elwha River on high, one-lane bridge.

5.4 Turn right on **State Route 112** as Elwha River Road ends. Grocery and cafe at mile 13.7.

14.3 Turn left on **Joyce-Piedmont Road** by Crescent High School as Agate Beach Road goes right. Crank over a summit at 17.7. Enter Olympic National Park at mile 18.2.

18.7 Turn right on unmarked side road toward Spruce Railroad Trail. Cross Lyre River at mile 19.3, and continue on unpaved road.

19.5 Go past Spruce Railroad Trail parking area, turn right by trail sign, and walk bicycles up wood-framed gravel path to old truck trail. Turn left on truck trail for 0.3 mile, follow footpath down to old railroad grade, and continue for 3.5 miles. Railroad grade is rideable except for diversion around collapsed tunnels and occasional rockfalls and erosion breaks.

23.6 Continue on **Camp David Jr. Road** and **North Shore Road** as Spruce Railroad Trail ends. Pavement resumes at mile 28.0.

28.5 Turn right and crank uphill on **U.S. 101**. *Note: Last food supply before Sol Duc Hot Springs is left and 0.2 mile downhill on U.S. 101 at Fairholm.*

30.3 Turn left on **Soleduck Valley Road** toward Sol Duc Hot Springs.

30.5 Turn right on side loop to Soleduck Valley information display. Loop road continues and rejoins main road.

30.6 Park entrance kiosk: entrance fee $1.00 per bicycle. Short trail leads right at 37.6 to Salmon Cascades on Soleduck River.

42.6 Turn right across Soleduck River to Sol Duc Hot Springs Resort; cabins, restaurant, hot mineral pools, and fresh-water pool. *Note: Sol Duc Campground is another 0.5 mile along Soleduck Valley Road.*

SECOND DAY

0.0 Leave Sol Duc Hot Springs Resort, cross Soleduck River, and turn left on **Soleduck Valley Road**.

12.5 Turn right on **U.S. 101** as Soleduck Valley Road ends. Pass Fairholm grocery and snack bar at 14.4. A side road goes left to Olympic National Park's Lake Crescent Lodge at 21.2.

22.1 ***CAUTION!! BAD LONGITUDINAL GRATING IN CENTER OF SHOULDER!*** Climb to east summit at mile 24.6. Grocery and cafe at mile 26.2.

32.9 Cross the Elwha River and immediately turn right on **Olympic Hot**

Springs Road by Elwha Resort, then left on **Little River Road**. Crank (or walk) up steep hill.

36.6 Continue on **Black Diamond Road** as Little River Road turns right, unpaved, toward Hurricane Ridge Road. Cross U.S. 101 on high bridge at 41.2 and continue on **Pine Street** in Port Angeles.

41.8 Turn left on **West 8th Street** at stop sign. Cross canyon on high bridge.

42.4 Turn left toward airport on **C Street**.

42.9 Turn right on **West 16th Street** toward Clallam County Fairgrounds.

43.8 Turn left on **L Street**.

44.1 Turn right into entrance of William R. Fairchild International Airport. End of tour by terminal at 44.7.

79 HOOD CANAL BRIDGE–FORT WORDEN

STARTING POINT: Wolfe Property State Park. Take State Route 104 to west end of the Hood Canal Bridge, turn right on Paradise Bay Road 0.7 mile, then turn right on Seven Sisters Road 0.5 mile to the park.

DISTANCE: 62 miles. Can be combined with Tour 82 for a 117-mile overnight tour starting from Seattle.
TERRAIN: Strenuous hills.
TOTAL CUMULATIVE ELEVATION GAIN: 3950 feet.
RECOMMENDED TIME OF YEAR: All seasons.
RECOMMENDED STARTING TIME: 8 A.M.
ALLOW: 8 hours.
POINTS OF INTEREST
Fort Worden State Park
Wild rhododendrons

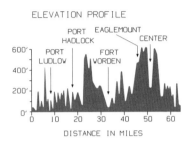

ELEVATION PROFILE

Two starting point options are available for this tour. For a long day ride or short overnight, cyclists can park cars at the parking lot of the Wolfe Property State Park. For a moderate length overnight, this ride can be started from the Colman Ferry Terminal in Seattle by incorporation of Tour 82. Overnight tours to Fort Worden should not be undertaken without adequate forethought and planning. The 50-unit, fully equipped campground is full to capacity throughout the summer, although the park manager has indicated that he will endeavor to squeeze in individuals or small groups of cyclists when vehicular sites are full. Fort Worden has no group camp, and campsites cannot be reserved. For families or small groups, the youth hostel offers comfortable lodging. For less spartan quarters, the former officers' homes beside the parade grounds may be reserved à la motel units at motel prices. Large groups may be able to arrange to occupy the barracks, complete with meals, at lower per-person costs. Port Townsend also has motels, B&Bs, and restaurants. Many bicyclists and cycle groups, however, find the nearby Old Fort Townsend State Park, with its group camp and individual campsites, a better choice for overnight camping during the vacation season.

Fort Worden has a lengthy history as a defense installation, beginning with the construction of its big gun emplacements just before the turn of the century. By 1904 it had become the headquarters for the defense of Puget Sound, with extensive rifle and mortar batteries on the sandy hill above Point Wilson. Today a veritable labyrinth of concrete tunnels and passageways competes with grass, trees, and vines to produce a fascinating place for exploration. The headquarters of the Puget Sound coastal defense fortification during World Wars I and II was designated as Fort Worden, with Fort Flagler and Fort Casey occupying two other stations of the crossfire triangle. In 1957 it was purchased by the state of Washington and used by the Department of Institutions as a diagnostic and treatment center. The

State Parks and Recreation Commission took over in 1972, and dedication as a state park followed in 1973. Its many buildings and barracks are fine examples of classic military architecture. Contrast to the military structures is provided by Alexander's Castle, a red brick building with high battlements, built in the 1880s by the rector of one of Port Townsend's churches. The campground straddles the spit that runs out to the Coast Guard Station on Point Wilson, where waves from the strait lash at the beach and wind-blown firs resemble palm trees, presenting a scene not unlike that of a coral atoll in the South Pacific. The Coast Guard Lighthouse Station, automated in 1989, is closed to the public.

As Fort Worden represents the ultimate in military installations at the turn of the century, so Port Townsend exhibits the opulence of the early civilian residents and the transitory financial successes of the business community. Many beautiful, well-preserved Victorian mansions, built in the late nineteenth century, remain today as fine architectural examples of an earlier, elegant way of life. Several homes and buildings are listed in the National Historical Register. Take a complete tour past the homes and buildings. During September the Port Townsend Chamber of Commerce sponsors an open house tour of many of these handsome, venerable mansions.

Flora embellishing the roads along this tour deserve special mention. The native rhododendron can be seen at many places in late May and early June. Serviceberry, Scotch broom, yellow lupine, and pink roses mingle with many other flowers of the montane forest belt. Although few flora are active during winter, the protective shield of the Olympics allows the sun to blossom forth on many of Seattle's rainy winter days.

MILEAGE LOG

0.0 Leave Wolfe Property State Park and head out **Seven Sisters Road**.

0.5 Turn right on **Paradise Bay Road**.

6.4 Turn right on **Oak Bay Road** as Paradise Bay Road ends. Grocery, deli, and cafe here, and grocery on the right at 8.4.

15.1 Continue straight on Oak Bay Road (**State Route 116**) as Flagler Road goes right. *Note: Fort Flagler State Park is right 8.5 miles on Flagler Road.*

16.0 Turn right at flashing red light toward Port Townsend on **Irondale Road** in Port Hadlock. A side road goes left at 17.3 to Jefferson County Irondale Park.

17.9 Turn right on **Rhody Drive** (**State Route 19**) as Irondale Road ends.

18.1 Bear left on **4 Corners Road** toward Discovery Bay. At 19.4 cross State Route 20 and continue on **Discovery Road**.

20.6 Turn left on **Cape George Road** toward Beckett Point and Cape George by old inn and Chevy Chase Golf Course. Start up a long hill, steep in places. The summit is reached at 22.2.

23.3 Turn right with Cape George Road toward Cape George as Beckett Point Road goes on to a dead end.

26.0 Turn left on **Cape George Wye**. Turn left again on **Hastings Avenue W.**, where rhododendrons appear.

28.7 Turn left on **Cook Avenue Extension** and descend steep hill.

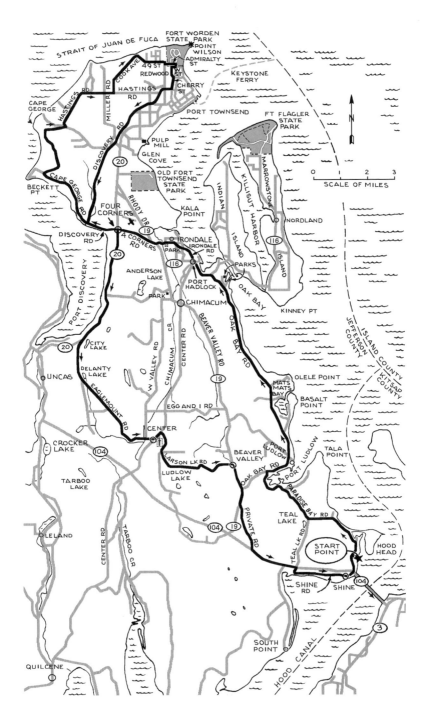

30.3 Turn right on **53rd Street** as Cook Avenue is barricaded ahead. Continue on **49th Street** as it enters from the left at mile 30.9. Jefferson County Fairgrounds appear on the right at mile 31.3. Road bends right at mile 31.5 and is renamed **San Juan Avenue**.

31.6 Turn left on **Admiralty Street**. The road swings right, then left, and is renamed **Spruce Street** and **W Street**.

32.0 Turn left into Fort Worden State Park on **Fort Worden Way** as Cherry Street goes right. Proceed past parade ground and turn right toward park office on **Eisenhower Avenue**.

32.3 Administration building, Fort Worden State Park. After lunch, return to this point and head west and south out main park entrance.

32.6 Turn right at park exit on **W Street**.

32.7 Turn left on **Redwood Street**, which shortly joins **Cherry Street**.

33.5 Turn right at stop sign on **F Street**. Road is shortly renamed **Discovery Road**.

34.5 Bear right on **19 Street** at stop sign. Cross Sheridan Street and continue as the road bends left and reacquires the name of **Discovery Road**.

39.7 Turn right on **State Route 20**. A broad, blacktop shoulder makes the highway traffic bearable. A long, moderately steep climb is rewarded by sweeping views of Discovery Bay.

44.1 Turn left on **Eaglemount Road** .

49.4 Bear left on **Center Road** toward Chimacum and Port Ludlow as Eaglemount Road ends at a wye.

49.7 Turn right and uphill on **Larson Lake Road** toward Port Ludlow. An easy climb is followed by a delightful, long, downhill run.

53.8 Turn right on **Beaver Valley Road** (**State Route 19**) toward Port Ludlow by Beaver Valley Grocery.

55.4 Turn left and downhill at Private Road sign and continue under iron gate. *Note: If road is marked closed for logging or extreme fire hazard, continue on Beaver Valley Road to S.R. 104.*

57.1 Turn left on **State Route 104** and continue on the wide, paved shoulder.

58.7 Turn right on **Shine Road** as Teal Lake Road goes left. Views of Hood Canal are followed by a very steep hill.

61.0 Cross State Route 104 and continue on **Paradise Bay Road**.

61.7 Turn right toward Wolfe Property State Park on **Seven Sisters Road**.

62.2 End of tour at Wolfe Property State Park.

80 EDMONDS–FORT FLAGLER

STARTING POINT: Parking along Admiral Street in Edmonds. Take exit 177 (State Route 104) when approaching from the south on I-5 or exit 181 (State Route 524) when approaching from the north. Follow signs to the ferry terminal in Edmonds. Turn left on Dayton Street at signal by ferry ticket kiosk, cross railroad tracks, and bear left along Admiral Street.

DISTANCE: 78 miles: first day, 35 miles; second day, 43 miles.
TERRAIN: Hilly.
TOTAL CUMULATIVE ELEVATION GAIN: 4400 feet: first day, 2200 feet; second day, 2200 feet.
RECOMMENDED TIME OF YEAR: All seasons.

RECOMMENDED STARTING TIME: 8 to 10 A.M.
ALLOW: 5 hours per day as an overnight, 10 hours for one-day ride.
POINTS OF INTEREST
Port Gamble National Historic Site
Fort Flagler

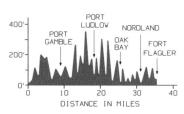

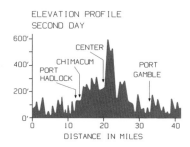

Fort Flagler State Park, in the precipitation penumbra of the Olympic Mountains, is rapidly becoming one of the area's more popular parks. A scant 50 miles from Seattle by road, it offers blue skies, beaches, hiking trails, a variety of overnight accommodations, and historic military museum attractions. Routes with moderate to low automobile traffic make this a fine bicycle objective. The route described here starts from Edmonds to allow a shorter ride but may be combined with Tour 82 for a Seattle starting point. Overnight accommodations at the park are varied. An open campground on the west beach concentrates the recreational vehicles well away from the tent campers, who are furnished secluded, wooded sites farther south atop a bluff. A rustic group camp area is available to groups by reservation with the park manager. An AYH hostel, dedicated in 1975 after conversion from a storage building by generous private contributions of time and labor, is presided over by resident house-parents. The hostel welcomes cyclists but cannot handle large groups. For groups of 30 or more, the park offers its old military barracks as an Environmental Learning Center. Heated in winter, these barracks offer beds in partitioned rooms with individual clothing storage to make overnight lodging enjoyable in all seasons. Cooking for large groups is made an easy task by the well-equipped kitchen and dining facilities. Although in heavy demand during the summer months, these accommodations are lightly used during the rest of the year and are ideal for a winter group bicycle tour. Reservations are available through the park manager. A hotel at the junction of Flagler Road and Oak Bay Road may better suit cyclists with more expensive tastes.

Once the accommodations are settled, many park attractions invite investigation. Trails through the forest, along the beach, and along the bluff offer miles of hiking. Views of Port Townsend, Whidbey Island, and the San Juans are unusual in their scope. A few of the old fortifications have been restored and are open to investigation, but the majority are posted as unsafe for public access. A long sand spit stretches westward around the end of Indian Island, attracting clam diggers at low tide. A row of old wooden pilings stretching toward Port Townsend from the end of the spit is said to be the remains of a submarine net installation.

These are a few of the many attractions of the park. The tour route to the park is a worthwhile trip on its own and is described in the mileage log and other Jefferson County tour descriptions.

MILEAGE LOG

FIRST DAY

0.0 Ferry terminal, Edmonds. Buy ferry ticket and proceed to bicycle staging area near end of pier.

0.2 Disembark ferry at Kingston and follow **State Route 104 West**.

4.2 Turn right with S.R. 104 at traffic light as State Route 307 (Bond Road) continues on to Poulsbo.

8.0 Proceed straight on **Rainier Avenue** in Port Gamble as highway swings left. Signs along sidewalk in front of old houses display historical data.

8.2 Port Gamble Store; groceries, hardware, seashell museum. Green lawn, picnic tables, shade trees, view. Restrooms in post office on

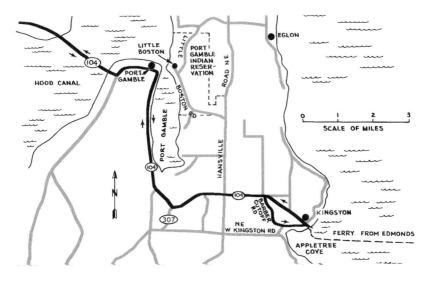

corner. Old cemetery on hill. Proceed out to highway on **Puget Way**. Turn right on highway toward Hood Canal Bridge.

9.5 Turn right with **State Route 104** at junction with State Route 3 and proceed across Hood Canal Floating Bridge. A bikeway of friction-surfaced steel plates provides safe passage across the bridge deck gratings, but be careful of draw span joints.

11.7 Turn right on **Paradise Bay Road**. Follow main thoroughfare as it charges up and down several hills.

17.3 Turn right on **Oak Bay Road** as Paradise Bay Road ends by a shopping center with grocery, cafe, and deli. Resort and restaurant below on right at 18.0. Grocery store at 19.2 as road acquires a wide, paved shoulder. *Note: Portage Way and Cleveland Street lead right to Jefferson County parks fronting on Oak Bay at 25.3. Pit toilets and picnic tables but no potable water.*

25.7 Turn right on **State Route 116** (**Flagler Road**) toward Fort Flagler State Park at a major intersection. Freewheel down steep hill and cross bridge over Portage Canal. Port Hadlock Lions Park on right at 26.6; nominal lunch stop. Old orchard trees and picnic tables, but no potable water. After lunch continue across Indian Island toward Fort Flagler. A chain link fence on the left forms a perimeter security barrier for the Keyport U.S. Naval Station Indian Island Annex. A dirt road disappears to the right and down to a Jefferson County day-use park along the beach.

28.7 Cross causeway and turn left at wye with bike route sign on Flagler Road and S.R. 116. The road climbs along a bluff, offering long views of Killisut Harbor. Nordland Grocery and Post Office at 31.1; last grocery before state park. Enter Fort Flagler State Park at 33.7.

34.4 Turn left toward camping area at crossroads in park. *Note: To visit the park office, hostel, or barracks, do not turn but proceed straight.* Group camp area on the left at 34.4 may be reserved by contacting the park manager; telephone: (360) 385-1259.

35.4 Tent camping area entrance; secluded campsites, restrooms, water. Road continues down to beach picnic area, food concession, and RV camping area.

SECOND DAY

0.0 Tent campground entrance, Fort Flagler State Park. Turn east toward park exit.

1.3 Turn right at crossroads in park and continue on **State Route 116** (**Flagler Road**) at park exit.

4.1 Turn left on **East Beach Road** toward East Marrowstone and East Beach Park.

4.4 Turn right on **East Marrowstone Road**. A short gravel road leads to Jefferson County East Beach Park. At 7.3 follow the main thoroughfare as it swings right, climbs a hill, and is renamed **Robbins Road**.

8.0 Swing right with thoroughfare on **Beach Drive**, and then left at Nelson's Corner past the island entrance planting wye onto **Flagler Road** (**State Route 116**) as it crosses the causeway to Indian Island.

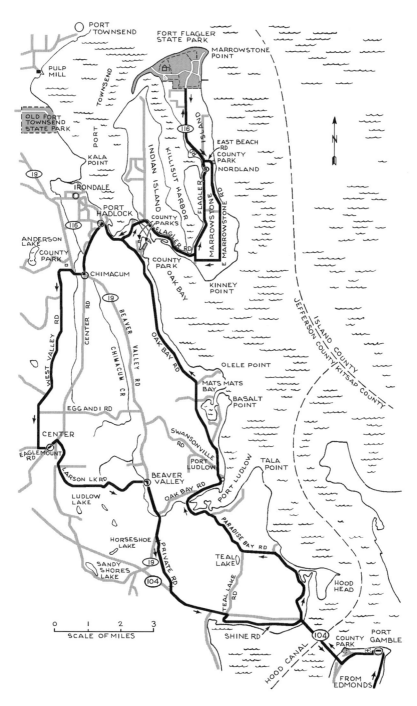

Continue across Indian Island and across the Portage Canal Bridge.

11.0   Turn right on **Oak Bay Road** with S.R. 116 toward Port Townsend.

11.9   Turn left on **Chimacum Road** toward Chimacum in Port Hadlock as S.R. 116 continues on.

13.4   Turn right on **State Route 19 (Rhody Drive)** at Chimacum junction as Center Road continues on. *Note: A county sign advises cyclists against shortening tour by turning left on Beaver Valley Road. An alternative is offered of continuing along shoulder of Center Road.* A cafe on the left at 13.6 features homemade pies.

13.9   Turn left on **West Valley Road**. Jefferson County Chimacum Park at this corner; many wild rhododendrons. Water faucet by corner of shelter. The road climbs the west side of the valley and offers occasional view points. Forest closes in with typical montane forest vegetation. The road continues down to a branch of the valley, crosses Chimacum Creek, and begins to climb again.

19.5   Turn left on **Eaglemount Road** as West Valley Road ends. A grove of birch trees appears out of place in these surroundings.

19.7   Turn left on **Center Road** at wye by grocery as Eaglemount Road ends.

20.0   Turn right on **Larson Lake Road** toward Port Ludlow and begin a long, moderate ascent. The road eventually crests and furnishes a refreshing downhill plunge.

24.1   Turn right on **Beaver Valley Road (State Route 19 South)** toward Port Ludlow and State Route 104 by corner grocery as Larson Lake Road ends.

25.8   Turn left and downhill by Private Road sign and continue under iron gate on old roadway. *Note: If road is marked closed for logging or extreme fire hazard, continue on Beaver Valley Road to S.R. 104.*

27.4   Turn left on **State Route 104** toward the Hood Canal Bridge and continue on wide, paved shoulder.

29.0   Turn right on **Shine Road** and cycle along edge of Hood Canal. The road climbs a wall, then winds down to the highway again.

31.3   Turn right on **State Route 104** and cross the Hood Canal Bridge.

33.1   Turn left toward Kingston with S.R. 104. Port Gamble at mile 34.2. (See First Day, mile 8.2, for facilities.) Continue toward Kingston.

38.2   Turn left with S.R. 104 at traffic light as State Route 307 goes right.

40.8   Bear right on **N.E. Barber Cutoff Road**.

41.8   Turn left at stop sign on **N.E. West Kingston Road**.

42.2   Turn right on **State Route 104** at stop sign and idle down to the ferry landing. Board ferry and return to Edmonds.

42.8   Edmonds Ferry Terminal; end of tour.

81 TOANDOS PENINSULA

STARTING POINT: Old South Point ferry landing. Take South Point Road south from State Route 104, three miles west of the Hood Canal Floating Bridge, and drive to road's end. Park in northwest corner of abandoned ferry traffic holding area.

DISTANCE: 36 to 54 miles.
TERRAIN: Strenuous hills.
TOTAL CUMULATIVE ELEVATION GAIN: 2600 feet to 4000 feet.
RECOMMENDED TIME OF YEAR: Mid-May for rhododendron bloom; otherwise any season.
RECOMMENDED STARTING TIME: 9 A.M.
ALLOW: 5 to 8 hours.
POINTS OF INTEREST
Native rhododendrons
Views of Hood Canal

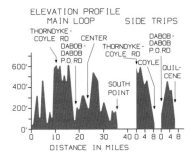

Talk to almost any Washington State resident about the Toandos Peninsula and you will get a blank stare or a quizzical expression. This ten-mile-long peninsula, jutting into Hood Canal just south of the Hood Canal Bridge, was logged several decades ago and until recently has been ignored by all but a few summer residents. Now, with the increasing demand for waterfront, its precipitous sides are being sought out for residential property. Roads have been regraded and surfaced to make this an interesting, but hilly tour.

South Point, hardly more than a ferry slip even before the opening of the Hood Canal Bridge, is a wide, paved area extending to the water's edge, the paint stripes and numbers of the ferry waiting lanes still showing on the pavement. A weathered tavern presides over the area. From here the route climbs along the water before heading sharply inland, where it plays roller coaster and elevator with the ridges, creek valleys, and inlets. Occasional glimpses of Hood Canal are afforded from the ridge tops, but otherwise the views are screened by dense forest. Rhododendrons appear as the peninsula road is approached, but for a spectacular display, at least a mile or two of the side trip down the peninsula should be taken. The flowering evergreen shrub grows in profusion here, from a few inches in height in the mowed area by the road to 15 or 20 feet tall back in the forest. Navigation aids along the roadside, apparently erected for naval tests in Dabob Bay, now are screened from that body of water by the tall, growing fir trees.

Food concessions and other amenities that civilization has to offer must be earned by an extra 12 miles and 800 feet of climbing over the intervening hill to and from Quilcene. The valley of the Tarboo then beckons as the road climbs gradually toward Center, where the road begins the climb over the last major ridge. More rhododendrons decorate the hillside as a long, swooping, downhill run leads to Beaver Valley and a small grocery ever popular with bicyclists. After a short, gradual climb out of the valley, the rest of the ride seems all downhill.

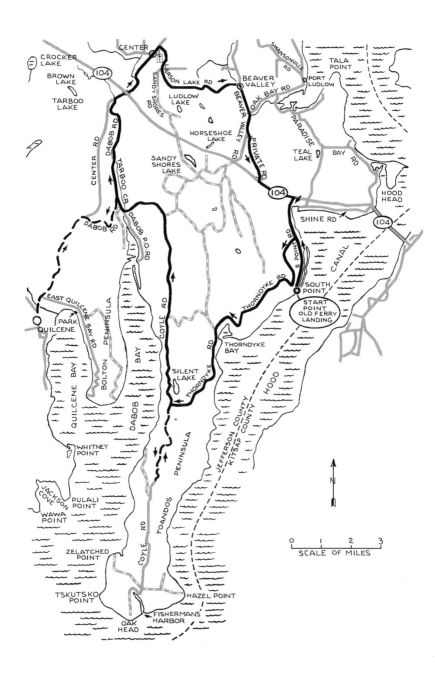

MILEAGE LOG

0.0   Starting from South Point, head out of old ferry holding area on **South Point Road**.

1.6   Turn sharp left on **Thorndyke Road** and wind uphill. Stay on oiled road as gravel roads branch to the side. Several long, steep hills.

10.0   Turn right on **Coyle Road** as Thorndyke Road ends. *Note: Optional side trip goes left two to three miles for greatest rhododendron display.* A gravel drive on right at mile 10.9 leads abruptly down to Silent Lake. No facilities except for primitive boat launch.

17.8   Turn right on **Dabob P.O. Road** as Coyle Road ends.

18.2   Bear right on **Dabob Road** as it comes in from the left. *Note: Optional side trip left to Quilcene, 12 miles round trip, for cafe or city park lunch.*

21.7   Turn right on **Center Road** at a stop sign as Dabob Road ends and go under State Route 104.

24.1   Turn right on **Larson Lake Road** and crank up moderate grade, topping a summit at mile 26.3.

28.2   Turn right on **Beaver Valley Road** as Larson Lake Road ends by Beaver Valley Store. Continue toward S.R. 104 as Oak Bay Road goes left at 29.4.

29.8   Turn left and downhill at milepost 8 on Private Road and continue under iron gate. *Note: If road is marked closed for logging or extreme fire hazard, continue on Beaver Valley Road to S.R. 104.*

31.5   Turn left on **State Route 104** as private road ends.

32.6   Turn right on **South Point Road**.

35.7   Back at starting point.

KITSAP COUNTY

Bainbridge Island, site of the annual Chilly Hilly bicycle spectacular, has become a popular area for Seattle people to cycle. Tour 82 in northern Kitsap County uses the island as a stepping stone to other places and, in effect, other times as it visits Indian village sites, early lumbering towns, and old ferry terminals. This ride is also valuable as an "escape route" from Seattle to Canada, Skagit County, and points east. Other routes in southern Kitsap are detailed in *Bicycling the Backroads of Southwest Washington*.

"You sure this is the right road?"

82 WINSLOW–PORT GAMBLE–POULSBO

STARTING POINT: Washington State ferry terminal at Pier 52 in Seattle. Take ferry to Winslow, Bainbridge Island.

DISTANCE: 51 miles. Can be taken by itself or combined with Tours 59, 79, and 80 for overnight or multi-day tours starting from Seattle.

TERRAIN: Hilly.

TOTAL CUMULATIVE ELEVATION GAIN: 3300 feet.

RECOMMENDED TIME OF YEAR: All seasons.

RECOMMENDED STARTING TIME: Catch 8 A.M. ferry.

ALLOW: 8 hours or overnight, staying at Kitsap Memorial State Park, or B&Bs on Big Valley Road or in Poulsbo.

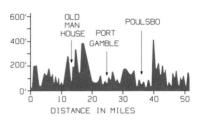

POINTS OF INTEREST

Old Man House State Historic Site
Chief Seattle's Grave
Port Gamble National Historic Site

Poulsbo waterfront
Suquamish Museum
Bloedel Reserve

A long, rural bicycle route that leaves from downtown Seattle is just one of the many features of this Kitsap County ride. Miles of seascape open up along Bainbridge Island and the Kitsap Peninsula. Ducks paddle and dive near shore, allowing easy identification. Great blue herons frequent the coves and bays; many make their home in a rookery in a marshy forest on north Bainbridge Island. Harbor seals swim and feed near Port Gamble. Even the big pileated woodpeckers find resonant old tree snags on which to sound out a drum-roll mating call.

A potpourri of historical facts and places relates to a variety of peoples and occupations in close geographic proximity. Western American Indians made their homes along the shores and inlets of Puget Sound. The Old Man House State Historic Site and the Suquamish Museum describe the Indian way of life when white settlers first appeared. Chief Seattle's grave in Suquamish is carefully tended and enclosed with replicated native artifacts.

The harvest and sale of timber, financed by East Coast interests, opened up small Puget Sound shipping ports such as Port Gamble, which once was the "company town" of Pope and Talbot. With old elm trees brought around Cape Horn still lining its streets, Port Gamble has changed little over the years and today is preserved as a national historic site. The old homes, showing their owners' pride, are painted and well maintained. Signs relate interesting facts for each well-preserved home and building. The mill, operating for many decades, closed its doors and was auctioned off and dismantled in the spring of 1996. Another timber interest, the Bloedel family, is represented by the Bloedel Reserve, where many acres of forest, ponds,

155

and gardens are tended meticulously by a team of full-time gardeners. The reserve is open to the public by reservation at (206) 842-7631.

Poulsbo, near the end of Liberty Bay, presents an entirely different flavor and influence. It was first settled in 1883 by Norwegian families and even today resembles a fishing village deep in the fjords of Norway. The residents take pride in their Scandinavian background and share their arts and crafts and food with the public at the Viking Festival held annually around May 17, the Norwegian Independence Day.

MILEAGE LOG

0.0 Colman Ferry Terminal, Seattle, Pier 52. Board ferry for Winslow.

0.1 Ferry terminal, Winslow, Bainbridge Island. Leave the ferry dock and head uphill.

0.4 Turn right on **Winslow Way East** at the first traffic light.

0.6 Turn left on **Ferncliff Avenue N.E.** and continue uphill. Road enters the countryside as driveways disappear into the forest or dive down to the water.

2.3 Bear left with roadway as signs proclaim **N.E. Lofgren Road**.

2.6 Turn right on **Moran Road N.E.** as Lofgren ends.

2.9 Turn right on **N. Madison Avenue** toward Manitou Beach. Busy State Route 305 appears on the left.

3.0 Bear right on **Manitou Beach Drive N.E.** Route follows along the beach for a mile, then bends sharply left and uphill. Seattle is silhouetted against the eastern sky. The road is renamed **N.E. Valley Road** at mile 4.3.

4.5 At top of hill turn right on **Sunrise Drive N.E.** toward Fay Bainbridge State Park, on the right at mile 7.2.

7.3 Road bends sharply left at bottom of a dip and becomes **N.E. La-Fayette Avenue**. Pass Kane Cemetery at mile 7.5 on the right. During late spring the hill in this cemetery is a good vantage point for observing and hearing great blue herons in their rookery across the road. The big nests sit atop alder trees.

7.8 Turn left on **Euclid Avenue**.

7.9 Turn left on **Phelps Road N.E.** at stop sign. At 8.4 continue through Frog Rock intersection on Phelps Road past this cleverly painted landmark.

8.6 Turn right on **N.E. Hidden Cove Road**. Road proceeds along a long, narrow cove.

10.0 Turn right on **State Route 305**; heavy traffic. On the far side of Agate Passage Bridge at 11.9 a sign announces Entering Port Madison Indian Reservation. An Indian totem pole records a family history.

12.0 Turn right on **Suquamish Way N.E.** toward Suquamish and Indianola.

13.3 Turn right on **Division Avenue** toward Old Man House State Historic Site. Restaurant and grocery at this corner.

13.7 Bear left on **McKinistry Street**.

13.8 Cross **Angeline Avenue** to a small parking area. Historic site is down the hill. Visualize the scene of yesteryear, hike the short trail to

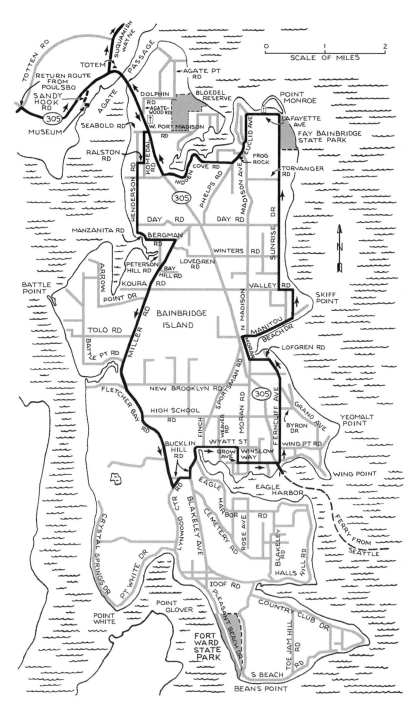

SCALE OF MILES

0   1   2

TOTTEN RD

SUQUAMISH WAYNE

PASSAGE

AGATE

TOTEM

RETURN ROUTE
FROM
POULSBO

SANDY
HOOK
RD

305

MUSEUM

SEABOLD RD

DOLPHIN
RD

AGATE-
WOOD RD

AGATE PT
RD

BLOEDEL
RESERVE

W. PORT MADISON
RD

POINT
MONROE

LAFAYETTE
AVE

FAY BAINBRIDGE
STATE PARK

RALSTON
RD

HENDERSON RD

KOMEDAL
RD

HIDDEN

COVE RD

PHELPS RD

MADISON AVE

EUCLID AVE

FROG
ROCK

TORVANGER
RD

305

DAY   RD

DAY RD

SUNRISE DR

MANZANITA RD

BERGMAN
RD

WINTERS   RD

N

PETERSON
HILL RD

LOVEGREN
RD

BAY
HILL RD

BATTLE
POINT

ARROW

POINT DR

KOURA
RD

MILLER RD

BAINBRIDGE
ISLAND

N MADISON RD

VALLEY   RD

SKIFF
POINT

TOLO RD

MANITOU BEACH DR

BATTLE PT RD

LOFGREN RD

FLETCHER BAY RD

NEW BROOKLYN RD

SPORTSMAN RD

MORAN RD

305

FERNCLIFF AVE

GRAND AVE

YEOMALT
POINT

HIGH SCHOOL
RD

FINCH

WEAVER
RD

WYATT ST

BYRON
DR

WING PT RD

BUCKLIN
HILL
RD

GROW
AVE

WINSLOW
WAY

WING POINT

LYNWOOD CTR RD

EAGLE

HARBOR

BLAKELEY AVE

CEMETERY RD

EAGLE
HARBOR

ROSE AVE

RD

FERRY FROM SEATTLE

CRYSTAL SPRINGS DR

PT WHITE DR

BLAKELEY
HILL RD

HALLS

POINT GLOVER

IOOF RD

PLEASANT BEACH DR

COUNTRY CLUB DR

POINT
WHITE

FORT
WARD
STATE
PARK

TOE JAM HILL RD

S BEACH

BEANS POINT

the beach, then retrace the route back to Suquamish Way.

14.2 Cross Suquamish Way on **Division Avenue**. About 100 yards farther turn right on **South Street** toward Chief Sealth Grave.

14.4 Turn left by St. Peters Church toward Chief Sealth Grave. Chief Seattle's grave is surrounded by a post and beam structure with decorative dugout canoes. Return to **Division Avenue N.E.** and turn right.

15.0 Turn left on **N.E. Columbia Street**. Route continues through rolling, forested terrain. Road name changes to **Port Gamble Road N.E.** at 15.9. Horse and cow pastures interrupt the forest landscape.

21.2 Turn left on **State Route 104** as Port Gamble Road ends. Wide, paved shoulders.

23.8 Enter Port Gamble National Historic Site.

24.1 Proceed straight on **Rainier Avenue** as highway swings left.

24.3 Park bicycles for a short break in park by flagpole overlooking Hood Canal in Port Gamble. Store with delicatessen and interesting sea-shell museum; post office with restrooms nearby. Continue out to highway on **Puget Way**. Turn right on **State Route 104** toward Hood Canal Bridge.

25.6 Continue straight on **State Route 3** as S.R. 104 goes right over Hood Canal Bridge.

28.6 Turn left on **Big Valley Road**. *Note: Kitsap Memorial State Park is a few yards farther on S.R. 3 and to the right on Park Street.* Enjoy five miles of pleasant, rural, traffic-free cycling. Bed-and-breakfast on right at mile 30.0; telephone (360) 779-4628.

33.4 Turn right on **Bond Road N.E.** as Big Valley Road ends, crossing State Route 305 at traffic light at mile 33.8.

34.3 Turn left at stop sign on **Front Street N.E.** as Bond Road ends. To avoid heavy left-turning traffic, use left-hand sidewalk along Front Street and cross at next pedestrian crosswalk. Climb hill above Liberty Bay and freewheel down the hill into picturesque Poulsbo; shops, restaurants, and bakery. Delightful waterfront park on Liberty Bay.

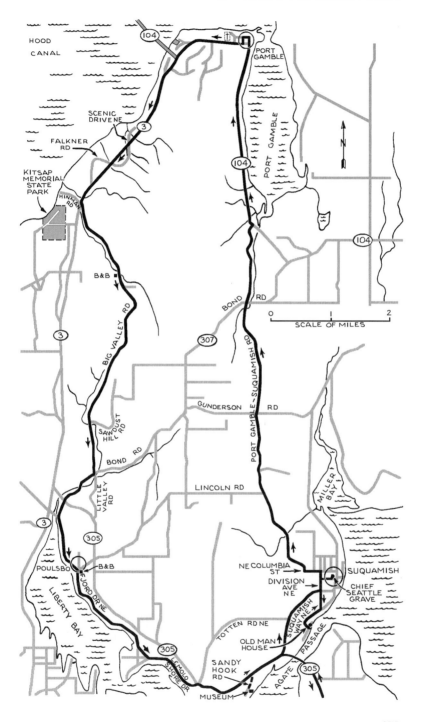

35.4 Leave town, bear left and uphill on **Hostmark Street N.E.**, and turn right on **Fjord Drive N.E.** Bed and breakfast at this corner, telephone (360) 779-1600. Road is renamed **Lemolo Shore Drive** at 37.0. Road bends away from waterfront by Lemolo Market at 37.4.

38.5 Turn right on broad, paved shoulder of **State Route 305**. *Note: Sandy Hook Road goes right at mile 39.7 to the Suquamish Museum and Tribal Center. Numerous displays of Indian artifacts, culture, and interaction with white settlers. A recommended side trip.* Cross Agate Pass Bridge at mile 40.3. *Note: Agatewood Road N.E. goes left 0.6 mile to Bloedel Reserve at mile 41.1; fee and reservation required.*

41.3 Turn right on **N.E. Seabold Road**, then left on **Komedal Road**.

41.8 Turn right on **N.E. Ralston Road** by Seabold Community Club.

41.9 Turn left on **Henderson Road N.E.**, which shortly is renamed **Manzanita Road**. Ride through forest to the waterfront at Manzanita. Route bends sharply left, climbs a steep hill, and becomes **N.E. Bergman Road**.

43.7 Turn right on **N.E. Miller Road** as Bergman Road ends.

46.2 Continue on **Fletcher Bay Road** as Miller Road ends; Island Center Park and Community Hall on right at 47.5.

48.1 Turn left on **Lynwood Center Road** at stop sign as bicycle route signs continue right. Road is renamed **Bucklin Hill Road**.

48.5 Turn left with Bucklin Hill Road as Blakeley Avenue goes right.

48.8 Bear left on **Eagle Harbor Drive**.

49.0 Road turns corner, changes name to **Wyatt Street N.E.**, and heads up a long, steep hill.

49.7 Turn right on **Grow Avenue N.E.** at top of hill.

49.9 Turn left on **Winslow Way West**.

50.4 Turn right at traffic light toward ferry terminal. Board ferry at mile 50.7.

50.9 End of tour at Coleman Ferry Terminal in Seattle.

"I think it's a little high now."

ISLAND COUNTY

Many bicyclists visiting Whidbey Island regard it only as a stretch of highway shoulder between Clinton and Deception Pass. The tours in this section, however, present quite a different story. Many unusual features of the island are not to be found elsewhere, and many state, county, and city parks dot the shores. Museums, cemeteries, buildings, forts, homesteads, and military installations bring up visions of historic scenes from the past. In July, the creamy-white panicles of the oceanspray shrub put on a floral display all over the island. A word of caution, however: this island has steep hills, and low gearing is advantageous. With this preparation, come see what the highway travelers have missed.

83 FORT CASEY–OAK HARBOR

STARTING POINT: Picnic area parking, Fort Casey State Park, Whidbey Island. From the north, take State Route 20 west to Deception Pass and the Keystone ferry. From the south, take the Mukilteo ferry to Clinton and follow State Routes 525 and 20 to the Keystone ferry terminal. Proceed north on Engle Road past the terminal and the Fort Casey State Park campground; turn left uphill by the entrance to Seattle Pacific University's Camp Casey campus.

DISTANCE: 42 miles.
TERRAIN: Hilly.
TOTAL CUMULATIVE ELEVATION GAIN: 2400 feet.
RECOMMENDED TIME OF YEAR: Any season.
RECOMMENDED STARTING TIME: 9 to 10 A.M.
ALLOW: 6 hours.
POINTS OF INTEREST
Fort Casey Historical State Park
Crockett Blockhouse
Whidbey Island State Game Farm
Chief Snakelin's Grave
Coupeville Museum
Alexander Blockhouse and Indian canoes in Coupeville
West Beach
Sunnyside Cemetery
Ebey's Landing

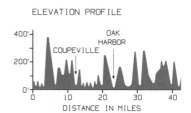

As set forth in the Constitution of the United States, providing for the common defense has always been an important concept to Americans. And so it was to the early settlers on Whidbey Island. They arrived in the 1850s and staked out their claims to the land. Periodic attacks by the fierce Haida Indians from the north, previously limited in their focus to the non-warlike local Skagit Indians, prompted settlers to build blockhouses around their homes for refuge and defense of their property. Colonel Isaac Ebey lost his head in one of these attacks. Three of the old blockhouses, built in 1855, remain today and can be viewed and examined by bicyclists as they pedal along this 42-mile loop ride in central Whidbey Island.

At the turn of the century, the United States was in the process of fortifying its major harbors. Fort Casey on Whidbey Island became one of the three coastal defense forts constructed to protect the entrance to Puget Sound, the others being Fort Flagler and Fort Worden. All three of these army fortresses, though long since obsolete, were solidly built. The gun and mortar emplacements at Fort Casey remain almost without blemish or observable wear to provide a study of historical significance. One of the authentic, big, "disappearing" rifles presents a picture of skilled precision workmanship in polished brass and steel.

Twentieth-century fortifications now command the skies over Whidbey Island as naval airplanes based at nearby Ault Field fly practice sorties.

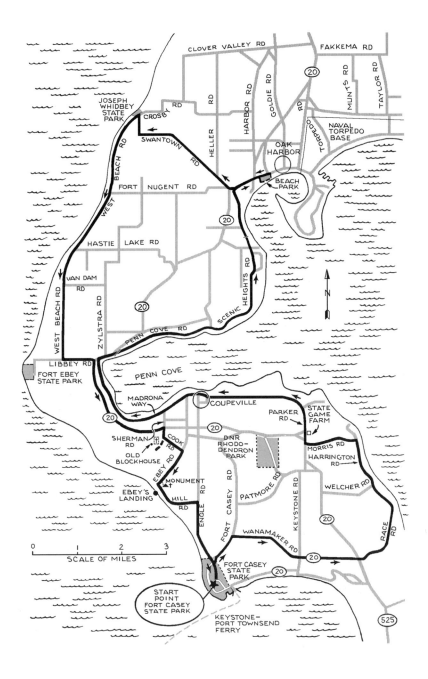

CLOVER VALLEY RD · FAKKEMA RD · MUNTS RD · TAYLOR RD
GOLDIE RD · HARBOR RD · HELLER RD · RD
20
TORPEDO
NAVAL TORPEDO BASE
OAK HARBOR
JOSEPH WHIDBEY STATE PARK
CROSBY
SWANTOWN RD
BEACH RD
WEST BEACH RD
FORT NUGENT RD
BEACH PARK
20
HASTIE LAKE RD
SCENIC HEIGHTS RD
VAN DAM RD
N
ZYLSTRA RD
20
PENN COVE RD
WEST BEACH RD
LIBBEY RD
FORT EBEY STATE PARK
PENN COVE
MADRONA WAY
COUPEVILLE
PARKER RD
STATE GAME FARM
20
SHERMAN RD
COOK RD
OLD BLOCKHOUSE
EBEY RD
DNR RHODO-DENDRON PARK
MORRIS RD
HARRINGTON RD
WELCHER RD
MONUMENT
EBEY'S LANDING
HILL RD
ENGLE RD
FORT CASEY RD
PATMORE RD
KEYSTONE RD
20
RACE RD
WANAMAKER RD
20
0   1   2   3
SCALE OF MILES
FORT CASEY STATE PARK
20
START POINT FORT CASEY STATE PARK
KEYSTONE–PORT TOWNSEND FERRY
525

163

The historic importance of this vast tract of central Whidbey Island is recognized by its inclusion in Ebey's Landing National Historical Reserve. The registered area stretches along both shores of Penn Cove on the east side of the island to Partridge Point on the west for the northern boundary. Its southern edge is near Admiralty Head and the Keystone ferry landing. Our bicycle tour rolls over much of the territory and touches base at a number of the historic sites, structures, and fortresses.

MILEAGE LOG

0.0 Picnic area at Fort Casey State Park. Leave park and head north on **Engle Road** past Seattle Pacific University's Camp Casey Campus.

0.7 Turn right on **Fort Casey Road**. Crockett Blockhouse of 1855 stands by the road 0.4 mile beyond this corner.

1.5 Turn right on **Wanamaker Road** past acres of field crops.

3.1 Turn left on **State Route 20**.

4.4 Cross junction of S.R. 20 with S.R. 525. Continue uphill on **Race Road** and proceed downhill past Race Lagoon. The road changes name to **Harrington Road** at mile 7.0 as Welcher Road goes left. At mile 7.9 the road bends left and becomes **Morris Road**.

9.4 Turn right on **State Route 20**, then immediately bear right on **Parker Road** to Whidbey Island State Game Farm at mile 9.5: visitors welcome, interesting live game displays, public restrooms. *Note: At mile 9.8, as Parker Road bends left, a dirt road leads into the forest on the right to a fenced monument marking the grave of Chief Snakelin and two other chiefs of the Snoqualmoo Indian tribe.* Rhododendrons grow in the forest as the route tops a hill before plunging down into Coupeville, Island County seat. At mile 11.9 the road bends left, then right, and is renamed **N.E. 9th Street**.

12.2 Turn right on **N.E. Gould Street**, then left on **Front Street** along the waterfront in Coupeville. Pass several restaurants and shops.

12.6 Turn left on **N.W. Alexander Street** for a visit to the city museum, Alexander Blockhouse, and Indian dugout canoes.

12.7 Turn right on **Coveland Street**.

12.8 Bear left on **Madrona Way**. *Note: Coveland Street continues by Coupeville City Park, where a slice from a huge fir log is ring-dated with its beginnings 200 years before Columbus discovered America.* Views of Penn Cove aquaculture (mussel culture) pens at mile 13.2.

16.0 Turn right on **State Route 20**. Busy traffic, 30-inch shoulder.

16.6 Turn right past barrier by Old San de Fuca Store on **Penn Cove Road**, which hugs the northern rolling shoreline of Penn Cove. Indian potlatches were held in this cove. The road name changes to **Scenic Heights Road** at mile 18.5 by public beach access. Large clumps of *Mahonia aquifolium* (tall Oregon grape) grow along the roadside but give way to pastureland at the top of the hill. The sandy peninsula below was once an Indian burial ground. Continue around traffic barrier at mile 21.1.

22.5 Turn right on **State Route 20** and freewheel downhill into Oak Harbor. Fast food concessions, corner grocery.

23.4 Turn right on **80th N.W. Street** at first traffic light, pass a trailer camp on the left, and turn left at a wye on **350 Avenue S.W.** into Oak Harbor Beach Park. Restrooms, picnic tables, and shelters. Continue through park across footbridge or around lagoon bathing area to **70th N.W. Street** and turn left.

23.6 Turn left on **W. Pioneer Way** at traffic light. A bakery wafts enticing odors from a block to the right of this intersection.

23.9 Go straight at traffic light as **State Route 20** joins from the right. (Beware of Right Turn Only lane.) The tensions of an uphill grind on a busy, otherwise shoulderless road are eased by the presence of a sidewalk.

24.5 Turn right at traffic light on **Swantown Road** as S.R. 20 makes a left turn.

27.4 Turn left on **West Beach Road** as Swantown Road ends by Joseph Whidbey State Park (Picnic tables, restrooms, ocean view, beach access). Another public access to the beach appears on the right just before the road climbs a long, steep hill and runs along the bluff. A strawberry farm at mile 32.7 stretches across the rolling plateau.

33.5 Turn left on **Libbey Road** as West Beach Road ends. Signs point right to Fort Ebey State Park, 1.6 miles.

34.1 Turn right on **State Route 20** as Libbey Road ends. Wide, four-foot shoulders. Rhododendrons form thick groves among the trees.

36.8 Turn right on **Sherman Road**. Field crops spread over Ebey Prairie below.

37.1 Turn left on **Cook Road** as Sherman Road ends. *Note: For more history, turn right and uphill into Sunnyside Cemetery. James Davis Blockhouse, Coupe and Ebey headstones. Peruse the old gravestones and take in the commanding view before returning to Cook Road.*

37.6 Turn right on **Ebey Road**. Interesting old house built in 1892 stands at this corner. *Note: As the road starts downhill toward the beach, a trail on the left leads to the edge of the bluff where a monument commemorating Ebey's death is placed.* Beware of sharp left turn at base of hill.

38.6 Ebey's Landing; beach access. Head uphill on **Hill Road**. At the top of the hill, trees form a canopy over the road.

39.8 Turn right on **Engle Road** as Hill Road ends. Views of Port Townsend across Admiralty Inlet.

41.6 Turn right and uphill at entrance to Fort Casey State Historical Park.

41.8 Back to picnic area parking lot; end of tour.

84 FREELAND–FORT CASEY

STARTING POINT: Parking area by Island County Park near Freeland on Whidbey Island. Take Freeland Avenue exit from State Route 525 near Freeland and follow it to its end, then right on Shoreview Drive downhill to the park. Whidbey Island can be reached by ferry from Mukilteo or via State Route 20 and Deception Pass.

DISTANCE: 38 miles.
TERRAIN: Moderate to strenuous hills.
TOTAL CUMULATIVE ELEVATION GAIN: 2250 feet.
RECOMMENDED TIME OF YEAR: Any season.
RECOMMENDED STARTING TIME: 9:30 A.M.
ALLOW: 6 to 8 hours.
POINTS OF INTEREST
Fort Casey State Park military installations
Crockett Blockhouse

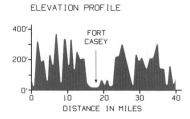

Story has it that an elderly native of south Whidbey Island suffered a medical emergency that caused him to lose consciousness. As he was being taken to the hospital he woke up and, seeing beautiful scenery, wondered aloud if he was in heaven. The reply, of course, was, "No, this is just a part of Whidbey Island you have not seen before."

This ride up the central portion of Whidbey Island makes the story believable. Although several roads are posted as scenic drives for the benefit of visiting auto tourists, the traffic is generally negligible. From the steep hills and dales of Honeymoon Bay and North Bluff, the flat accretion dike along Crockett Lake, and the bluffs at Fort Casey to the forested escarpment along Smugglers Cove Road, the scenery and views are fabulous. This is not all without price, however. Generally to obtain a view one must climb, and this ride is no exception. The route starts near sea level by a small hill in Freeland and begins a trajectory not unlike that of a yo-yo. This up-and-down terrain continues all along Honeymoon Bay and North Bluff roads with rapid changes in scenery. At Greenbank, a grocery, post office, and fire hall form a cultural nucleus for the nearby waterfront residents, and the Greenbank Winery offers a wine-tasting opportunity. The hills finally level out as the road stretches along Crockett Lake. At this point, with destination in sight and level road ahead, the bicycle tourist may often round the curve and slam into a strong southwesterly wind. Fort Casey, however, is a beautiful park, wind or no wind, and a delightful place for a picnic lunch plus an hour or so of exploring the old gun emplacements and ammunition bunkers. After lunch, as the route starts back, the Crockett Blockhouse presents a bit of Washington State history of earlier vintage than the Fort Casey fortifications. After looping around a small lagoon in Admirals Cove, where tame ducks and geese panhandle for lunch leftovers, the road switchbacks up a hill to the highway. A quick dash along the wide shoulder leads to Smugglers Cove Road and thence to South Whidbey Island State

Park. Although offering little of interest up by the road, this park has a fine beach at the bottom of a steep foot trail. Other than a few final hills, the remaining route back to Freeland is relatively uneventful.

MILEAGE LOG

0.0   Parking area by Island County Park in Freeland, Whidbey Island. Head west over a hill on **Shoreview Drive**.

0.7   Turn right on **Honeymoon Bay Road** and proceed up a long, moderate hill. The road changes name to **Resort Road** at mile 4.3.

6.1   Turn right on **State Route 525** and continue on shoulder.

7.9   Pass the Greenbank grocery and post office and bear right on **North Bluff Road** past the Greenbank Winery. At the top of a particularly steep hill, the road name changes to **Houston Road**.

12.7   Turn right on **State Route 525** as Houston Road ends.

14.1   Turn left on **State Route 20** as S.R. 525 ends. Follow highway and Keystone Ferry signs to Fort Casey State Park.

17.6   Continue past the ferry terminal and the state park campground and continue on **Engle Road**.

18.1   Turn left at the state park entrance and continue uphill to the Fort Casey State Park picnic area for lunch. After lunch and a leisurely tour of the fort's facilities, return to this point and continue north on Engle Road.

19.0   Turn right on **Fort Casey Road**. Crockett Blockhouse appears on the right after 0.3 mile.

19.8   Turn right on **Wanamaker Road**.

21.4   Turn right onto **State Route 20** as Keystone Road comes downhill from the left.

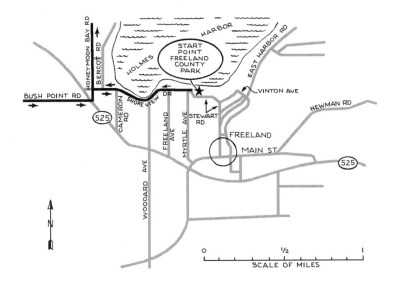

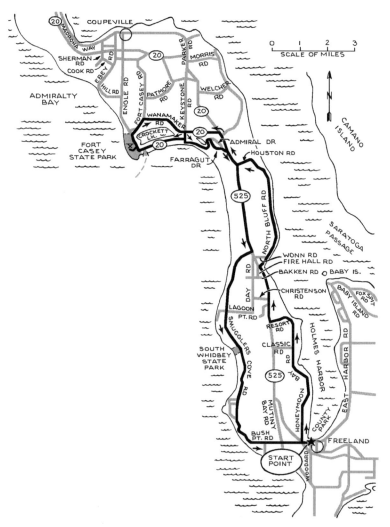

21.9 Continue straight on **Keystone Road** as the highway goes right. Follow road past small lagoon, around hairpin turn, and uphill.

23.2 Turn right on **Farragut Drive**, then left on **King Drive**, and then right again on **Admiral Drive**. Good views of Admiralty Bay.

24.0 Turn right on **State Route 525** and continue on shoulder.

28.1 Turn right on **Smugglers Cove Road**. South Whidbey State Park on right at mile 32.5. Pit toilets at parking lot; a long, steep trail leads down to the beach. The road rounds a corner at mile 34.6 and changes name to **Bush Point Road**.

37.4 Continue across State Route 525 on **Honeymoon Bay Road**, then turn right almost immediately on **Shoreview Drive**.

38.2 Back at starting point.

85   SOUTH WHIDBEY #1

STARTING POINT: Mukilteo State Park, Snohomish County. Take I-5 to exit 189 (Mukilteo) and follow signs to the park and Whidbey Island ferry. Park in unmarked stalls along east edge of the park. Read sign at south end of park by restrooms.

DISTANCE: 35 miles.
TERRAIN: Hilly.
TOTAL CUMULATIVE ELEVATION GAIN: 2800 feet.
RECOMMENDED TIME OF YEAR: Any season.
RECOMMENDED STARTING TIME: 8 to 10 A.M.
ALLOW: 6 hours.
POINT OF INTEREST
Pioneer-motif shops in Langley

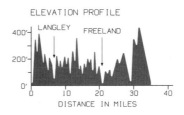

The scenic roads and pathways of the southern tip of Whidbey Island are too many and varied to be fully appreciated in a single visit. We therefore offer two tours. This South Whidbey #1 tour ventures north to Saratoga and west to Freeland before returning to Clinton; South Whidbey #2 (Tour 86) explores the southern communities of Glendale and Maxwelton, returning by way of Langley to Clinton. Both rides are hilly, each offering a vigorous workout.

Small farms and forest mark the gently rolling route to Langley, site of Island County's annual fair held in August. Perched on the edge of an erosion bluff, Langley, fighting the sea in order to keep the main street from eroding into the sound, constructed a concrete sea wall in 1975. Stairs connect a topside boardwalk and garden with the rocky, sandy beach that stretches in front of the sea wall, and beach walks are possible at low tide. Interesting pioneer-motif shops, offering tempting caloric foods for energy-hungry bicyclists, line First Street.

Magnificent clumps of oceanspray decorate the roadsides along Saratoga Road, their filmy, off-white, panicle inflorescence reaching a peak during July. Evergreen huckleberry grows in profusion, its sweet, dark berries standing out against the small, shiny green leaves. Sword ferns and salal add their carpet of green to the fir and alder forest. Nettles also like the soil conditions on Whidbey Island. They grow everywhere. When leaving the roadway, cyclists must take care to keep away from their stinging leaves.

Marine views along Holmes Harbor open up as the route follows the roller-coaster roads close to the water near Freeland. Here Island County's Freeland Park offers a seaside picnic lunch stop. Several cafes nearby offer shelter in exchange for meal purchases when the weather is not conducive to an outside picnic lunch.

As a little stream rushes beside it, French Road climbs the narrow valley between two steep hills. Foxglove and ferns help anchor the soft ground on the less precipitous cuts. Bicyclists get a few glimpses of Deer Lake before the route returns to Clinton and plunges downhill to the ferry landing.

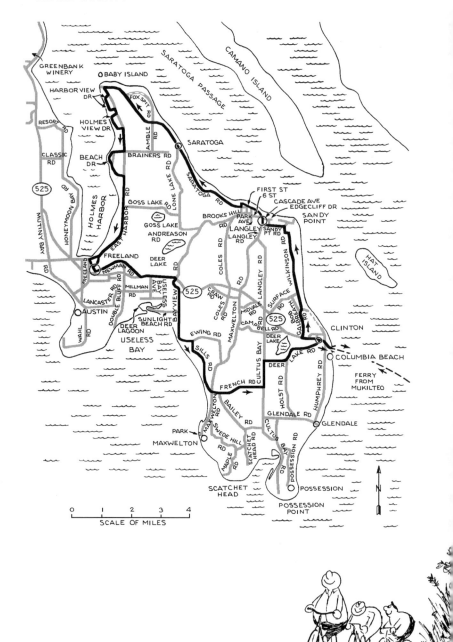

GREENBANK
WINERY

BABY ISLAND

SARATOGA PASSAGE

CAMANO ISLAND

HARBOR VIEW
DR

FOX SPIT RD

RESORT RD

HOLMES
VIEW DR

SARATOGA

CLASSIC
RD

525

BEACH
DR

BRAINERS RD

AMBLE RD

LONE LAKE RD

SARATOGA RD

MUTINY BAY

HONEYMOON BAY RD

HOLMES
HARBOR

GOSS LAKE RD

EAST HARBOR RD

GOSS LAKE

ANDREASON
RD

DEER
LAKE

FIRST ST
6 ST
CASCADE AVE
EDGECLIFF DR

BROOKS HILL

PARK
AVE

LANGLEY

LANGLEY
RD

SANDY
POINT

SANDY PT RD

HAT
ISLAND

FREELAND

NEWMAN RD

FREELAND RD

MILLMAN
RD

USELESS BAY AVE

BAYVIEW RD

525

COLES
RD

COLES
RD

CRAW
RD

LANGLEY RD

WILKINSON RD

SURFACE RD

LANCASTER RD

DOUBLE BLUFF RD

AUSTIN

WAHL RD

SUNLIGHT
BEACH RD

DEER
LAGOON

MAXWELTON RD

MIDVALE RD

CAMPBELL RD

525

DEER
LAKE

BOB HALL RD

GALBREATH RD

CLINTON

COLUMBIA BEACH

USELESS
BAY

EWING RD

SILLS RD

CULTUS BAY

DEER LAKE RD

DEER

HOLST RD

HUMPHREY RD

FERRY
FROM
MUKILTEO

FRENCH RD

BAILEY RD

GLENDALE RD

GLENDALE

MAXWELTON RD

SWEDE HILL RD

SCATCHET HEAD RD

CULTUS BAY RD

POSSESSION RD

PARK

MAXWELTON

MAPLE RD

SCATCHET
HEAD

POSSESSION
POINT

POSSESSION

N

0   1   2   3   4
SCALE OF MILES

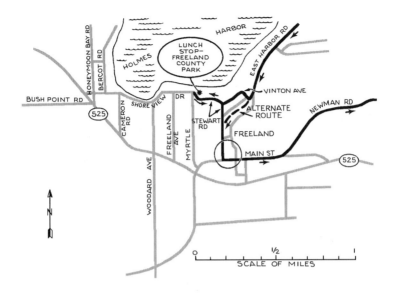

MILEAGE LOG

0.0   Mukilteo State Park parking lot. Purchase ferry tickets at ticket booth on hill and proceed to bicycle staging area by waiting room. Board ferry with passengers.

0.2   Leave ferry and proceed uphill on main thoroughfare.

0.9   Turn right on **Bob Galbreath Road**.

1.7   Bear right on **Wilkinson Road** as Galbreath heads up a hill.

2.5   Turn right with Wilkinson Road at stop sign.

4.9   Turn left with thoroughfare on **Sandy Point Road**.

5.8   Turn right on **Camano Avenue** by Island County Fairgrounds. A carved wooden sign welcomes visitors to Langley.

6.2   Turn right toward City Center on **Cascade Avenue** in Langley as Sixth Street continues on. Road shortly is renamed **First Street**. At 6.5 a stairway by a totem pole and flower plantings leads down to the water's edge.

6.8   Turn left on **De Bruyn Avenue** as First Street ends, then turn right on **Saratoga Road** as Second Street goes left.

13.7   Turn left on **East Harbor Road** as Baby Island Road goes on to dead end.

13.8   For scenic diversion, turn right on **Harbor View Drive** and ride through residential area with views of Holmes Harbor, returning to **East Harbor Road** at 14.6.

14.7   Turn right on **Holmes View Drive** for another diversion, rejoining **East Harbor Road** at 15.5.

16.4   Turn right on **Brainers Road** for last scenic diversion. Turn left on **Beach Drive** at bottom of hill. Turn right again on **East Harbor Road** at mile 17.9 after a strenuous climb.

20.9   Turn right and downhill on **Vinton Avenue** as Cherry Street goes left. *Note: For cafe lunch, continue into Freeland on East Harbor Road.*

21.1   Turn right on **Stewart Road**.

21.3   Turn right to picnic tables along waterfront in Island County Freeland Park. Return via Stewart Road to East Harbor Road.

21.6   Bear right on **East Harbor Road**.

21.8   Turn left on **Main Street**. Freeland Cafe here specializes in homemade clam chowder.

22.2   Turn left on **Newman Road**.

24.0   Turn left on **State Route 525** and continue along shoulder.

25.4   Turn right on **Bayview Road**.

27.6   Turn right on **Sills Road**. Cross Maxwelton Road at stop sign at bottom of hill at mile 29.5 and continue on **French Road**. *Note: Dave MacKie Island County Park is 1.1 miles right on Maxwelton Road. Sandy beach, view.* After 0.5 mile the road starts up a long hill.

31.5   Turn left on **Cultus Bay Road**.

32.4   Turn right on **Deer Lake Road**.

33.2   Turn left with Deer Lake Road as Holst Road goes right.

34.6   Turn right at wye on **Deerlake Street** as highway appears ahead, bear right on highway, and freewheel down to ferry landing.

35.4   Back at starting point.

86   SOUTH WHIDBEY #2

STARTING POINT: Mukilteo State Park, Snohomish County. Take I-5 to exit 189 (Mukilteo) and follow signs to the park and Whidbey Island ferry. Park in unmarked stalls along east edge of the park.

DISTANCE: 26 miles.
TERRAIN: Hilly.
TOTAL CUMULATIVE ELEVATION GAIN: 1950 feet.
RECOMMENDED TIME OF YEAR: Any season.
RECOMMENDED STARTING TIME: 9 to 10 A.M.
ALLOW: 6 hours.
POINTS OF INTEREST
Island County Dave Mackie Memorial
    Park in Maxwelton
Sea wall in Langley

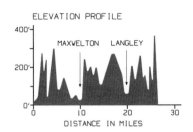

Although this is a short ride, it has much scenery to recommend it and enough hills to provide a challenge. As the route climbs out of Clinton, the homes stacked on the hillside at Columbia Beach give way to pastureland and dense forest along Humphrey Road. A steep plunge leads to the water level at Glendale.

Glendale, which enjoys semi-isolation, presents a picture of retreat to a secluded beachfront where a few homes share the magnificent view of Puget Sound. As the road winds up a creek canyon, salal, evergreen huckleberry, and sword ferns carpet the ground in the filtered light of the dense forest. The slower pace of island life is reflected by the languid smoke plumes from chimneys of old log cabins surrounded by gnarled orchard trees. Occasional newer forest abodes appear on the hillsides.

At Maxwelton, a park along the beach provides an opportunity to relax and enjoy the views of Point No Point, Foulweather Bluff, and the distant Olympic Mountains across Puget Sound. If the visibility happens to be poor, the foghorn at Point No Point expresses its displeasure. A regular sequence of flashing beacons dances across Admiralty Inlet after dark, reaching northward toward Useless Bay. Great blue herons frequent the shallow water in search of morsels, and loons and diving ducks join in the exercise.

In Langley, a totem pole and wooden benches by flower beds mark the top of a wooden staircase that descends to the beach, where a concrete sea wall has been constructed to hold back the erosion of the city's shoreline. Embossed Indian motifs in the sea wall blend the past with the present. Gulls and crows add their distinctive touch to a walk along the sandy, rocky beach. Langley's pioneer origins are reflected in the restoration of shops to the architectural styles of the nineteenth century.

Sheep, horses, and cattle complete the pastoral scenes along Wilkinson Road. Ferry traffic on the state highway signals the end to this delightful trip on Washington State's largest island.

MILEAGE LOG

0.0 Mukilteo State Park parking lot. Backtrack up the hill to the ticket booth, purchase ferry tickets, and proceed to bicycle staging area by pedestrian waiting room. Board ferry and sail to Clinton.

0.4 Just beyond toll booth at Clinton, turn left on narrow, one-way road.

0.5 Turn right at stop sign on **Berg Road**.

0.6 Turn left on **Humphrey Road**, which narrows and enters forest.

3.1 Glendale on the sound. Views of Mt. Rainier and Mt. Baker. Turn right with **Glendale Road** as it follows a creek up a narrow ravine. Dense forest closes in on both sides.

4.0 Turn left with Glendale Road as Holst Road continues on.

4.6 Turn left on **Jewett Road** and start downhill.

5.4 Turn right on **Cultus Bay Road**. Bailey's Corner Store here, good snack stop.

6.0 Turn left on **Bailey Road** and continue downhill.

8.2 Turn left on **French Road** by a fire station as Bailey Road ends.

8.6 Turn left on **Maxwelton Road** by a church.

9.8 Island County's Dave Mackie Memorial Park in Maxwelton: restrooms, sandy beach, boat ramp, far-reaching views. Enjoy a snack or early lunch, then return to French Road intersection.

11.1 Turn left on **Sills Road** as French Road goes right. Sills Road heads steeply uphill before leveling off among tall, arching alder trees. Ivy covers the trees and fences in places as the route heads downhill again.

13.0 Turn left onto **Bayview Road** as Sills Road ends and Ewing Road goes right. Route climbs a short hill and passes an old holly farm. Views of Useless Bay open up to the west.

15.3 Cross State Route 525 and continue on Bayview Road. Lone Lake appears on the left just before the route starts uphill, enters forest, and becomes **Brooks Hill Road**. As it enters Langley, the road is renamed **Third Street**.

19.2 Turn left on **De Bruyn Avenue**. Follow road downhill and around to **First Street** in downtown Langley along the waterfront. First Street is renamed **Cascade Avenue** and **Camano Avenue** as the route heads south and east out of town along the edge of the cliff.

20.2 Turn left on **Edgecliff Drive**.

20.5 Turn right on **Decker Street** as Edgecliff is marked Dead End.

20.7 Turn left on **Sandy Point Road** as Decker ends.

21.3 Turn right with the scenic drive on **Wilkenson Road** as Sandy Point Road ends. The road name spelling soon changes to **Wilkinson**.

23.6 Turn left with Wilkinson Road as Bob Galbreath Road continues on.

24.5 Turn left on **Bob Galbreath Road** as Wilkinson Road ends. Mt. Baker dominates the North Cascades and Mt. Rainier appears on the southern horizon as route tops a hill before entering Clinton.

25.3 Turn left on **State Route 525**, coast downhill to the ferry landing and take the ferry to Mukilteo.

26.2 End of tour in parking lot of Mukilteo State Park.

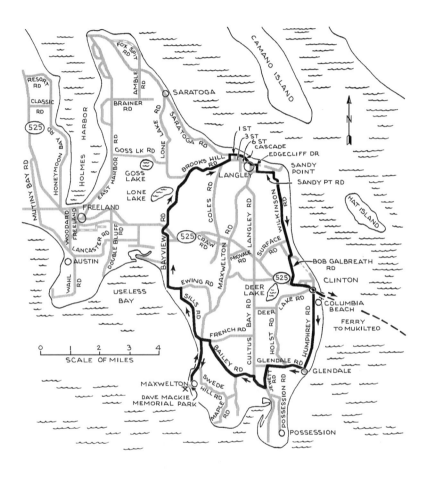

KING AND SNOHOMISH COUNTIES

This area is always popular for bicycle routes because of its proximity to the state's main population centers. Although covered extensively in *Bicycling the Backroads Around Puget Sound*, several interesting rides remain for inclusion in this volume. Hidden natural spectacles such as Twin Falls invite the inquisitive cyclist. The breath-taking descents of Klein Hill (Cougar Mountain) and Seattle Hill (Woodinville-Snohomish) are not unlike a good mountain ski run. Other routes add to the ever-popular repertoire of Snohomish Air Base, Monroe, and Fall City starting points. Versatile King County still has a few surprises to the south, but they are presented in *Bicycling the Backroads of Southwest Washington*.

"Registration, running lights, life vests?"

87 CONWAY HILL

STARTING POINT: Fishing access on Lake McMurray in Skagit County. Turn right on McMurray Lake Lane toward Lake McMurray Resort from State Route 9, nine miles north of Arlington, and follow signs to fishing access parking area.

DISTANCE: 26 miles.
TERRAIN: Moderate to hilly.
TOTAL CUMULATIVE ELEVATION GAIN: 1100 feet.
RECOMMENDED TIME OF YEAR: Any season.
RECOMMENDED STARTING TIME: 9 to 10 A.M.
ALLOW: 4 to 5 hours.
POINTS OF INTEREST
None outstanding

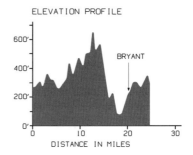

Although this Skagit–Snohomish County ride has no particularly outstanding points of interest or significant historic places to visit, it offers beautiful forest and countryside scenery from smooth, traffic-free, blacktop roads.

Our route circles the hill that straddles the Skagit–Snohomish County line east of Conway, west of Pilchuck Creek, north of Arlington, and south of Mt. Vernon. We call it Conway Hill, but in past years it had the rather affectionate nickname of "starvation ridge," as it is certainly harder to make a living farming on the ridge than in the fertile Skagit Valley below.

The roadside forest is especially attractive in the fall, when the scarlet vine maple and brilliant yellow bigleaf maple shimmer like jewels set against the velvet green trees and bright blue skies. Springtime brings special aromas that only the newly awakened growing things can produce, such as the pungent odor of skunk cabbage and the unique fragrance of the black cottonwood (balm of Gilead). Tasty blackberries tempt the taste buds on a warm summer day. Many varieties of warblers sing forth in springtime; song sparrows fill the woods with their lovely songs all year long, while the Swainson thrush lends his particular melody to the forest only during the three months of summer.

MILEAGE LOG

0.0 Fishing access on Lake McMurray. Proceed out to the highway.

0.5 Turn right on **State Route 9** and head northwest. Views of Lake McMurray.

1.7 Turn left with **State Route 534** toward Conway. Route heads uphill and through a swampy meadow before heading downhill again.

4.9 Turn left on **English Road** as Lake 16 Road goes right to public fishing. Old maps show this site, now a small residential area, was the location of the English Logging Company.

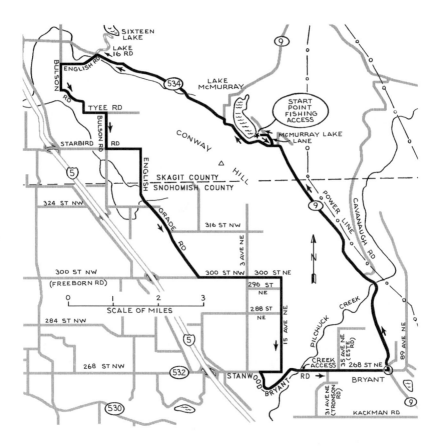

5.8 Turn left on **Bulson Road** as English Road comes to an end. There may be no road signs. The road zigs and zags through a forest of cedar, alder, and cottonwood trees before emerging into upland meadows.

7.6 Turn right and downhill with Bulson Road as Tyee Road goes on to a dead end.

8.4 Turn left on **Starbird Road**.

9.1 Attack a short, steep hill before the road turns south and is renamed **English Grade Road**. Route enters a dense cedar, alder, and maple forest that is carpeted with salmonberries and salal. The road contours the hillside with a continuous, gradual slope, as the name—which refers to an old logging railroad grade—implies. Leave Skagit County, enter Snohomish County.

12.3 Turn left on **300 Street N.W.** as English Grade Road ends. Road changes name from 300 Street N.W. to **300 Street N.E.** at mile 13.4. Local agricultural activities include a horse-breeding ranch and strawberry and raspberry farms.

14.1 Turn right on **15 Avenue N.E.** as 300 Street goes on to a dead end. Views of North Cascades. Freewheel down long hill. Road bends right at 16.1 and becomes **268 Street N.E.** and finally **Bjorndahl Road** as alder trees form an archway over the road.

16.5 Turn left on **Stanwood-Bryant Road** toward Bryant as Bjorndahl Road ends. Continue downhill. At 17.6 cross Pilchuck Creek. Access roads to the creek on far side of bridge; possible picnic lunch stop but no sanitary facilities. A deep pool partially diked off from the creek invites a quick dip.

19.7 Turn left on **State Route 9** by Bryant Store. *Note: Ride may be lengthened by turning right 3.5 miles to Arlington cafes.* Cross Pilchuck Creek on narrow bridge at mile 21.7. At mile 24.6 a small fountain flows from a pipe on the right just after the road crosses the Skagit County line. The fountain provides a refreshing cold drink of water on a hot summer day.

25.6 Turn right on **McMurray Lake Lane** toward Lake McMurray Resort.

26.0 Back to start of ride on the shore of Lake McMurray.

"...but it doesn't bother my bicycling!"

88 MONROE–LAKE ROESIGER

STARTING POINT: Monroe Riverside Park on State Route 203 by the Skykomish River. Take exit 194 (U.S. 2) from I-5 to Monroe and S.R. 203 to the park on the south edge of town; or take exit 23A (State Route 522) from I-405 to Monroe, then right on U.S. 2 and S.R. 203. Park cars on old concrete pavement near the river.

DISTANCE: 37 miles.
TERRAIN: Hilly.
TOTAL CUMULATIVE ELEVATION GAIN: 1300 feet.
RECOMMENDED TIME OF YEAR: Any season.
RECOMMENDED STARTING TIME: 10 A.M.
ALLOW: 4 to 5 hours.
POINT OF INTEREST
Lake Roesiger Snohomish County Park

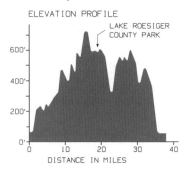

ELEVATION PROFILE

This bicycle ride travels the hills and valleys immediately north of Monroe in Snohomish County. Moss and licorice ferns envelop bigleaf maple trees along the upper reaches of Woods Creek. Sword ferns and other wild plants grow in crevices of attractive rock outcroppings. Only occasionally do unsightly logged-off areas appear along the route to spoil the otherwise pleasing forest setting. Older clearcuts have been replanted and now exhibit tall stands of rapidly growing Douglas fir.

On a hot summer day a dip in the lake at Lake Roesiger Snohomish County Park provides a refreshing pause after a morning of hill climbing. Lake Roesiger Park also allows the avid bird watcher to observe the many different ducks that frequent the lake during the winter. An early spring ride brings the unmistakable aroma of skunk cabbage and unexpected rapid changes of weather, which may vary from clear, sunny skies to rain to snow pellets to real snow sticking to the roads—all on the same day.

The opportunity to look for red-tailed hawks, great blue herons, and ruffed grouse that frequent this hill country is another attraction of this relatively short but moderately strenuous ride north of Monroe.

MILEAGE LOG

0.0 Monroe Riverside Park in Monroe. Head north on **State Route 203 (Lewis Street)**.
0.5 Turn right on **Main Street** at traffic light.
0.9 Cross railroad tracks and U.S. 2 at traffic light and continue on **Owens Road** (Some places marked **Old Owen Road**).
2.8 Bear left on **Florence Acres Road**.
5.0 Turn left on **259th Avenue S.E.**
5.2 Turn left on **132 Street S.E.**

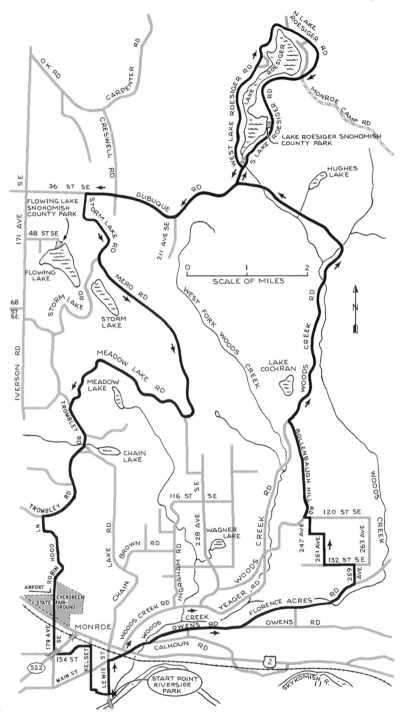

SCALE OF MILES

5.7 Turn right with thoroughfare on **251st Avenue S.E.** Follow thorough-fare around several turns as the road is renamed several times, eventually becoming **120th Street S.E.**

6.8 Turn right on **Bollenbaugh Hill Road** as 120th Street ends.

8.4 Turn right on **Woods Creek Road** as Bollenbaugh Hill Road ends. Cross Woods Creek at mile 11.0. Enter a small valley and head uphill through forest.

13.6 Turn right on **Lake Roesiger Road** as Dubuque Road goes on.

13.8 Bear left on **West Lake Roesiger Road** and bicycle up and down short hills along the western shore of Lake Roesiger. Cabins and permanent residences crowd the shoreline.

16.7 Turn sharp right at stop sign and proceed uphill on **North Lake Roesiger Road**. Lake Roesiger Store appears on the right at mile 18.1 as route heads downhill. Monroe Camp Road leads into forest on the left to Boy Scout Camp Brinkley.

19.2 Turn right into picnic area entrance to Lake Roesiger Snohomish County Park. Camping area is up in the forest on the left. The campsites are the walk-in variety, with sturdy, varnished, triangular tables typical of other Snohomish County parks. Enjoy a leisurely picnic lunch, then continue south along Lake Roesiger on **South Lake Roesiger Road**.

20.4 Turn right on **Dubuque Road** and head downhill as South Lake Roesiger Road ends.

23.4 Turn left on **Storm Lake Road**. Pass grocery at mile 24.6.

24.7 Turn left on **Mero Road** as Storm Lake Road bends right.

28.0 Turn right at stop sign on **Meadow Lake Road** as Mero Road ends.

30.9 Bear left on **Trombley Road** at a stop sign as Meadow Lake Road ends.

33.2 Turn left on **Robin Hood Lane**. Descend long, steep hill as road name changes to **179th Avenue S.E.** Go by Evergreen State Fairgrounds. Cross U.S. 2 at a traffic light at mile 35.0.

35.6 Turn left on **154th Street S.E.** and go under State Route 522 elevated roadway. Road is renamed **Blueberry Lane**.

36.3 Turn right on **N. Kelsey** as Blueberry Lane ends. Cross W. Main Street in Monroe and continue on **S. Kelsey**.

37.0 Turn left on **Terrace Street** as Kelsey ends.

37.1 Turn right on **S. Sams Street** as Terrace ends, then immediately turn left on **Sumac Drive**.

37.3 Cross State Route 203 (Lewis Street) and turn right into parking lot of Riverside Park. End of ride.

89 BOTHELL–SNOHOMISH

STARTING POINT: Sammamish River Trail parking area in Bothell. Take I-405 to Exit 24, Beardslee Boulevard. Follow Beardslee Boulevard and Main Street into Bothell. Turn left at stop light on 102 Avenue and cross bridge to parking area.

ALTERNATE STARTING POINT: Snohomish Airport, Snohomish. Take I-405 to east State Route 522 turnoff near Woodinville, follow State Route 522 east to Snohomish turnoff, then State Route 9 into Snohomish; or take I-5 to Everett and U.S. 2 to Snohomish. Park along the edge of the parking area closest to the railroad tracks and near the road.

DISTANCE: 32 to 36 miles.
TERRAIN: Moderate.
TOTAL CUMULATIVE ELEVATION GAIN: 1600 feet.
RECOMMENDED TIME OF YEAR: All seasons. Horseshoe Grange dinner in Cathcart featured on the second Sunday of every month.
RECOMMENDED STARTING TIME: 9:30 to 10 A.M.
ALLOW: 5 hours.
POINTS OF INTEREST None outstanding

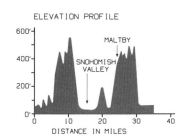

As the Seattle–Everett metropolitan complex continues to grow, the urban-suburban fringe gradually creeps out into what once was rural farmland. This tour explores the fringe, or transition phase, of southern Snohomish and northern King counties, where farms are driven out by skyrocketing real estate taxes and taken over by country homes, industry, and shopping centers.

Although the traffic of busy I-405 rushes by along its eastern boundary, Bothell retains the atmosphere of a small town where city hall, small businesses, and homes line its narrow streets. On its outskirts, lush green farmland is rapidly being covered by business parks.

Appaloosa, Arabian, Morgan, Quarter horse—just name your breed of horse and it probably inhabits the fields, pastures, or corrals of the habitations around Canyon Park and north to the Snohomish Valley. This upland country exhibits a variety of soil conditions ranging from gravelly, rocky land to peat bog near Thomas Lake along Seattle Hill Road. Horse ranches dominate the landscape with a few dog kennels thrown in for good measure. Beef cattle occupy only a small percentage of the available pastureland.

Subject to periodic flooding, the Snohomish Valley stretches for many miles between Everett, Snohomish, and Monroe, presenting acres of green grass, plowed fields, tall cornstalks, or flooded land, depending on the capriciousness of Northwest storms. The smooth, green slopes of a golf course covering a hillside above the valley south of Snohomish enhance the pastoral scene of Holstein-Friesian cows grazing in the valley below. Only the sound of small airplanes landing and taking off from the nearby Snohomish Airport breaks the spell of a completely rural area. The field provides hangars for numerous small airplanes. Skydivers take to the silk in the skies over the field and, with colorful parachutes flying, zero in on a landing target. A good vantage point for watching the display is in the Air Base Cafe over a bowl of soup or a piece of homemade pie. In addition to getting good food, the patronage is a small way of saying "thank you" for the privilege of parking for our bicycle tours.

Monthly Sunday dinners at the Horseshoe Grange in Cathcart have become a favorite for bicycle tour groups as well as a large clientele of automobile-borne families. Beef pot roast with "all the fixin's" plus home-made pie are served up family-style in a fashion to satisfy even the hungriest of cyclists.

Wild ducks of many varieties fly into Lake Beecher and the swampy area by Evans Creek, while chickens and geese scratch and hunt for food in the yards of homes along Fales Road. Small creeks, rushing full of water in the rainy season, dwindle to slow trickles during the drier summer months. As it nears Woodinville, the route diverts past diminutive Summit Lake, dives down a steep hill, and skirts the busy downtown area. It then follows the Sammamish River Trail past an industrial complex, goes under the I-405/SR-522 interchange maze, crosses North Creek, and returns to Bothell. Small trailer homes line the river near Bothell and keep the local resident duck and goose populations well supplied with food. Ducks frequently waddle along the trail and are quite unconcerned as the bicyclists whiz by only inches away.

MILEAGE LOG

0.0 Leave parking lot and turn left on **102 Avenue N.E.** Cross the Sammamish River.

0.1 Turn right on **Main Street** and bicycle through downtown Bothell. Road changes name to **Beardslee Boulevard**, then to **112 Avenue N.E.** as it leaves Bothell.

1.1 Turn right on **N.E. 195 Street** and cross I-405 on an overpass. Enter a fertile valley taken over by business parks.

1.3 Turn left at traffic light on **North Creek Parkway** and cycle through business park.

1.9 Cross North Creek and turn left on bikeway through the business park.

2.3 Turn right on bikeway along **240th Street S.E.**

2.4 Turn left on **35th Avenue S.E.**

3.2 Turn right on **228th Street S.E.** as 35th Avenue ends.

3.4 Turn left on **39th Avenue S.E.**

4.9 Turn left on **Maltby Road** as 39th Avenue ends, then right at the next intersection on **York Road**, which is shortly renamed **35th Avenue S.E.** *Note: For a shortcut to the Horseshoe Grange, turn right on Jewell Road at mile 5.0 and follow alternate route on map.*

8.4 Bear right on **Seattle Hill Road**. Pass Tri-Way Grange 1093.

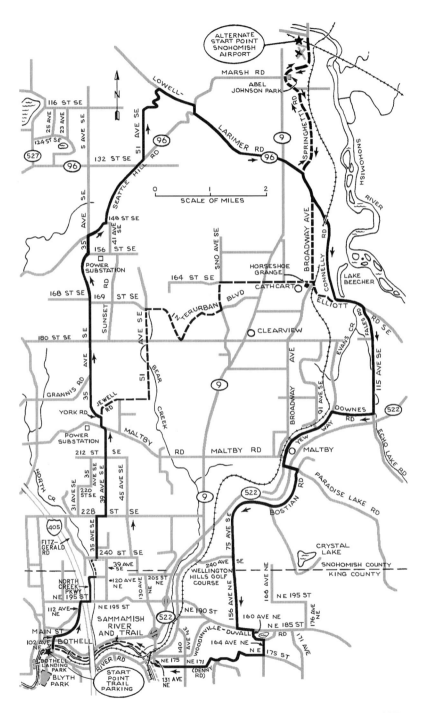

ALTERNATE
START POINT
SNOHOMISH
AIRPORT

MARSH RD

ABEL
JOHNSON PARK

116 ST SE

25 AVE
23 AVE

5 AVE SE

51 AVE SE

LOWELL-

LARIMER RD

96

9

SPRINGHETTI RD

96

124 ST SE

527

96

132 ST SE

SNOHOMISH RIVER

SEATTLE HILL RD

148 ST SE
41 AVE SE

35 AVE SE

156 ST SE

POWER
SUBSTATION

SCALE OF MILES

SNO AVE SE

164 ST SE

HORSESHOE
GRANGE

CATHCART

BROADWAY AVE

CONNELLY RD

LAKE
BEECHER

168 ST SE

169 ST SE

SUNSET RD

INTERURBAN BLVD

ELLIOTT

EVANS CR

FALES RD

115 AVE SE

180 ST SE

AVE SE

51

BEAR

CREEK

CLEARVIEW

9

BROADWAY AVE

91 AVE SE

DOWNES RD

522

GRANNIS RD

35 AVE SE

JEWELL RD

YORK RD

ECHO LAKE RD

POWER
SUBSTATION

MALTBY

RD

MALTBY RD

MALTBY

YEW WAY

212 ST SE

35 AVE SE

39 AVE SE

45 AVE SE

9

522

BOSTIAN RD

PARADISE LAKE RD

NORTH CR

31 AVE SE

220 ST SE

228 ST SE

405

FITZ-
GERALD
RD

35 AVE SE

240 ST SE

39 AVE
SE

NORTH
CREEK
PKWY
NE 195 ST

120 AVE
NE

205 ST
NE

130 AVE NE

75 AVE SE

240 AVE NE
WELLINGTON
HILLS GOLF
COURSE

CRYSTAL
LAKE

SNOHOMISH COUNTY
KING COUNTY

166 AVE NE

NE 195 ST

176 AVE NE

112 AVE
NE

NE 195 ST

522

NE 190 ST

156 AVE SE

160 AVE NE

NE 185 ST

171 AVE

MAIN ST

102 AVE
NE

BOTHELL

BOTHELL
LANDING
PARK

BLYTH
PARK

SAMMAMISH
RIVER
AND TRAIL

RIVER RD

START
POINT
TRAIL
PARKING

NE 175

140 AVE NE

131 AVE
NE

NE 171
(DENNY RD)

WOODINVILLE-DUVALL

164 AVE NE

RD

NE 175 ST

8.8   Turn left with Seattle Hill Road (**40 Avenue S.E.**) as 148th Street S.E. continues on. At mile 10.0 cross 132nd Street S.E. and continue on Seattle Hill Road as it starts down a steep hill.

10.2 Turn left on **51st Avenue S.E.**, which bends right at mile 11.0 and becomes **116th Street S.E.**, and finally **56th Avenue S.E.**

11.6 Turn right at the bottom of the hill on **E. Lowell-Larimer Road**, which joins **State Route 96** at mile 12.3. Cross State Route 9 at traffic light and continue on **131st Street S.E.** The road is renamed **Broadway Avenue** as it turns a corner and starts uphill. *Note: To visit the Snohomish Airport and Cafe, turn left on Springhetti Road at mile 14.7.*

15.2 Turn left on **Connelly Road**. Road goes downhill and under a railroad trestle. *Note: To visit the Horseshoe Grange, continue on Broadway 1.5 mile to Cathcart. Head down Elliott from nearby intersection after dinner.*

17.2 Bear left on **Elliott Road** as Connelly Road ends. Cross Evans Creek. Dairy farm on hillside to the right. Lake Beecher and swamp on the left.

17.6 Turn right on **Fales Road** (**115 Avenue S.E.**) and head uphill along a creek gorge. Waterfalls are visible through the trees.

19.6 Turn right with **Downes Road** just before Fales Road butts into State Route 522.

CUSTOMER COPY

4833 9000 0028 0103

JERRY RICHART   02/98 ✓

BARNES AND NOBLE
1915   BELLEVUE   WA
5464881697   053097

5268056

QUAN.	CLASS	DESCRIPTION	PRICE	AMOUNT
1		049515(763		13.00
		0898850772		14.75
1				24.45
		-30%		
			SUB TOTAL	22.20
			TAX	1.92
			TIPS MISC.	
			TOTAL	24.20

DATE 5-30-6

AUTHORIZATION

REG/DEPT.

REFERENCE NO.   SERVER   CLERK

FOLIO/CHECK NO.

SALES SLIP

IMPORTANT: RETAIN THIS COPY FOR YOUR RECORDS

PURCHASER SIGN HERE
X _____

Cardholder acknowledges receipt of goods and/or services in the amount of the Total shown hereon and agrees to perform the obligations set forth in the Cardholder's agreement with the issuer.

20.4 Turn left on **Yew Way** as Downes Road ends. As road approaches Maltby it is sandwiched between S.R. 522 and railroad tracks.

21.9 Bear left with thoroughfare, cross S.R. 522, and immediately turn right on **Bostian Road**, which parallels the highway before veering south and acquiring the alias of **75th Avenue S.E.**, and finally **156 Avenue N.E.** as it enters King County.

25.6 Turn left on **Woodinville-Duvall Road N.E.** at traffic light and continue on wide paved shoulder.

26.0 Turn right on **160th Avenue N.E.**, which bends left and is renamed **N.E. 180th Street**.

26.4 Turn right on **164th Avenue N.E.** and head uphill.

26.7 Turn right on **N.E. 175th Street**, which tops a summit and becomes **N.E. 173rd Street** as it descends the other side.

27.8 Keep right with thoroughfare as side roads go left. Road is renamed **146th Place N.E.**, and finally **N.E. 171st Street**. Cross busy 140th Avenue N.E. at traffic light at mile 28.4.

29.0 Turn left, just before buildings N and Q, through apartment parking lot and past tennis courts to paved access trail. Turn right on the **Sammamish River Trail** as access trail ends. Turn left on the trail bridge across the Sammamish River at mile 30.9.

31.5 Back at trail parking area. *Note: For lunch stop for alternate starting point, continue on trail to footbridge to Bothell Landing Park; food concessions nearby.*

90 AVONDALE–ECHO LAKE

STARTING POINT: Parking lot of Farrell McWhirter Park, City of Redmond. Take I-5 to State Route 520 (exit 168B) in Seattle. Follow State Route 520 to the Sammamish Valley and continue on Avondale Road. Turn right on Novelty Hill Road at the third traffic light, then left on Redmond Road. Turn left into entrance of McWhirter Park.

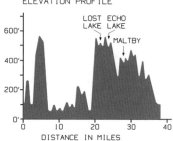

ELEVATION PROFILE

DISTANCE: 36 miles.
TERRAIN: Moderate to strenuous hills.
TOTAL CUMULATIVE ELEVATION GAIN: 1900 feet.
RECOMMENDED TIME OF YEAR: Any season.
RECOMMENDED STARTING TIME: 9 to 10 A.M.
ALLOW: 5 to 6 hours.
POINTS OF INTEREST
None outstanding.

Topographic maps are most revealing. They not only show where the cliffs, lakes, rivers, forest, logged-off areas, and roads are located, but they also show many houses and other buildings. A comparison of old maps with updated ones shows the extent and direction of spreading urbanization into the previously undeveloped countryside. A forested plateau rising to 600 feet elevation separates the small, confined Bear Creek Valley at the north end of Lake Sammamish from the broad, expansive valley of the Snoqualmie River. Roads and houses are slowly but inexorably threading their way across Bear Creek Valley and extending long fingers onto the western slope of this plateau. Many acres of forest still remain, however, providing a buffer between the suburban sprawl and the delightfully rural river valley. Further hope for the future of the flood plain of the Snoqualmie Valley is offered by the King County moratorium on rezoning of farmland to other uses.

Our bicycle ride ascends the divide, plunges down to the floor of the Snoqualmie Valley, and follows it for a number of miles before climbing the northern edge of the plateau to Lost Lake and Echo Lake and returning to Avondale.

Lost Lake and Echo Lake, stocked annually with fingerling trout, are just two of many small lakes nestled among the hills and ravines of the plateau country above the Snoqualmie Valley. Several homes along the shores share the pleasant, tranquil setting.

A fall ride provides bicycle riders a chance to observe salmon spawning, as Bear Creek is one of the few small, gravel-bed streams still producing natural runs of salmon. Beavers enjoy felling the willow trees that grow alongside and occasionally build dams that cause trouble. Department of Wildlife animal control agents must then trap the beavers and transport them to territory farther removed from suburbia. Yes, King and Snohomish counties still have their rural areas and wild animals. Here is a short trip to such environs.

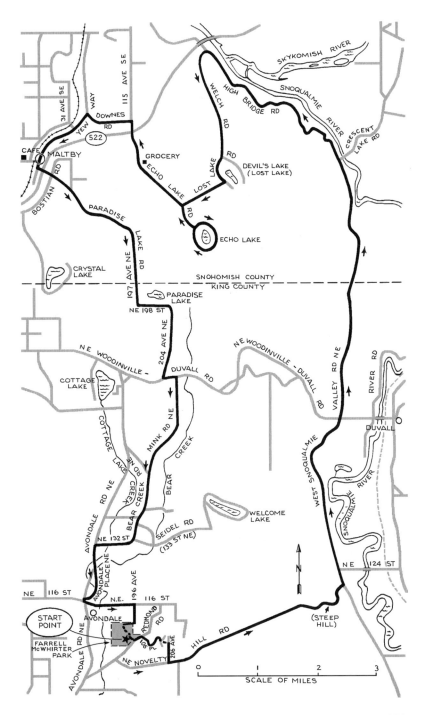

MILEAGE LOG

0.0 Leave Farrell McWhirter Park parking area, go out entrance drive, and turn left on **Redmond Road N.E.**

0.2 Turn right on **N.E. 106 Place** toward Overlake School. Continue straight uphill at 0.8 as side road goes right into Overlake School campus.

0.9 Bear right at road fork, then immediately left through bollards on dirt trail.

1.0 Turn right on **206 Avenue N.E.** as dirt trail ends.

1.4 Turn left on **N.E. Novelty Hill Road** as 106 Avenue ends.

4.4 Check brakes and descend the eastern slope of the hill carefully, as the grade is steep and has several sharp switchbacks.

4.8 Bear left on **West Snoqualmie Valley Road N.E.** at stop sign at bottom of Novelty Hill. Enjoy the pastoral scenes as the road proceeds north along the edge of the Snoqualmie Valley. At 7.7 cross Woodinville-Duvall Road and continue north past dairy farms. Enter Snohomish County at 10.1.

12.1 Continue straight and uphill on **High Bridge Road** as Crescent Lake Road goes over the Snoqualmie River on the right. Hillside farms, bucolic scenery, Hereford and Limousin cattle.

15.6 Turn hard left and uphill on **Welch Road** toward Lost Lake Road. High Bridge Road is still going downhill here, and the turn comes just before it plunges under S.R. 522; so be prepared.

17.6 Turn right with **Lost Lake Road** as Welch Road turns left. Lost Lake fishing access on left at mile 18.2; requires conservation license.

19.0 Turn left on **Echo Lake Road** as Lost Lake Road comes to an end. Pass a gas company compressor station and circumnavigate Echo Lake. Echo Lake fishing access at mile 20.1; conservation license required. Continue around lake and downhill on Echo Lake Road. Watch out for dogs on this downhill run. Pass Rainbow General Store at mile 21.6; store park area available for picnic lunch.

22.9 Cross State Route 522 and immediately turn left on **Downes Road**.

23.8 Turn left on **Yew Road** as Downes Road ends. Industrial buildings march along the railroad track on the right as route enters Maltby. *Note: Maltby Road goes right to Maltby Cafe at mile 25.0.*

25.2 Turn left with thoroughfare, cross S.R. 522 at traffic light, and proceed on   **Paradise Lake Road**. Housing development soon gives way to pastures and forest. At mile 28.1 route re-enters King County, where the road assumes in succession the names of **197 Avenue N.E.**, **N.E. 198 Street**, and eventually **204 Avenue N.E.** This is numeromania!

30.2 Turn left on **N.E. Woodinville-Duvall Road** as 204 Avenue ends.

30.4 Turn right on **Mink Road N.E.**

32.2 Turn left on **Bear Creek Road N.E.** and stay with it as Seidel Road goes left at 33.4. As the road swings right it is renamed **N.E. 132 Street**.

33.7 Cross Cottage Lake Creek and turn left on **Avondale Road N.E.**

34.4 Bear left on **Avondale Place N.E.**

34.8   Rejoin **Avondale Road N.E.** Stay on left shoulder and turn left on **N.E. 116 Street** toward Overlake School.
35.5   Turn right on **196 Avenue N.E.** Ignore Dead End sign.
35.8   Turn right into Farrell McWhirter Park.
36.0   Turn left at base of hill and proceed through gate on asphalt-surfaced trail. Park menagerie at mile 36.3.
36.4   End of tour in east parking lot.

"...with steep switchbacks, requiring much braking."

91   PINE LAKE

STARTING POINT: Olive Taylor Quigley Park in Fall City, on the Redmond–Fall City Road. Take I-90 to exit 22 (Preston); proceed through Preston to Fall City.

DISTANCE: 35 miles.
TERRAIN: Half hilly, half flat.
TOTAL CUMULATIVE ELEVATION GAIN: 1350 feet.
RECOMMENDED TIME OF YEAR: Any season.
RECOMMENDED STARTING TIME: 10 A.M.
ALLOW: 4 to 5 hours.
POINTS OF INTEREST
Beaver Lake King County Park
Pine Lake King County Park
Carnation Research Farm
John MacDonald Memorial Park

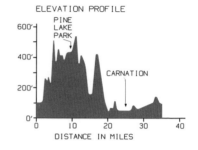

ELEVATION PROFILE

DISTANCE IN MILES

On this ride from Fall City to Pine Lake, the plateau and hills east of Issaquah demand strenuous effort of bicyclists, while the Snoqualmie Valley between Fall City and Carnation rewards them with miles of pleasant, relaxing cycling.

Our starting point, Olive Taylor Quigley Park along the banks of the Snoqualmie River in Fall City, once boasted large hop-drying sheds during the early days of farming in the valley when hops were a principal agricultural crop. Although the hop sheds and vines are long gone, the scene is still green with carefully tended pastures and occasional row crops. Olive Taylor Quigley, a Fall City pioneer, was said to be the first white person born in the upper Snoqualmie Valley. She died in 1974 at the ripe old age of 98. Her uncle, James Taylor, a prospector, homesteaded the townsite of Fall City in 1869.

The recent inrush of residential development to the Pine Lake Plateau has brought heavy traffic to several of its previously enjoyable backroads. A cross-plateau bicycle/pedestrian trail, financed by the 1979 King County Forward Thrust bond issue, is several years behind schedule in its planning, due to public outcry against portions of the proposed routes ("Not in my backyard!"). The trail should eventually provide a pleasurable alternative to the busy roads.

Carnation Farm's founding dates back to the turn of the century. The research and development carried on here has done much to make dairy farming the successful industry it is today. The farm, open for delightful tours of its dairy and gardens for decades, closed its doors to the public in 1996.

Lush green pastures cover the bottom land along the Snoqualmie River, providing food for the many dairy and beef cattle. Acres of strawberries and corn thrive in the loamy soil around Carnation and Fall City. But it was not always so. These river-bottom lands were once covered with trees, swamp flora, and underbrush. A Herculean effort was required, clearing trees and stumps and draining the marshes, before the land could be farmed. The hills and plateau area between Fall City and Issaquah are for the most part still covered with the natural vegetation of the Northwest forest belt. Evergreens include Douglas-fir, hemlock, and cedar, while bigleaf maple, vine maple, and alder are the principal deciduous trees. In places the road appears to bore a tunnel through the trees as they arch overhead. Sword ferns line the banks along the way to Ames Lake, with salal, salmonberry, and spiraea crowding in to form a true jungle of the temperate climate.

Today bicyclists can enjoy the fruits of the labors of their pioneer ancestors as they pedal through the river-bottom farmland. Only when they picture the hillside forest covering the valley, however, can the visitors fully appreciate the labors of the early farmers.

MILEAGE LOG

0.0 Olive Taylor Quigley Park in Fall City. Cross the Redmond–Fall City Road and continue on **335 Place S.E.**

0.2 Turn right on **S.E. 44 Place**.

0.4 Turn left on **332 Avenue S.E.** as 44 Place ends.

0.7 Road swings right and becomes **Issaquah–Fall City Road**. Follow it through pastures and strawberry fields, eventually climbing the forested hillside. At 3.3 turn left with Issaquah–Fall City Road as S.E. 40 Street goes downhill to the right. Many small streams rush down the hillside. At 4.2 ascend a summit, dive into a small valley, cross a creek, and climb back up again.

5.8 Cross Duthie Hill Road as Issaquah–Fall City Road turns left. Cross roadside berm and turn right on asphalt-surfaced trail. Keep right at 5.9 as left fork goes into Klahanie residential area. The trail bends left at mile 6.1 and parallels S.E. Issaquah–Beaver Lake Road.

6.6 Turn right across roadway on **E. Beaver Lake Drive S.E.** as 256 Avenue S.E. goes left into Klahanie. Pass public fishing access at mile 7.2. The road bends right at mile 9.5 and is renamed S.E. 24 Street. King County Beaver Lake Park on the left; picnic shelter, portable toilets, water, lake frontage, trails.

10.9 Turn left on **228 Avenue S.E.**, then immediately right into Pine Lake Park.

10.2 In the picnic area are tables, a shelter, restrooms, and food concession. A swimming beach and boat launch are nearby. A concrete pier provides a good duck-feeding vantage point. After lunch, proceed back out entrance road.

11.5 Turn left at the park exit. The road dips, then climbs a moderately steep hill to a summit at 12.1. Pass several country homes and plunge down a long hill. At the summit, the Seattle skyline interrupts the western horizon.

13.5 Turn right on **N.E. 8 Street** by the Sammamish Highlands Shopping Center; grocery and food services.

14.5 Turn left on **244 Avenue N.E.** as 8 Street is marked Dead End. Proceed down and up several short hills before heading steeply down to the Fall City Road.

16.2   Turn right on **Redmond–Fall City Road (State Route 202)**. Grocery/delicatessen at mile 16.4.

16.9   Bear left and uphill on **N.E. Ames Lake Road**. It starts up a moderately steep incline but gradually becomes a comfortable low-gear grade as it follows the canyon of a little stream. The road attains a summit at mile 18.3 and begins a slow, easy descent. At 19.3 the road is renamed **Ames Lake–Carnation Road N.E.** and starts downhill. Cross a bridge over the outlet stream from Ames Lake, pass W. Snoqualmie Valley Road as it branches left, and emerge into farmland.

22.2   Continue on **Carnation Farm Road** as Ames Lake–Carnation Road is renamed. The road turns a corner, follows along Sikes Lake (a good spot to see ducks), and passes Carnation Farm. At mile 23.3 the top of the hill beyond Carnation Farm is a fine site for viewing the fields and buildings of the farm.

24.3   Turn right on **310 Avenue N.E.** immediately after crossing the Snoqualmie River. Dikes of gravel separate the road from the river. A small farm appears on the left just before the road swings left past acres of strawberries and becomes **N.E. 60 Street**.

25.3   Turn right on **320 Avenue N.E.**

25.6   Turn left on **N.E. 55 Street** as 320 Avenue ends, then right on **Carnation-Duvall Road N.E. (State Route 203)**. A picturesque old cemetery appears on left at town limits of Carnation at mile 25.8. Old masonry obelisk still shows the old town name of Tolt. Continue through Carnation. Grocery stores and cafes offer their services.

26.4   Turn right on **N.E. 40th Street** for a visit to John MacDonald Memorial Park at mile 26.9; picnicking, camping, and restrooms with hot showers. The confluence of the Tolt and the Snoqualmie rivers is a favorite spot for steelheaders. Return on N.E. 40 Street.

27.3   Turn right on **State Route 203**, cross the Tolt River, and turn right on **N.E. Tolt Hill Road** across the Snoqualmie River.

28.5   Turn left on **West Snoqualmie River Road N.E.** as Tolt Hill Road continues on uphill. Warning signs with covered legends imply that water may cover this road during flood season. Deep ditches line the sides of the road, separating it from the thick marshland vegetation of alders, vine maple, salmonberry, skunk cabbage, spiraea, and occasional tall cedar trees. Clematis vines cover supporting trees with a decoration of white flowers in spring and fluffy white seed pods in fall. Road bends left at 30.8 as name changes to **East Main Street**, then bends right and becomes **West Snoqualmie River Road S.E.**

32.6   Turn left on **S.E. 24 Street** as West Snoqualmie River Road ends. Changing its name at each turn, the road threads its way through the farmland along the Snoqualmie River, finally turning right and becoming **324 Avenue S.E.**

34.3   Turn left on **State Route 202 (Redmond–Fall City Road)**.

35.2   Back at Olive Taylor Quigley Park in Fall City, the starting point.

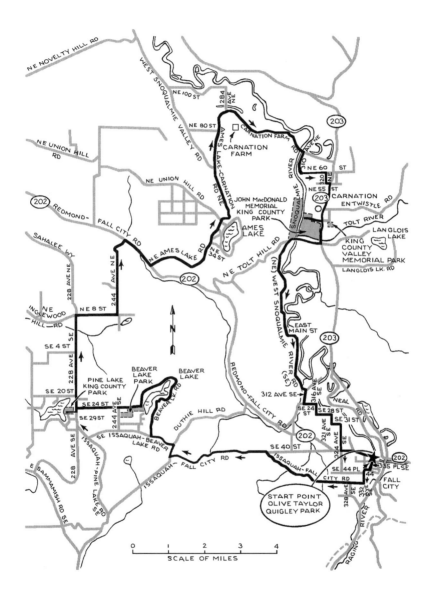

92 COUGAR MOUNTAIN

STARTING POINT: Coalfield King County Park. From I-405, take exit 5 (State Route 900) to Coalfield. Turn south (right) on 164 Avenue S.E. by tavern/cafe ½ mile to park. Park in parking lot along fence.

DISTANCE: 24 miles.

TERRAIN: One long, steep hill, the rest flat by comparison.

TOTAL CUMULATIVE ELEVATION GAIN: 1250 feet.

RECOMMENDED TIME OF YEAR: Any season.

RECOMMENDED STARTING TIME: 10 A.M.

ALLOW: 4 hours.

POINTS OF INTEREST
Cougar Mountain Zoological Park
King County Regional Wildland Park
Boehm's Candy Kitchen in Issaquah

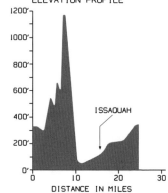

ELEVATION PROFILE

Three mountains play a prominent part in this bicycle ride, but Cougar Mountain, directly east of Lake Washington, gets top billing. The route climbs up its western side and takes in the far-reaching view toward Seattle and Puget Sound with the Olympics beyond. Our route follows Issaquah Creek up the valley separating Squak and Tiger mountains, two rather precipitous, sparsely populated foothills of the Cascades. The three mountains have one thing in common—large deposits of low-grade soft coal. In years gone by, the mining of this mineral played an important part in the economy of Issaquah and the smaller communities of Coalfield and Newcastle. At the turn of the century, along with other coal mines in southern King County, these mines supplied the coal used in the homes, industries, and steam locomotives of the greater Seattle area.

Much to the delight of bicyclists, the land developers have been slow to wrest this area from its quiet state. Horses, sheep, and cattle graze the pastures in the small valleys of May Creek and Issaquah Creek. The larger valley at the southern end of Lake Sammamish near Issaquah, however, is slowly but surely disappearing under a covering of asphalt and concrete. I-90 cuts a giant swath across its middle. Restaurants and motels spring up along the highway. Lake Sammamish State Park, a protected green area in this spreading blight, preserves 432 acres for recreational use.

Homes climb nearly to the top of the western and northern sides of 2000-foot Cougar Mountain. The King County Park Department claims the summit, having acquired the land from the army when it was abandoned as a Nike base. The park has been expanded greatly by the acquisition of several old coal-mining claims, and a large number of foot and horse trails have been established. Bicycles, however, are excluded from the trails. Near the northern base of the mountain, the Cougar Mountain Zoological Park specializes in threatened and endangered species.

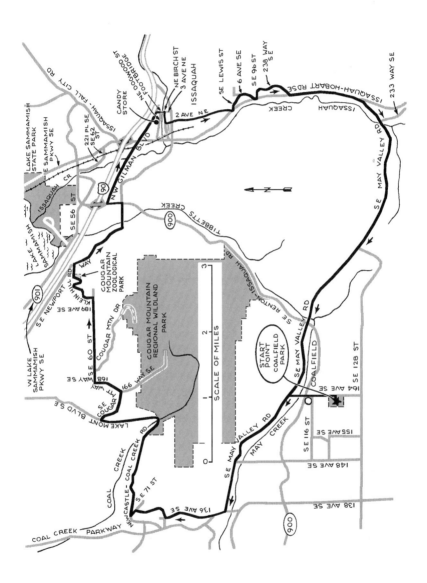

Mixed deciduous-evergreen forests of the western Washington lowland belt line the roadsides along the Newcastle–Coal Creek Road. The lengthening days of late winter are greeted by delicate clouds of pink and white blossoms of flowering trees along May Valley Road, while numerous bushes of the wild, red-flowering currant welcome the rufous hummingbirds back to their northern nesting grounds in early spring. White osoberry bushes bloom even earlier. In summer and fall, old neglected fruit trees still produce apples and plums. Easily accessible blackberry vines are always loaded with berries for the taking on a summer ride.

Additional tasty snacks are available at Boehm's Candy Kitchen in Issaquah. Located just off I-90 at the east end of town, this little Bavarian-style structure has attracted customers for many years. The delicious homemade chocolates and creams are a real treat.

MILEAGE LOG

0.0 Parking area, Coalfield King County Park. Head north (left) on **164th Avenue S.E.** Cross State Route 900 at mile 0.6. Road is renamed **S.E. May Valley Road** as it bends left at mile 0.8.

3.0 Turn right on **Coal Creek Parkway S.E.** as May Valley Road ends.

3.1 Bear right on **136 Avenue S.E.** and wind uphill as Coal Creek Parkway continues on.

4.0 Turn right on **S.E. 79 Place** at stop sign as 134 Avenue continues on with sidewalks. Road is shortly renamed **136 Avenue S.E.**

4.7 Turn left with 136 Avenue S.E. as S.E. 71 Place goes right.

4.8 Turn right on **Newcastle–Coal Creek Road** as 136 Avenue ends. At 6.5 cross Coal Creek as road is renamed **Lakemont Boulevard S.E**. Cougar Mountain King County Wildland Park trailhead on right.

7.2 Turn right on **S.E. Cougar Mountain Way** and head uphill for 1.2 miles as the thoroughfare is renamed **168 Way S.E.** and **S.E. 60 Street**. Summit of route at mile 8.4 as S.E. Cougar Mountain Drive goes steeply uphill to the right 1.2 miles to another trailhead for King County's Cougar Mountain Wildland Park. Views of the Olympics in the distance and the Renton area directly below. Plunge downhill with S.E. 60 Street. Good brakes are absolutely necessary.

9.6 Turn left very sharply at **180 Avenue S.E. (Klein Hill Road)** as 60 Street is marked Dead End. Brake around sharp curves and switchbacks. Road changes name to **190 Avenue S.E.**, **S.E. 56th Street**, **194 Avenue S.E.**, and **S.E. 54th Street**. Cougar Mountain Zoological Park appears on the right at mile 10.5.

10.7 Turn right on **S.E. Newport Way** at stop sign at bottom of hill as 54 Street ends.

11.8 Turn left at traffic light on **State Route 900 (Renton-Issaquah Road)**.

12.2 Turn right at traffic light on **N.W. Gilman Boulevard**. Sidewalk available along this busy, four-lane road. Fast-food enterprises and the fashionable Gilman Village offer lunch opportunities. Cross Issaquah Creek at mile 13.1.

13.6   Cross Front street at traffic light in Issaquah.

13.8   Turn into Boehm's Candy Kitchen for delicious chocolates. Continue east along Gilman Boulevard to cross a creek on a narrow footbridge.

14.1   Turn right on **N.E. Birch Street**, then left on **2nd Avenue N.E.** *Note: For a brown-bag lunch in Issaquah's delightful city park, continue on Birch Street to its end, then left on trail along railroad tracks. Railroad museum and old logging equipment on display.*

15.1   Bear left across opposing Do Not Enter lane onto sidewalk and continue around corner as 2nd Avenue ends, then turn left on **S.E. Lewis Street** and right on **6th Avenue S.E.**

15.3   Bear left around a corner on the unpaved left shoulder of **Issaquah-Hobart Road S.E.** and continue on **S.E. 96 Street**. Bear right on **238 Way S.E.** as S.E. 96 Street turns to gravel. Llama farm on the left.

16.1   Turn left on **Issaquah-Hobart Road S.E.** and continue on wide, smooth shoulder.

17.6   Turn right at traffic light toward Coalfield and Renton on **S.E. May Valley Road**. Cross S.E. Renton-Issaquah Road (S.R. 900) at 21.6.

22.8   Turn left on **164 Avenue S.E.** as May Valley Road ends. Cross State Route 900 at mile 22.9 by tavern/cafe.

23.5   Back at starting point at Coalfield King County Park.

93 TWIN FALLS

STARTING POINT: Si View King County Park in North Bend. Take exit 31 (North Bend) from I-90. Turn right at traffic light on N.E. North Bend Way. Drive east through town and turn right on Orchard Drive.

DISTANCE: 12 miles. Can be combined with Tours 10 through 17 for rides of arbitrary length.
TERRAIN: Flat to moderate.
TOTAL CUMULATIVE ELEVATION GAIN: 370 feet.
RECOMMENDED TIME OF YEAR: Avoid winter weather when freezing level is below 1200 feet.
RECOMMENDED STARTING TIME: Suit yourself.
ALLOW: 3 hours.
POINT OF INTEREST
Twin Falls Natural Area

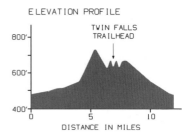

ELEVATION PROFILE

DISTANCE IN MILES

Combine this short, moderately strenuous bicycle ride with the relatively short hike to Twin Falls and you have a pleasant morning or afternoon outing. But if a leisurely, enjoyable bicycle ride is all that interests you, this Twin Falls ride has all the necessary elements: low-traffic roads, deep forest, and mountain stream scenery.

Our ride begins at Si View King County Park in North Bend and traverses the bases of two major local landmarks. Mt. Si, a prominent 4190-foot mountain, rises to the north, and Rattlesnake Ridge extends across the southern edge of this upper Snoqualmie River Valley.

The semi-deserted, divided roadways of old U.S. 10, displaced and cut off by construction of I-90, now are suitably low in traffic for enjoyable bicycling. The former eastbound roadway is now the shortest and allows a delightful diversion through the semi-isolated community of Maloney Grove. As the roadway ends, another seemingly forgotten road is taken past the site of Tanner Mill, serving the North Bend community for many decades and now demolished. Still more backroads explore the area north of the old highway, revealing a truckers' service area and eventually making a straight downhill run to the South Fork Snoqualmie River. Here, if the ride seems too short, a side trip up Edgewick Road to its end offers rewarding scenery.

Twin Falls Natural Area originally had its entrance above the falls on U.S. 10. Construction of I-90 closed this access, and for many years only the very determined of hikers visited the twin falls of the South Fork Snoqualmie River. Then, in 1989, a new access road was completed from the south, and a new trail and trailhead were established. The restrooms now have doors installed, and the trail and falls are superb. Be prepared, however, to lock and leave bicycles at the trailhead, as they are prohibited on the trail.

The short ride back to North Bend on the former westbound U.S. 10 roadway may have light to moderate traffic, but it is a good downhill grade and brings the trip to a quick ending.

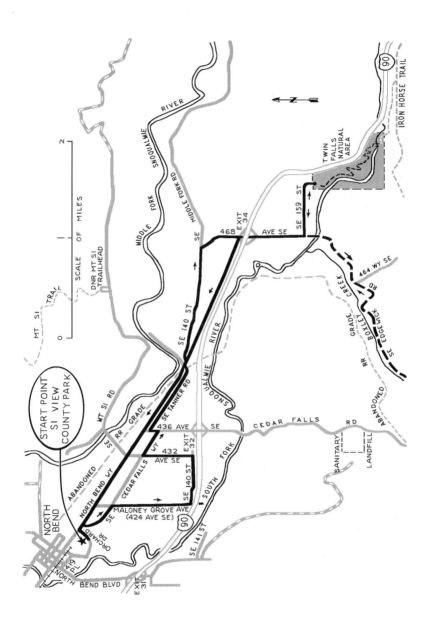

MILEAGE LOG

0.0 Starting from parking area by Si View King County Park, head left (northeast) on **S.E. Orchard Drive**.

0.3 Turn right on bicycle lane along **S.E. Cedar Falls Way** as Orchard Drive ends. The bike lane reverts shortly to a wide, paved shoulder.

0.7 Turn right on **Maloney Grove Avenue S.E.**

1.5 Turn left on **S.E. 140 Street** as 424 Avenue S.E. continues on to a dead end.

2.1 Turn left on **432 Avenue S.E.**

2.6 Turn right at stop sign on **S.E. Cedar Falls Way**.

3.0 Turn left at stop sign on **436 Avenue S.E.** as S.E. Cedar Falls Road goes right.

3.1 Turn right on **S.E. Tanner Road**.

3.7 Turn right on **S.E. North Bend Way** as Tanner ends.

4.0 Turn left on **S.E. 140 Street**.

5.1 Bear right with thoroughfare on **468 Avenue S.E.** as S.E. Middle Fork Road continues on, marked Dead End. Pass truck stop, restaurant, motel. Continue under I-90 at mile 5.7.

6.3 Turn left on **S.E. 159 Street**. *Note: 468 Avenue S.E. continues on under the name of Edgewick Road, 2.2 miles to a dead end; a scenic, uphill ride.*

Public restrooms

6.8 Twin Falls Natural Area trailhead, Olallie State Park. Pit toilets; bicycles prohibited on trail. Lock bicycles and walk trail 1.5 miles to falls viewing platform and bridge over falls. *Note: Trail continues on another mile to Iron Horse Trail, the old Milwaukee Railroad grade.* Retrace route to trailhead, mount bicycles, and ride back out S.E. 159 Street.

7.3 Turn right on **468 Avenue S.E.**

8.1 Go under I-90 and immediately turn left by truck stop on **S.E. North Bend Way**. *Note: S.E. Mt. Si Road goes right to the DNR Mt. Si trailhead at mile 10.6.*

11.6 Turn left on **S.E. Orchard Drive** in North Bend.

11.9 Back to starting point at Si View King County Park.

"...said it was okay then!"

ALPHABETICAL INDEX OF TOURS

MILEAGE INDEX–DAY TOURS

MILEAGE INDEX—OVERNIGHT AND MULTI-DAY TOURS

TOUR JUNCTIONS

Note: Rides 1 through 54 are found in Bicycling the Backroads Around Puget Sound, ***and 94 through 139 in*** Bicycling the Backroads of Southwest Washington ***(The Mountaineers, Seattle, Washington).***

Tour Junction	Tour Numbers	Tour Junction	Tour Numbers
Abbotsford, B.C.	57, 58	Hartford	28, 33
Agate Passage	42, 82	Hickson	68, 70
Alger	67, 68, 69	Issaquah	15, 92
Anacortes	39, 40, 41, 72	Kalaloch	76
Arlington	30, 31, 32, 34, 35	Keystone	
Avondale	18, 19, 90		38, 59, 77, 79, 83, 84
Bay View	59, 69, 70, 71	La Conner	36, 38
Bellingham	59, 64, 67, 69	Lake McMurray	35, 73, 87
Birch Bay	60, 61, 62	Lake Roesiger	24, 28, 29, 88
Blaine	55, 56, 60	Lake Sammamish State Park	92
Bothell	89	Langley	59, 85, 86
Carnation	12, 13, 14, 16, 91	Lynden	56, 63, 64
Center	79, 80, 81	Maltby	89, 90
Chimacum	77, 80	Maple Falls	59, 65
Clear Lake	70, 73, 74	Marysville	33, 38
Coalfield	5, 92	Mission, B.C.	57, 59
Concrete	34, 74	Monroe	17, 23, 24, 25, 88
Conway	36, 38, 73, 87	Mt. Vernon	36, 70, 71, 73
Coupeville	38, 59	Mukilteo	22, 38, 59, 85, 86
Custer	60, 62	Nordland	77, 80
Darrington	34	North Bend	10, 93
Deception Pass	38, 59, 72	Oak Harbor	59, 83
Deming	59, 65, 66	Park	68
Dungeness Park	59, 75	Port Angeles	59, 78
Duvall	16, 17, 90	Port Gamble	59, 80, 82
Eaglemount	59, 79	Port Ludlow	59, 81
Edison	59, 69, 70, 71	Port Townsend	77, 79, 83, 84
Edmonds	43, 59, 80	Seattle	20, 42, 44, 82, 94, 95
Everett	21, 22, 38	Sedro Woolley	34, 70, 74
Everson	58, 63, 64, 65	Sequim	59, 75
Fall City	11, 12, 15, 91	Snohomish	21, 22, 23, 24, 89
Ferndale	61, 62, 63	Stanwood	30, 37, 38
Fort Langley, B.C.	56, 59	Sumas	57, 58, 59
Freeland	38, 59, 84, 85	Swartz Bay, B.C.	59
Grand Mound	51, 124	Tsawwassen, B.C.	55, 59
Granite Falls	28, 29, 31	Victoria, B.C.	59
Grapeview	108	Winslow	42, 82
Hadlock	77, 79, 80	Woodinville	18, 89
Harrison Hot Springs, B.C.	57, 59		

Other titles you may enjoy from The Mountaineers:

BICYCLING THE BACKROADS AROUND PUGET SOUND,
Fourth Edition, *Erin & Bill Woods*

BICYCLING THE BACKROADS OF NORTHWEST OREGON,
Second Edition, *Erin & Bill Woods*

BICYCLING THE BACKROADS OF SOUTHWEST
WASHINGTON, Third Edition, *Erin & Bill Woods*

BIKING THE GREAT NORTHWEST: 20 Tours in Washington,
Oregon, Idaho, and Montana, *Jean Henderson*
Collection of multi-day tours, many of them loops, for great
Northwest cycling vacations. Includes mileage logs and notes
on terrain, history, scenic highlights, and cycling smarts.

MOUNTAIN BIKE ADVENTURES IN WASHINGTON'S NORTH
CASCADES AND OLYMPICS, Second Edition, *Tom Kirkendall*
60 of the best off-road bike trails from Interstate 90 north to the
Canadian border, plus the Olympics.

MOUNTAIN BIKE ADVENTURES IN WASHINGTON'S
SOUTH CASCADES AND PUGET SOUND, Second Edition,
Tom Kirkendall
Covers the region from Interstate 90 south to the Columbia
River, offering trails to suit both novice and experienced
mountain bikers.

MOUNTAIN BIKE EMERGENCY REPAIR, *Tim Toyoshima*
Pocket-sized handbook shows how to perform temporary
trailside repairs with few or no tools, and then make permanent
repairs with proper tools.

WASHINGTON'S RAIL TRAILS: A Guide for Walkers,
Bicyclists, Equestrians, *Fred Wert*
Detailed guide to all rail-trails, with usage tips for walkers,
mountain bikers, in-line skaters, and equestrians.

THE MOUNTAINEERS, founded in 1906, is a nonprofit outdoor activity and conservation club, whose mission is "to explore, study, preserve, and enjoy the natural beauty of the outdoors. . . . " Based in Seattle, Washington, the club is now the third-largest such organization in the United States, with 15,000 members and five branches throughout Washington State.

The Mountaineers sponsors both classes and year-round outdoor activities in the Pacific Northwest, which include hiking, mountain climbing, ski-touring, snowshoeing, bicycling, camping, kayaking and canoeing, nature study, sailing, and adventure travel. The club's conservation division supports environmental causes through educational activities, sponsoring legislation, and presenting informational programs. All club activities are led by skilled, experienced volunteers, who are dedicated to promoting safe and responsible enjoyment and preservation of the outdoors.

If you would like to participate in these organized outdoor activities or the club's programs, consider a membership in The Mountaineers. For information and an application, write or call The Mountaineers, Club Headquarters, 300 Third Avenue West, Seattle, Washington 98119; (206) 284-6310; clubmail@mountaineers.org

The Mountaineers Books, an active, nonprofit publishing program of the club, produces guidebooks, instructional texts, historical works, natural history guides, and works on environmental conservation. All books produced by The Mountaineers are aimed at fulfilling the club's mission.

Send or call for our catalog of more than 300 outdoor titles:

The Mountaineers Books
1001 SW Klickitat Way, Suite 201
Seattle, WA 98134
1-800-553-4453 / e-mail: mbooks@mountaineers.org